AMERICAN CARNAGE

THE WARS OF DONALD TRUMP

Melvin A. Goodman

O pus
Self-Publishing
WASHINGTON DC

Copyright © 2019 by Melvin A. Goodman

ISBN: 978-1-162429-206-4

Cover Design: David L. Ekedahl

All rights reserved. This book or any portion thereof may not be reproduced or used in any manner whatsoever without the express written permission of the author except for the use of brief quotations in a book review.

Published through Opus Self-Publishing Services
Located at:
Politics and Prose Bookstore
5015 Connecticut Ave. NW
Washington, D.C. 20008
www.politics-prose.com / / (202) 364-1919

ALSO BY MELVIN A. GOODMAN

Whistleblower at The CIA: An Insider's Account of the Politics of Intelligence

National Insecurity: The Cost of American Militarism

The Failure of Intelligence: The Decline and Fall of The CIA

Bush League Diplomacy: Putting the Nation at Risk (With Craig Eisendrath)

The Phantom Defense: America's Pursuit of the Star Wars Illusion (With Craig Eisendrath and Gerald Marsh)

The Wars of Eduard Shevardnadze (With Carolyn M. Ekedahl)

The End of Superpower Conflict in the Third World

Gorbachev's Retreat: The Third World

To Lini and our magical grandchildren:

Alex, James, Matthew, Julia, Willa, Quinn, Eleanor, Elke, Eoin, Zoe, Knox, and "Gandalf"

CONTENTS

Introduction

1 | TRUMP'S CABINET: TRUMP'S WAR ON PUBLIC SERVICE   1

2 | DONALD TRUMP'S WAR ON DIPLOMACY   28

3 | TRUMP'S WAR ON NATIONAL SECURITY POLICY   59

4 | DONALD TRUMP'S WAR ON INTELLIGENCE   87

5 | TRUMP'S WAR ON GOVERNANCE   113

6 | TRUMP'S WAR ON SCIENCE   145

Conclusion | TRUMP'S CARNAGE: WHAT CAN BE DONE?   172

"I've had a lot of wars of my own. I'm really good at war. I love war…"
    –Donald Trump, Campaigning in Iowa, 2015.

"Donald Trump is a chaos candidate, and he would be a chaos president."
    –Jeb Bush, 2016.

American Carnage

INTRODUCTION

The supporters and detractors of President Donald Trump agree on one thing: he is at war. His supporters, led by Stephen Bannon, boast that Trump is at "war with the elites; war with the permanent political class; war with the opposition party media, tech oligarchs, the Antifa anarchists."[1] They contend that Trump is president to "take on the vested interests in this country for hard working Americans."

Trump's opponents agree that he is at war or at least perpetually embattled with everyone (but Russian President Vladimir Putin) and with American governance, and argue that his verbal and political assaults are harming our democracy. President Trump has no understanding or patience for governance.

Trump's war against the Department of Justice and the justice system itself is undermining the foundations of our rule of law. His war against the intelligence community is designed to politicize intelligence, which will compromise our national security. His anti-intellectual campaign against science and reason undermines departments and agencies designed to improve the lives of Americans and others. But what of real war? Will we find that he favors that too? If Trump says he loves war, perhaps we should believe him.

At the halfway mark of Trump's first term in the White House, the casualties in Trump's wars are beginning to mount. A government shutdown began in December 2018 over the cost of a wall on the Mexican border, which would

---

[1] Ashley Parker, "Trump as the arbiter of truth," *The Washington Post*, August 31, 2018, p. 6.

represent 1/10th of one percent of the federal budget. There was a roller coaster ride on the New York stock exchange due to threats to fire the chairman of the Federal Reserve and the implications of the trade and tariff war with China. Secretary of the Treasury Steven Mnuchin's response to the shutdown and the stock market plunge was a family vacation in Mexico.

There was bureaucratic chaos over Trump's plan to withdraw forces from Syria and Afghanistan. Secretary of Defense James Mattis and the special envoy for policy against the Islamic State, Brett McGurk, resigned in protest against the withdrawal. National Security Adviser John Bolton contradicted the notion of an imminent Syrian withdrawal, but Bolton and Secretary of State Mike Pompeo gave different interpretations of Trump's goals in the Middle East.

There was unprecedented turbulence in the President's Cabinet. Several departments were led by "acting" secretaries, including the Department of Justice. Mick Mulvaney, the budget director, is "acting" chief of staff and "acting" director of the Consumer Financial Protection Bureau. Following the sudden resignation of the ambassador to the United Nations, Nikki Haley, Trump appointed a former Fox News personality, Heather Nauert, to the post. She had to withdraw her nomination.

Nauert, formerly press spokesman at the Department of State, joined several Fox News veterans in the administration, including former top communications adviser, Bill Shine, and Fox News contributor John Bolton, who heads the National Security Council. The so-called "adults" in the White House are gone, replaced by loyal subordinates who offer no resistance or challenge to the president. There has been more than 40 percent turnover among senior staff in the White House, and the president explains that "I'm speaking with myself, number one, because I have a very good brain and I've said a lot of things."

Trump's assault on governance is lost in the cacophony of charges that are related to the work of Special Counsel Robert Mueller; the trials of cronies such as Paul Manafort and Michael Cohen; and the financial payoffs to women who have had affairs with the president. This book documents the significant damage being inflicted on American governance each and every day of the Trump presidency. Eventually, the nation will have to rebuild its institutions if it is to regain its rightful place in the international community. It will be difficult and costly to rebuild the institutions of government, and the Mueller investigations; the trials; and the salacious tales will offer no recompense for the damage.

The conventional wisdom in the United States has been that someone with the character and personality of a Donald Trump could not be elected—that the political guardrails of our democracy would prevent it, and that filters at various levels would block his route to the White House. Demagogues in the past, narcissists and bullies such as George Wallace, Joseph McCarthy, and Huey Long garnered a great deal of political support without clearing the last hurdles to the presidency. But 63 million Americans voted for Donald Trump. This book is concerned with exploring the Trump administration's debasement of our government and warning about the difficult task of rebuilding that lies ahead. It offers suggestions on what needs to be done.

* * *

DONALD TRUMP IS NOT THE FIRST ILL-EQUIPPED PRESIDENT IN AMERICAN history, but he is the most ignorant, most cynical, most dishonest, and possibly the most unstable. He claims a special standing in the pantheon of U.S. presidents because of his unique combination of misogyny, crassness, and self-absorption. No previous president has been caught with his hand in the till. For the first time in the modern era, we have a president who refuses to release his income tax returns and has surrounded himself with grifters who have been indicted. A national security advisor, Michael Flynn, and a campaign director, Paul Manafort, were forced to resign because of dishonorable connections to Russia and Ukraine, respectively. Ethics issues forced the resignation of the Secretary of Health and

iii

Human Services, the Secretary of the Interior, and the director of the Environmental Protection Agency; several other cabinet secretaries face accusations regarding their personal ethics.

And for the first time in history, a federal judge, Peter J. Messitte, has ruled that a suit can proceed against the president for violating the foreign and domestic emolument clauses in the Constitution. Messitte ruled on a case brought by the Attorneys General of Maryland and the District of Columbia, who accused Trump of "unprecedented" profits from foreign interests. The Founding Fathers wanted presidents to live off their federal income; no previous president held the kind of financial interests that Trump holds.

For the first time in our history, the United States has a president who has been shunned at home and abroad. Shortly before his death in August 2018, Senator John McCain made clear that President Trump was not welcome at his funeral. Earlier in the year, the family of Barbara Bush asked the president not to attend her funeral. U.S. athletes and artists are making a regular practice of not accepting invitations to attend ceremonies at the White House. The president skipped the honors ceremony at the Kennedy Center in 2017 and 2018 because he knew he would not be welcome. When President Trump was in the United Kingdom in June 2018, Queen Elizabeth was the only member of the royal family to meet with him. It was an awkward encounter as Trump violated protocol and walked in front of the Queen.

Trump's closest advisers, such as Rudy Giuliani and Stephen Miller, enforce Trump's worst instincts. No adviser was closer to President Trump during his campaign and the early days of his administration than Stephen Bannon, a onetime naval officer and Goldman-Sachs investment banker, and a "white supremacist." Bannon rose to prominence in the conservative movement by producing propaganda documentaries that promoted the Tea Party; blamed the economic recession on minority-lending programs; and praised former vice presidential candidate Sarah Palin.

Bannon's deputy during his short stay in the White House was Stephen Miller, a former congressional staffer for then Representative Jefferson Beauregard Sessions, who became one of the most controversial Attorneys General in history. Bannon and Miller are masters of anti-Muslim rhetoric; they orchestrated the Muslim Ban, a controversy that dominated the first months of the Trump presidency. They support a conspiracy view of Islam that does not accept the faith as a religion but as a political ideology that rivals Naziism, fascism, and communism. They co-authored a speech for Trump in the presidential campaign that turned on tropes of white nationalism and anti-Semitism. Sessions and Miller are responsible for the inhumane policy of separating parents from their children that began in April 2018.

Chapter One deals with one of the Trump administration's most egregious features, the mediocrity and mendacity of the White House staff as well as Cabinet secretaries committed to weakening the departments and agencies they lead. The first secretary of health and human services was fired for the misuse of federal funds. The first administrator of the Environmental Protection Agency was forced out for the same reason. The Director of the Veterans Administration was fired for blocking privatization of the VA. The Secretary of the Department of Housing and Urban Development was admonished for extravagance in furnishing his own office as his agency was cutting housing benefits for the nation's poor.

Chapter Two discusses Trump's assault on traditional American diplomacy. Trump's national security team has no strategy or coherent approach to stabilizing the international situation or strengthening our place in the global community. Trump has worsened the international environment by engaging in unilateral disengagement. He has turned his back on the Iran nuclear accord, the Trans-Pacific Partnership, and the Paris climate accord. Trump has referred to African countries as "shitholes" and asserted that Africans will never leave their huts. To Trump, illegal immigrants are "animals."

His national security team has no interest in traditional diplomacy. National Security Adviser Bolton is hostile to international agencies, such as the United Nations and the International Criminal Court, and to disarmament treaties such as the Intermediate-range Nuclear Forces Treaty. The rhetoric of Secretary of State Mike Pompeo is particularly bellicose. He may have left the U.S. Army several decades ago, but his soldierly carriage remains threatening. Bolton and Pompeo are dangerous Trump-whisperers.

Chapter Three deals with Trump's impulsive and irrational views that amount to an assault on the conventional wisdom regarding national security policy. Trump uses his Twitter account to announce major troop withdrawals from war zones. There is no consultation with the national security team, and no deliberations within the National Security Council. Summit meetings take place with heads of state without proper preparation. Some international meetings are attended by the commander in chief; others are ignored. Meetings with allies become acrimonious; meetings with adversaries are benign. There is no official record of the five meetings between Presidents Trump and Putin over the past two years.

Chapter Four deals with Trump's assault on the intelligence community, an assault that is threatening and unprecedented. Even before his inauguration, Trump compared the Central Intelligence Agency to the Gestapo in Nazi Germany. The former director of national intelligence and the former director of the CIA have been particularly vilified, and the latter had his security clearance revoked. Other institutions, such as the Federal Bureau of Investigation, are similarly maligned.

Chapter Five examines Trump's assault on domestic governance, particularly the decimation of environmental regulations that were the foundation of the U.S. effort to rein in global warming. In a 90-day period in 2018, the Trump administration attacked the rules on carbon dioxide pollution from vehicle tailpipes; coal-fired power plants; and the burning of methane gas from oil and gas wells. Trump attacked the legacy policies of the Obama administration, a fixation for the president. The stewards for policy at the Departments of Energy, Interior, and Education have been part of the campaign against Obama's legacy.

Chapter Six deals with Trump's anti-intellectual orientation, which led to an administration that is occupied by "science deniers." The role of science is being undermined at the important regulatory agencies, particularly the Environmental Protection Agency, and many of the professional cadre at these institutions have retired or gone elsewhere. The EPA has lost its entire scientific advisory council. The president himself waited more than a year and a half before appointing a science adviser, a key position in the executive branch.

The government shutdown in December 2018-January 2019 hurt the thousands of scientists among the hundreds of thousands of furloughed federal workers. Research projects were disrupted or delayed, and there was great uncertainty regarding new research. The closure of the National Science Foundation, a funding agency, had a major impact on research.

The book concludes with "What is to be Done" to reverse the assault on our key institutions and the meanness of Trump's social and economic policies. Bipartisan commissions will be required to do a serious accounting of the damage to governance and our participatory democracy. There were problems that existed before the election of Trump, such as the social and economic inequality in the United States, and the high cost of health insurance and a college education. A college education should not be a debt trap for American students. Meanwhile, we have a president who says that he loves the "poorly educated." Inequality led to a lack of trust in government that allowed a demagogic authoritarian to be nominated and elected.

* * *

THE FIRST TWO YEARS OF THE TRUMP ADMINISTRATION RESEMBLED THE LAST two years of Richard Nixon's presidency, defined by the Watergate scandal. Nixon and Trump share a political and personal paranoia; both referred to the investigations of their administrations as "witch hunts." The deep-seated insecurity and paranoia of Nixon and Trump have been well-documented. Soviet Ambassador Anatoly Dobrynin reported to the Kremlin in the fall of 1969 that Nixon was "growing angry, sarcastic, paranoid and agitated." Robert Mueller's investigations have made Trump agitated. Nixon and Trump with their fragile personalities lashed out often; Nixon did so privately and verbally; Trump's frustrations are on display in numerous tweets.

Neither Nixon nor Trump were able to get close to people; perhaps a basic insecurity was the driving force that led each to the presidency. Both lacked self-assurance. They used stark language in their inaugural speeches to describe what was wrong with the United States. Nixon bewilderingly told "My fellow Americans" that the "long dark night for America is about to end;" Trump referred to "American carnage."[2] Subsequently, both men retreated behind a wall of privacy in the White House. Dwight Chapin, a key White House staffer for Nixon, described the president in a fashion that could be applied to Trump. "When you get in tight and close and everything else and you're fighting him and you're fighting his people and you're coming at him," Chapin remarked, "and its them vs. we—he falls apart."[3] Is Trump falling apart?"

A disturbing trait that Nixon and Trump share is racism. Nixon's list of enemies had common denominators—race and ethnicity. Liberal Jews ranked high on this list; Nixon found Jews obnoxious. He referred to the Irish as mean drunks and to Mexicans as thieves; the inferiority of blacks was a constant. "Most

---

[2] *New York Times,* January 23, 1969; January 22, 2018.

[3] John A. Farrell, "Richard Nixon: A Life," New York: Doubleday, 2017, p. 385.

viii

of them [blacks] basically are just out of the trees," Nixon told one young appointee, Donald Rumsfeld.[4] President Nixon was critical of the Brown vs. the Board of Education decision in 1954 to integrate the public school system. In a memorandum to his senior aides, he wrote that "segregated white education is probably superior to education in which there is too great a degree of integration of inferior black students with white students."

John Dean, Nixon's White House aide, revealed to a congressional committee that Nixon had an "enemies list." An internal White House memorandum in August 1971 described the "available federal machinery to screw our political enemies." A few weeks later, Nixon's special counsel, Charles Colson, prepared a list of 20 people to be screwed, including labor leaders, Democratic fundraisers, and journalists. CBS reporter Daniel Schorr was identified as a "real media enemy," and columnist Mary McGrory, who won a Pulitzer Prize for her writings on Watergate, was cited for her "daily hate Nixon articles."

Trump is less secretive about his enemies. He targeted dozens of former officials, particularly in the judicial and intelligence communities, who have criticized his presidency or played a role in the investigation of Russian interference in the 2016 presidential election. Trump would not even permit his White House staff to release a sympathetic statement following the death of Senator John McCain in August 2018.

Nixon viewed Democrats as a distant elite dominated by lawyers, writers, and professors. He believed that he could capture the "little guy" by linking these groups to the "jaundiced values of the campus and the newsroom."[5] Trump waged a "dog-whistle" campaign to garner the votes of the "little guy" and, like

---

[4] Farrell, "Richard Nixon," p. 400.

[5] Farrell, "Nixon," p. 200.

Nixon, believed that he could establish a "quality of oneness" with ordinary people.[6] He believed that he could "shoot someone on Fifth Avenue," and not face any consequences.

In attacking the press, Nixon and Trump targeted one of the most important guardrails of our democracy. James Keogh, a Nixon speechwriter and biographer, said that Nixon's "antipathy" toward the press was "very intense. Just a real visceral feeling.... He could not excise himself of it. It would burn on him."[7] Biographers for Nixon and Trump believed that neither man was ever "one of the boys," feeling disliked by the working press.

To Trump, the press is the "enemy of the people." His antipathy toward the press and his constant incantations of "fake news" have resonated not only with his base, but with a larger audience as well. The term "fake news" has been accepted by many within our borders and attracted attention from authoritarian leaders outside our borders as well. Trump has weakened the credibility of the mainstream media and, in doing so, has undermined faith in our democracy. Authoritarian leaders in Hungary, the Philippines, and Thailand are bleating "fake news" to attack the media in their countries.

The Washington Post was a fixation for Nixon and Trump. *Washington Post* cartoonist Herbert Block, better known as Herblock, was a constant irritant for Nixon. Trump carried his distaste for the *Post* to new levels, attacking *Post* owner Jeff Bezos and his company Amazon. Trump's attacks affected Amazon's value on the Dow Jones Stock Exchange. Trump threatened to have the U.S. Postal Service increase mailing rates for Amazon deliveries.

---

[6] William White, "Nixon: What Kind of President?" *Harper's*, January 1958, p. 31.

[7] Farrell, "Nixon," p. 203.

Nixon and Trump were hostile toward the CIA, which Nixon considered a "muscle-bound bureaucracy" with a "completely paralyzed brain."[8] He wanted a study to determine "how many people in CIA could be removed by Presidential action." He linked his contempt for the CIA to his contempt for elitism, ordering National Security Adviser Henry Kissinger to end "recruiting from any of the Ivy League schools or any other universities where either the university president or the faculty have taken action condemning our efforts to bring the war in Vietnam to an end."

A dangerous area of comparison between Nixon and Trump involves the "madman theory of history." According to H.R. Haldeman, Nixon's chief of staff, Nixon believed in a "Madman Theory."[9] Nixon wanted the Soviet Union to put pressure on North Vietnam to end the war and suggested that he should signal to the Kremlin 'for God's sake, you know Nixon is obsessed about Communism. We can't restrain him when he is angry—and he has his hand on the nuclear button.'"[10] In 1969, Nixon even ordered a "madman nuclear alert," code-named Giant Lance, in which B-52 bombers loaded with atomic weapons flew from bases in California toward the Soviet Union.

Trump employed the madman approach when he engaged in loose talk about preparing for military action against North Korea, Iran, and even Venezuela. His bizarre tactics were irresponsible attempts to scare Pyongyang and Tehran into negotiations. His withdrawal from the Iranian nuclear accord pointed toward the possible use of force. His denunciation of North Korean leader Kim Jong Un at the United Nations in 2017 as a "Rocket Man…on a suicide mission" had similar implications.

---

[8] Richard Reeves, "President Nixon: Alone in the White House," New York: Simon & Schuster, 2001, pp. 482-483.

[9] See H. R. Haldeman, "The Haldeman Diaries: Inside the Nixon White House," New York: Berkley Books, 1995.

[10] Haldeman, "Inside the Nixon White House," p. 179.

Trump stated that, if the United States were "forced to defend itself or its allies" it would have "no choice but to totally destroy North Korea." If Kim Jong Un is "Little Rocket Man," then we know who is "Big Rocket Man." Vice President Michael Pence, Secretary of State Pompeo, and National Security Adviser Bolton also used bellicose language to intimidate North Korean and Iranian leaders.

There is a major difference between Nixon and Trump, however. Nixon was making tactical use of the madman concept. In the case of Trump, there is the possibility of a genuine madman in the White House. For the first time in history, we have a commander-in-chief who is a malignant narcissist, a paranoid without impulse control. His delusional and hyperbolic tendencies are on frequent display. It's not a simple matter of Trump's lack of a "moral compass," but the absence of any compass whatsoever. It begs the question of whether the president is *compos mentes.*

Finally, the issue of impeachment faced Nixon and Trump, with Nixon resigning in August 1974 to beat the House of Representatives to the punch but Trump is confident that Republicans in the Senate would protect him. The echoes of Watergate were heard in Trump's first months in the White House. Just as Nixon leaned on a Justice Department official, Henry Petersen, to gather information on the Watergate investigation, Trump leaned on FBI director James Comey to learn if he was under investigation.

The firing of Comey brought immediate reminders of Nixon's firing of Attorney General Elliot Richardson in 1973, the infamous "Saturday Night Massacre." These firings were a pivotal point in the Nixon presidency, and Trump's advisors feared that the removal of Attorney General Jeff Sessions in November 2018 would be similarly pivotal. The "Saturday Night Massacre" contributed to the charge of obstruction of justice; similar moves by Trump could have the same result.

Unlike Watergate, which found key Republicans willing to press for the impeachment of Nixon, there was no sign of Republican willingness to pursue an aggressive congressional inquiry of Trump, let alone impeachment. Before the November 2018 congressional elections, the chairmen of the intelligence committees, Senator Richard Burr (R-NC) and Representative Devin Nunes (R-CA), were not moving in such a direction. The Democratic victory in the House of Representatives in November 2018 could lead to an impeachment referral to the Senate, where it would probably be defeated. Unlike Nixon's case, there is no sign of shame and little possibility of President Trump's resignation. President Gerald Ford pardoned Nixon; Trump's lawyers believe that, if the worst should happen, the president could simply pardon himself.

The Nixon and Trump crises were self-inflicted, the very definition of political tragedy. Nixon was facing one of the most one-sided victories in a presidential election in history but resorted to obstruction of justice, national security wiretaps, and misuse of the Internal Revenue Service and the CIA. Before completing his first year in office, Trump was being investigated for obstruction of justice, money-laundering, and contacts with Russian officials close to the Kremlin. Trump felt he was not being sufficiently protected by his Attorney General and the Department of Justice, and asked his aides "Where is my Roy Cohn," a name synonymous with the rise of McCarthyism in the 1950s and its dark political arts.

Nixon and Trump believed they were above the law. President Nixon will be forever identified with his musing to David Frost that "When the president does it, that means that it is not illegal." President Trump trumpeted in June 2018 that "I have the absolute right to PARDON myself." The fact that Trump believes "I have an absolute right to do what I want with the Department of Justice" threatens the rule of law in the United States.

The talk of impeachment and the Mueller investigation of Russian interference in the 2016 election and possible collusion between the Trump campaign and Russian officials have become serious distractions to Trump's wars against U.S. governance, the civil service, and the worlds of diplomacy, intelligence, and law enforcement. The mainstream media is preoccupied with interference with the presidential election, the relationship between Trump and Putin, and the emoluments received by the president. Meanwhile, our political culture and policy process have been corrupted.

Trump is pursuing tactics that degrade public trust in our institutions, and compromise our political culture and our democracy. Trump's assault on governance has produced a serious lack of trust in American institutions. The Trump administration is viewed as dangerous; Congress is seen as passive and dysfunctional; the Supreme Court seems positioned to protect the head of state; and key guardrails of democracy such as the press and law enforcement are being challenged. Large-scale gerrymandering has created uncompetitive congressional elections and undemocratic results, which the Supreme Court has yet to address. The victory of the Democrats in the 2018 congressional elections is a sign of resistance to the policies and politics of Donald Trump, but much work is needed to repair the damage of the past two years.

Trump's election is consistent with the decline in centrist and moderate governments throughout the Western world, marked by the Brexit decision in Britain in 2016; the rise of the far-right Alternative for Germany in 2017; and the emergence of right-wing movements in Europe. Europe has experienced turmoil before, and the United States has witnessed serious political division, particularly during the Vietnam War in the 1960s and 1970s. The current dysfunction rivals the instability and uncertainly of the post-Civil War period. Trump's tumultuous presidency is a demonstration of a dangerous level of pessimism, distrust, and cynicism in the United States.

This book is not concerned with porno stars and hush money, or Putin's politicking and the Mueller investigation; it is concerned with bringing to light

xiv

the regular debasement of the government and warning about the difficult task of rebuilding that lies ahead.

– 1 –

TRUMP'S CABINET:
TRUMP'S WAR ON PUBLIC SERVICE

"I would cite you to the Apostle Paul and his clear and wise command in Romans 13, to obey the laws of the government because God has organized them for the purpose of order."
—Attorney General Jefferson Beauregard Sessions, June 14, 2018 suggesting Biblical justification for the divine right of the United States to take children from immigrant parents and warehouse them in tent cities or abandoned Walmart stores.

"If they can make you believe absurdities, then they can make you commit atrocities."
—Voltaire

One of the most profound powers of the president is the appointment of officials to all departments and agencies of government as well as to the judicial and diplomatic arenas. The Senate is authorized to confirm many of these appointments, but it is rare for the confirmation process to reject a presidential nomination. Until 1883, with the passage of the Pendleton Act, the president even filled low level jobs within the federal bureaucracy, which encouraged corruption and graft. The Civil Service Commission was created to remove most federal jobs from the president's direct control, but presidential power remains enormous in this regard. Trump's woeful appointments have damaged public service and weakened governance.

The chaos of the first two years of the Trump presidency resembles the last two years of Nixon's presidency, but Nixon was intelligent, an experienced politician, and a policy guru. His appointments to high-level positions were respectable, and he introduced progressive plans for health care and environmental reform. Trump is doing his best to dismantle regulatory and environment regulation, and is fixated on reversing or revoking President Obama's legislation.

There was a startling difference between the personnel appointments of Nixon and Trump. A U.S. president can select nearly 4,000 individuals to occupy key policy positions. More than 1,000 of these individuals require Senate confirmation. Nixon's appointees were for the most part of the highest political caliber in terms of their expertise and their moderate political cast. President Trump's selections demonstrated his contempt for public service as he appointed the least qualified cabinet in American history. The unethical standards throughout the Trump administration has created the most corrupt government in U.S. history. Warren Harding's Teapot Dome scandal can now be relegated to a distant second place.

Nixon's appointees were stunningly competent. They included Henry A. Kissinger, one of the most powerful national security advisers in U.S. history, as well as Lawrence Eagleburger, William Rogers, and Elliott Richardson. The domestic choices were more impressive, including Democrats such as Daniel P. Moynihan and Richard Blumenthal as well as moderate Republicans such as Lamar Alexander, George Shultz, George Romney, and Elizabeth Dole. There were general officers in the Nixon administration (Alexander Haig and Brent Scowcroft), but they had civilian mentors in Kissinger and Eagleburger. There were no civilian mentors for Trump's general officers who had little experience with policymaking in Washington.

Nixon's appointment of moderates presaged reasonable and even progressive domestic policy even though the president was surrounded in the White House by ideologues such as Patrick Buchanan, John Dean, and Chuck Colson. These individuals did their best to push Nixon and his policies to the right and, on a personal level, fed his paranoia about the political opposition. Buchanan argued that President Nixon should destroy the Watergate tapes in order to save his presidency, and Colson argued for total obstruction of the Watergate investigation. Dean and Colson assembled the "enemies list" that included the conductor Leonard Bernstein as well as journalists Daniel Schorr, Mary McGrory, and Tom Wicker.

One of Nixon's greatest accomplishments in the domestic arena was the creation of the Environmental Protection Agency, which forged the president's reputation as a champion of the environment. The establishment of the EPA was a tactical move, designed to steal the thunder of Senator Edward Muskie (D-ME), who was the Democratic frontrunner for the 1972 election and a well-known supporter of the need for an environmental agency. Nixon did not start out as an environmentalist. He appointed Walter Hickel, the millionaire governor of Alaska, as Secretary of the Interior; Hickel was a crony of oil tycoons in his state. But Nixon and Hickel stopped the laying of the trans-Alaska pipeline that threatened the tundra; halted oil drilling in the Santa Barbara Channel following a major blowout; and pressed the Department of Justice to prosecute Chevron for fouling the Gulf of Mexico.

Nixon received more credit than he deserved with respect to environmental issues because it was the Democratic congress that forced environmental reform on him. Congress overrode Nixon's veto of the Clean Water Act of 1970 and Nixon's rejection of the Federal Water Pollution Control Act in 1972. Congress stopped Nixon's effort to permit detergents that were fouling the country's waterways. Nixon eventually named such environmentalists as William Ruckelshaus and Russell Train to manage EPA, but privately he referred to environmentalists as "clowns" talking "crap." Nixon believed that the Democrats were catering to environmentalists who were "nuts."[11]

Nixon's accomplishments shouldn't be confused with Lyndon Baines Johnson's Great Society, but he did set up the first Office of Consumer Affairs in the White House and approved a Consumer Product Safety Act. He supported the creation of Amtrak and signed Title IX legislation that banned sex discrimination in higher education and bolstered women's athletics. With a stroke of the pen, Nixon created the National Oceanic and Atmospheric Administration (NOAA), and signed the Clean Air Act of 1970. Citing the problems of his childhood, Nixon ordered federal agencies to transform surplus properties into parks for families to enjoy.

In economic policy, Nixon was no ideologue, entertaining policies that aggravated conservative Republicans. When his tight money policies produced signs of a recession, including higher interest rates and unemployment as well as a downturn in stock prices, Nixon shifted gears and announced, "I am now a Keynesian."[12] To conservative Republicans, this was akin to a Christian crusader saying, "All things considered, I think Muhammad was right." His policies led to the greatest quarterly gain in Gross National Product in seven years, sending Americans to the polls in 1972 with a sense of good feeling about the economy.

Unlike their immediate predecessors in the White House, Nixon and Trump shared a lack of support for civil rights, which John F. Kennedy and Lyndon B. Johnson considered the "moral presence of the presidency." Nixon and Trump ran thinly veiled racist campaigns, which skirted the blatant racism of a George Wallace or a Lester Maddox, but signaled to their supporters that their sympathies

---

[11] William E. Leuchtenburg, "The American President: From Teddy Roosevelt to Bill Clinton," New York: Oxford University Press, 2015, p. 493. John A. Farrell, "Richard Nixon: The Life," New York: Doubleday, 2017, p. 380.

[12] ibid, p. 495.

were not with improving schools and housing for the disadvantaged, let alone those of color. Even John Ehrlichman, his chief of domestic policy, conceded that Nixon "delivered a clear message that was hard to miss...[presenting] his views in such a way that a citizen could avoid admitting to himself that he was attracted by a racial appeal."[13]

Unlike Trump who held neoconservative and isolationist views, Nixon ignored the anger of conservative Republicans toward his foreign policy. Although considered the ultimate cold warrior, committed to rolling back the Iron Curtain in the east and the west, Nixon shocked his supporters with the creation of a strategic triangle that fostered closer bilateral relations between the United States and the Soviet Union as well as the United States and China. This triangle opened up numerous international opportunities that included the Treaty of Berlin, the Strategic Arms Limitation Treaty, and the Anti-Ballistic Missile Treaty. The strategic triangle placed the Soviet Union and China at a strategic disadvantage and compelled both Moscow and Beijing to improve relations with the United States. In this way, Nixon could enter the 1972 presidential election with claims of a more stable international situation.

Where Nixon sought expertise and experience in making important personnel moves, Trump sought loyalty and subservience. Where Nixon selected recognized luminaries in the field of international security for his national security team, Trump surrounded himself with general officers who lacked experience in dealing with arms control and disarmament as well as regional conflict. Trump professed an interest in improving relations with Russian President Putin, yet he appointed general officers hostile to dealing with the Kremlin. As a professor of international security at the National War College for nearly 20 years, I observed the anti-Russian attitudes of the officer corps, particularly general officers.

---

[13] See John Ehrlichman, "Witness to Power," New York: Simon & Schuster, 1982.

Nixon appointed one of the most accomplished national security teams in history; Trump can be credited with naming the most inexperienced and unqualified team. The appointments immediately raised questions regarding Trump's judgment and intelligence. In view of Trump's authoritarian personality and style, it was no surprise that he surrounded himself with authoritarians; for this, the Pentagon was the best recruiting ground.

Trump appointed retired and active-duty generals to key national security policy positions, receiving positive reviews from conservative and liberal commentators for doing so. Secretary of Defense James ("Mad Dog") Mattis was confirmed by a vote of 98 to 1, even though he had been out of uniform for only four years instead of the statutorily required seven. Trump was helped by the fact that Gallup polls revealed unparalleled support for the military across the political spectrum, registering high confidence from more than 70 percent of the people in numerous surveys. Even liberal Senator Richard Blumenthal (D-CT) remarked that placing generals in powerful jobs provided a "steadying hand on the rudder."[14] It is unfortunate that the United States reached the point where its political stability relied on the steady hand of general officers!

Trump's constant companion on the campaign trail in 2016, General Michael Flynn, became National Security Adviser for a brief period. There were numerous warnings to Trump about the selection of Flynn, including from President Barack Obama and New Jersey Governor Chris Christie, the transition manager at the time. Flynn lasted less than a month; he was forced to resign after lying to Vice President Pence about meetings with Russian officials on sensitive policy matters.

In his brief stewardship, Flynn restructured the National Security Council to ensure that there did not have to be a representative of the intelligence community at the table. Since the creation of the NSC 70 years ago, either the

---

[14] Charles Lane, "Our disturbing need for the generals," *The Washington Post*, April 18, 2017, p. 17.

7 | AMERICAN CARNAGE

Director of the CIA or the Director of National Intelligence attended principals' meetings to present the views of the intelligence community in the formation of policy making. And to make matters worse, Stephen Bannon, a pugnacious and polemical political adviser, was named a permanent member of the NSC. Bannon once stated that "Lenin wanted to destroy the state, and that's my goal, too. I want to bring everything crashing down, and destroy all of today's establishment."

Flynn militarized the NSC as never before. A conspiratorial thinker, who was unlikely to ensure that the president had the best possible advice from his Cabinet and his national security team, Flynn filled his staff with low-ranking officers. A former career Army officer, David Horan, was named a senior staffer dealing with strategy. A former Marine officer, Robin Townley, was appointed senior director for Africa, but could not get a security clearance. Another Marine intelligence officer, Matt Pottinger, was senior director for Asia. They were replaced soon after Flynn was forced to resign.

I talked to several colleagues from the intelligence community about Flynn's disastrous tour as Director of the Defense Intelligence Agency, but only one was willing to discuss Flynn on-the-record. Flynn arrived at DIA in 2012 for what was expected to be a three-year tour as director; the tour was cut short after two years because of the instability he created there. On three separate occasions, intelligence tsar General James Clapper warned Flynn that his management style was creating chaos, but it was a bizarre series of briefings on the Hill that led Clapper to insist that Flynn give up his post as Director and retire from the military. Clapper was acting on information from Flynn's deputy, David Shedd, and Shedd's predecessor, David Leatherwood, who cited Flynn's conspiratorial views on international issues and his intimidating managerial style that led to chaotic reorganization programs and the ouster of popular managers.[15]

---

[15] Flynn was often hostile to the conclusions of his intelligence officers, and preferred his own conspiratorial notions that his underlings referred to as "Flynn Facts." Flynn, however, was not alone in his conspiratorial views

Flynn's bizarre behavior during the campaign and the Republican convention, where he led chants of "Lock Her Up" against Hillary Clinton, was due to a combination of hubris and vengeance because of his firing from DIA. It was also telling that, after his retirement, Flynn, unlike so many generals, could not gain a high-level position at one of the military-industrial think tanks or "Beltway Bandits" as they are popularly referred to. Instead, he formed his own consulting company, and negotiated shady contracts with Russian and Turkish companies that were not reported to the Pentagon as required by the military. Flynn failed to register as a foreign agent until his financial dealings became well known and the subject of an FBI investigation.

Flynn was replaced as National Security Advisor by an active-duty Army General, H. R. McMaster, whose public remarks revealed little understanding of geopolitical issues. McMaster had never served a tour of duty at the Pentagon or in Washington. Unlike Flynn, who spent the campaign cheek by jowl with Trump, McMaster had never met the president before being summoned to Mar-a-Lago for the introduction to the American public. He lacked the stature to coordinate the positions of high-powered secretaries of state, defense, and treasury. Moreover, the three secretaries (Rex Tillerson, James Mattis, Steven Mnuchin, respectively) had no institutional memory for geopolitical decision making over the recent past, let alone an understanding of strategic statecraft. Another retired general, John Kelly, became secretary of homeland security.

When Reince Priebus was not up to the task of chief of staff for the president, Kelly was moved into the White House, completing the ring of general officers initially surrounding Trump. Even the Director of the CIA, former representative Mike Pompeo, had a military background, graduating from West Point in 1986 and serving in the military for 6 years.

---

toward Iran. Generals James Mattis and Stanley McChrystal had similar notions, and both had created problems for the Obama administration.

The appointment of professional military officers to key policy positions compromised the principle of military subordination to civilian political authority. General officers have command experience as well as operational and tactical experience, but are typically lacking in strategic or geopolitical insight, which requires international and diplomatic experience. General officers have a deep understanding of military issues, but limited insight into the non-military tools of strategic statecraft. A greater problem for our military class is its dearth of knowledge about the domestic political process, which is why the ten-month academic program at the National War College begins with a study of domestic politics and process.

When Secretary of State Alexander Haig claimed "I'm in charge here," in the wake of the shooting of President Ronald Reagan, he had no real idea of the chain of succession, according to one of my War College students who was with him that eventful day. Flynn testified that he received no warning from the FBI about the illegality of lying to FBI agents. Haig and Flynn might have benefitted from an academic year at the National War College.

The political awkwardness and liability of Trump's generals was obvious from the beginning. Any experienced political actuary would have predicted a short run for Flynn as head of the National Security Council, the most challenging inter-agency body in the U.S. government. The position requires a complicated skill set in diplomacy, negotiation, and international experience, all of which Flynn lacked. But no one expected that he would last only a month—forced to resign because of his lies to Vice President Pence and other high-level White House officials about his contacts with Russian Ambassador Sergei Kislyak, which violated the 1799 Logan Act. The Act criminalized negotiations by unauthorized persons with a foreign government that has disputes with the United States. Flynn, a career intelligence officer, should have known that his conversations with the Russian ambassador were being monitored by the National Security Agency.

Flynn's successor, H. R. McMaster became prominent because of the publication of his doctoral dissertation, *Dereliction of Duty: Johnson, McNamara, the Joint Chiefs of Staff, and the Lies That Led to Vietnam.*[16] McMaster's book argued that the Joint Chiefs of Staff failed to press the White House for greater force deployments in Southeast Asia. He ignored the fact that the war was decided long before the U.S. troop buildup in Vietnam; he stubbornly believed that a different strategy could have won the war.

The dereliction of duty was not the failure to tell truth to power, but the failure of general officers to speak the truth to themselves about the unwinnable war in Vietnam. McMaster missed the point in 2017 when he, along with other generals on the national security team, supported an incremental increase in American forces in Afghanistan, another unwinnable war. Both Vietnam and Afghanistan were fool's errands from the start, but the Joint Chiefs of Staff did not face reality in either situation.

Nevertheless, key pundits in the mainstream media, such as David Ignatius and Michael Gerson of the *Washington Post* and Nicholas Kristof and Thomas Friedman of the *New York Times,* believed that McMaster would stand up to Trump and his anti-establishment coterie in the White House. McMaster did not stand up to the president; he could not even hold his own against Secretary of Defense Mattis, a four-star general, who lorded it over McMaster, a mere three-star. Mattis also dominated Secretary of State Tillerson, a bureaucratic nihilist who was clueless about foreign policy, and Secretary of Treasury Mnuchin, a lackluster choice who lacked the stature and gravity to be a major voice on economic security.

There have been generals who have held their own as national security adviser (Brent Scowcroft and Colin Powell), but Flynn and McMaster were more in the

---

[16] See H. R. McMaster, "Dereliction of Duty: Johnson, McNamara, the Joint Chiefs of Staff, and the Lies that Led to Vietnam," New York: Harper Perennial, 1997.

mold of Admiral John Poindexter and Colonel Robert McFarlane who failed miserably in the Reagan administration. McMaster created a serious problem for himself with the president, similar to that created by Tillerson, who referred to President Trump as a "fucking moron" at a meeting at the Pentagon in July 2017. A week later, McMaster reportedly called the president an "idiot" and a "dope" with the mind of a "kindergartener," which violated a military code that doesn't allow an officer to criticize the president let alone engage in such vilification.[17] The following year, Chief of Staff Kelly lampooned the president's general intelligence as well as the "crazytown" at the White House. He managed to retain his job until December 2018.

Before McMaster was offered the job, President Trump tried to recruit retired Vice Admiral Robert Harward, who told close friends that the job was a "shit sandwich."[18] Unlike Flynn, a loyalist whose appointments to the NSC were referred to as "Flynnstones," McMaster believed that he could ameliorate the harsh ideology of the president. Harward had no such illusions.

Even McMaster gave up trying to educate the president and, instead, supported the president's bellicose thinking on key issues against Mattis and Tillerson. The latter, for example, initially favored diplomacy in dealing with the North Korean nuclear problem, but McMaster supported the president in pressing for military options. President Trump does not agree that the Russians interfered with the 2016 presidential election; accordingly, McMaster did not hold a principal's meeting or even a deputies meeting to develop a strategy against Russian interference. In February 2018, however, McMaster angered Trump when he finally told a conference in Munich, Germany, that the evidence of

---

[17] Joseph Bernstein, *"Sources: McMaster Mocked Trump's Intelligence at a Private Dinner,"* BuzzFeed, November 20, 2017.

[18] Patrick Radden Keefe, "McMaster and Commander: Can a national security adviser retain his integrity if the President as none?" *The New Yorker*, April 30, 2018, p. 36.

Russian interference was "incontrovertible." Not long after, John Bolton replaced McMaster at the National Security Council.

McMaster was particularly unhelpful on the Middle East, calling no high-level meetings to discuss policy toward Saudi Arabia, Syria, Yemen, and Qatar. The United States was facing problems in Syria, where the Russians were using a heavy hand and U.S. and Turkish forces were at odds over support for the anti-Assad coalition; in Yemen, where U.S. ally Saudi Arabia was conducting war crimes against innocent civilians; and in Qatar, where President Trump initially supported a Saudi campaign against a government that hosts the largest U.S. air base in the region. McMaster failed to join Mattis and Tillerson in trying to reverse Trump's decision to recognize Jerusalem as the capital of Israel and move the embassy there. The overall lack of policy coherence on the Middle East and the Persian Gulf ended Washington's influence there since assuming that role from the British in the 1960s.

To his credit, McMaster cleaned house at the National Security Council. In short order, he got rid of Bannon, the unpredictable ideologue, who never should have been placed in the NSC, and an unqualified deputy, K. T. McFarland, who the Trump administration tried to send to Singapore as an ambassador. McFarland's possible ties to the Trump campaign's contacts with the Russians placed her within the scope of the Mueller investigation. As a result, McFarland's name was withdrawn as ambassador. McMaster then moved against the most polemical ideologue on the White House staff, convincing chief of staff Kelly that, in addition to Bannon, Sebastian Gorka, another bloviating Islamophobe, had to go.

A protégé of General Flynn and a close colleague of the president's son-in-law, Jared Kushner, Ezra Cohen-Watnick, was also forced out. Cohen-Watnick was the NSC's senior director for intelligence and worked with the House Intelligence Committee to defend the president. Several months later, he was named to a high post on Attorney General Sessions' senior staff. The senior directors for strategic planning and for the Middle East, Rich Higgins and Derek Harvey, respectively, were sent packing. Both were Trump loyalists, with Higgins believing in the "deep state" and Harvey a well-known loose cannon in previous assignments.

Unlike Flynn, who lasted only a month as National Security Adviser, McMaster remained at the NSC for more than a year, which marked him as a survivor in view of the limited life expectancy in the Trump administration. In addition to having no allies in the White House, McMaster remained on active duty, unlike Brent Scowcroft who retired when named national security adviser. McMaster naively believed that remaining a general officer would insulate him from political pressure. He never developed a relationship with President Trump, who noted that "I'm the only one that matters" when it comes to foreign policy.[19] Unlike then CIA director Pompeo, who catered to Trump's style by providing "killer graphics" instead of substantive essays, McMaster did not dumb down his briefings to the president.

When McMaster wore out his welcome with the unpredictable president, Trump named Bolton to head the National Security Council. Trump, a scion of New York wealth, and his new national security adviser, the son of a Baltimore fire fighter, may not share a common background, but both have abrasive personalities and shirk the truth when it suits their purposes. Richard Nixon would never have named such an irresponsible figure to his national security team, but Bolton's unpredictability was a major attraction for Trump. When George W. Bush tried to name Bolton to be his Ambassador to the United Nations, the president had to settle for a recess appointment because not even a Republican-controlled Senate would confirm Bolton. The Bolton appointment,

---

[19] Keefe, "McMaster and Commander," p. 43.

making him the third national security adviser in Trump's first fourteen months in the White House, was Trump's most alarming personnel maneuver.

Bolton never had use for diplomacy in his professional career. He did his best to block the 1994 Agreed Framework with North Korea, which created a freeze in Pyongyang's plutonium program for nearly eight years. The collapse of that agreement in the Bush administration in 2002 led to the current crisis that finds North Korea with as many as 20 nuclear weapons. Bolton opposes diplomacy and summitry with North Korea and, several months before being named national security adviser, he wrote in the *Wall Street Journal* recommending an aerial attack on Pyongyang's nuclear facilities.[20] He opposed the Iran nuclear accord and argued that a preventive military attack was the correct approach.

Bolton foreswears cooperation with multilateral institutions and agreements; he is an exceptionalist who believes that belligerent unilateralism is the key to solving problems. In March 2015, he wrote that the best way to deal with Iran's nuclear program was to emulate Israel's 1981 attack on Saddam Hussein's Osirak reactor or its 2007 destruction of a Syrian nuclear reactor.[21] The attack on Osirak actually drove the Iraqi nuclear program underground, where it remained without monitoring until the U.S. invasion of Desert Storm in 1991 uncovered it.

Bolton can only worsen the Arab-Israeli conundrum; he opposes a two-state solution to the Israeli-Palestinian conflict, and identifies with anti-Muslim activists. He lacks the personality or inclination to be an "honest broker" in the NSC or to bring together high-ranking members of the national security team to hammer out options for the president. Bolton conducted no NSC principal's meetings before Trump's summit meetings with the heads of state of North Korea and Russia. The Paris climate accord, the Trans-Pacific Partnership, and the Iran

---

[20] John Bolton, *Wall Street Journal*, February 28, 2018, p. 17.

[21] John Bolton, *The New York Times*, March 13, 2015, p. 23.

nuclear accord were particular targets for Bolton's ire. He is an opponent of the United Nations and the International Criminal Court.

Just as Bush could not get Bolton confirmed in 2005, Trump could not have done so in 2018, so a Cabinet position was out of the question. By the time Bush left the White House, he concluded that "I don't consider Bolton credible."[22] No one played a more active role in politicizing the intelligence that misled the United States into the Iraq War than Bolton. Many former colleagues within the intelligence community have spoken privately about Bolton's efforts to distort intelligence on both Cuba and Syria while he was at the United Nations in order to buttress his hard-line positions. Bolton received the UN appointment only after Secretary of State Condoleezza Rice resisted White House pressure to make him her deputy. Years later, Secretary of State Tillerson refused to accept Bolton as his deputy.

Bolton has a well-earned reputation for kissing-up and kicking-down. His nasty treatment of underlings is legendary. Bolton is reminiscent of Winston Churchill's description of Secretary of State John Foster Dulles—"the only bull I know who carries his own china closet with him." Bolton's memoir was titled "Surrender Is Not an Option," and he branded the Foreign Service Officers in the State Department's East Asia and Pacific Affairs Bureau as "EAPeasers." Not even President Bush escaped Bolton's ire. In judging Bush's presidency, he noted the "ineffable sadness of an American presidency, like this one, in total intellectual collapse."

The Trump-Bolton team puts U.S. security at risk as it undermines U.S. influence around the world. The isolation of the United States in international affairs has increased the influence of Russia and China, two nations that have never served as reliable stakeholders in the global arena. Moreover, Moscow and

---

[22] Peter Baker, "Hawk Among Hawks Eager to Confront Foreign Adversaries," *The New York Times*, March 23, 2018, p. 18.

Beijing have forged their closest bilateral relationship in the past fifty years, which is their response to dealing with the uncertainty of Donald Trump. The Trump-Bolton combination is likely to create further discontinuity around the world.

Neither Mattis nor Kelly, the so-called adults in the room, distinguished himself in the first weeks of the Trump administration as secretaries of defense and homeland security, respectively. Kelly was AWOL in the disastrous declaration of the President's Muslim Ban of February 2017, which was overturned by a unanimous decision of the 9th Circuit Court of Appeals. Kelly clumsily handled the crackdown on immigrants, a policy that created chaos at home and abroad.

Mattis was humiliated by Trump, who drove to the Pentagon to announce the closing of U.S. borders to refugees fleeing the slaughter in Syria and suspending immigration from seven Muslim countries. Trump made a huge display of handing the pen used in the signing to the Secretary of Defense. With Mattis smiling over his shoulder, Trump established a religious test for refugees from Muslim countries and ordered that Christians and others from minority religions be granted priority over Muslims.

The photo opportunity was particularly embarrassing to Mattis, who emphasized in his confirmation that he favored cooperation with Muslim nations in dealing with the problem of radical Islam. He opposed vilifying the Muslim community, knowing that it would be used as a propaganda weapon for Muslim adversaries abroad. During his confirmation, he spoke with feeling about his opposition to such moves and explained that the coalition to stop international terrorism would be weakened by demonizing Muslims. Any policy aimed at the Muslim community puts U.S. military forces serving in the Middle East at greater risk. Additional embarrassment came in the form of a troop deployment on the border with Mexico in 2018 with Mattis truckling to the president by favorably citing U.S. efforts against Pancho Villa as a precedent for the president's actions.

The most important assignment for Trump's general officers was given to Kelly in July 2017, when he became Chief of Staff to bring stability to White House policies. There was no aspect of Kelly's background to suggest he had the ability to successfully fill the second most important position in the government. It was only a matter of months before his personal and political integrity were compromised, and he revealed himself as a right-wing ideologue. Kelly quickly aligned himself with Trump in the political and cultural wars that the president waged, particularly against immigrants. The longer he stayed in the job, the worse he performed.

In his short-lived stewardship of the Department of Homeland Security, Kelly moved to the right of the president on immigration issues. When the Trump administration began its internal debates on limiting immigration, there was a consensus for cutting in half the annual quota of 110,000; Kelly opined that "if it were up to him, the number [of immigrants] would be between zero and one."[23] (The administration ultimately settled on an annual cap of 45,000.) Under Kelly, the department targeted the most vulnerable of the immigrant community, the so-called "dreamers," the children of immigrants who had been raised in the United States. In March 2017, he threatened to walk out of a meeting with members of the Arab and Muslim communities in Dearborn, Michigan; they had been asking tough questions about the targeting of Muslims in the administration's travel ban.

Kelly targeted the immigration policy of the Obama Administration, which ignored undocumented immigrants who had no criminal record. He directed immigration officers to bring smuggling charges against individuals bringing children into the United States, arguing they were endangering children. Several months after Kelly left the Department of Homeland Security, immigration

---

[23] Peter Baker, "Once Seen as Calming Force, Kelly Amplifies Boss's Message," *The New York Times*, October 26, 2017, p. 1.

officials took into custody Rosa Maria Hernandez, a ten-year-old girl with cerebral palsy who had just undergone emergency surgery. She was brought to this country as an infant and hardly fit the description of "bad hombres" who Kelly promised to target. She faced deportation, which revealed the lack of humanity of Trump and Kelly.

When members of Congress began to push back against Kelly's aggressive policies, he berated them and told them to "have the courage and skill to change the laws" that they find objectionable or simply "shut up and support the men and women on the front lines."[24] In his private meetings with high-ranking Democrats, including Senator Charles Schumer and Representative Nancy Pelosi, Kelly was testy and contentious, revealing the arrogance of a bully.

Kelly revealed a racist nature in October 2017, when he defended President Trump, who was insensitive in a call to the widow of an African-American serviceman killed in Niger. Kelly targeted Rep. Frederica Wilson (D-FL), who had criticized the exchanges between the president and the war widow. He referred to her an as "empty barrel" and gave an erroneous description of a speech that Wilson made several years earlier. A tape of the speech showed Kelly lied, but he refused to apologize.

If more was known about General Kelly's role as Commander of the Southern Command, he might have faced more opposition in his congressional confirmation battle in 2017. He led military operations in Central America and the Caribbean, including the Guantanamo naval base and its infamous prison. This tour revealed his polemical views on immigration, so his combative role in fighting immigration reform was predictable. During tense negotiations in January 2018 to resolve immigration policy, Kelly roiled the waters when he

---

[24] Baker, "Kelly Amplifies Boss's Message," p. 18.

declared that some immigrants were simply "too lazy to get off their asses" to apply for legal status.

Kelly's worldview was more aligned with Trump than that of any other senior leader in the White House or the Cabinet, with the possible exception of Stephen Miller. He was the President's strongest backer of a wall on the border with Mexico, and compared Mexico to Venezuela, arguing that the United States must protect itself against the future collapse of both countries. Miller has become Trump's major speech writer, responsible for much of the president's bellicose language regarding immigrants and immigration.

In February 2018, Kelly hit a new low when he vigorously defended Rob Porter, the White House staff secretary, who was accused of physical abuse by his ex-wives as well as a recent girlfriend. Kelly defended Porter as a "man of true integrity and honor, and I can't say enough good things about him. He is a friend, a confidant and a trusted professional."[25]

Kelly's pathetic defense became more controversial when it turned out that it was written in part by Hope Hicks, then chief of communications for President Trump, who was Porter's girlfriend. Hicks had played a similar role in trying to write an apology for Corey Lewandowski, when he was Trump's campaign manager. When Hicks intervened to save the reputation of her boyfriend Corey, Trump chortled that she had "already done enough for him. You're the best piece of tail that he'll ever have," sending Hicks running from the Oval Office.[26] She resigned several months later.

The handling of the Porter disaster led many in the White House to rethink the view that Kelly's long service as a Marine would qualify him for the position

---

[25] Peter Baker and Maggie Haberman, "Unwelcome Attention for Man Who Came In To Calm Things Down," *New York Times*, February 9, 2018, p. 19.

[26] Michael Wolff, "Fire and Fury: Inside the Trump White House," New York: Henry Holt and Company, 2018, p. 204.

of chief of staff, particularly to a figure as unpredictable as Donald Trump. Even Leon Panetta, who was Bill Clinton's chief of staff and Kelly's former boss at the Pentagon as secretary of defense, was slow to recognize the general's lack of qualifications. Too many friends and associates of Kelly contended that his lack of experience in Washington "may not have attuned him to how the domestic abuse allegations against Mr. Porter would be perceived."[27] Kelly is not the only one in the White House without political and moral antennae.

The remaining appointments to the national security team also lacked the skills needed for decision making. The appointment of Rep. Pompeo (R-KS), a West Point graduate, to be Director of CIA was particularly worrisome. Like Flynn and Miller, Pompeo is a polemicist and Islamophobe who favored the Muslim ban and opposed the international nuclear accord with Iran. His leading characteristic was his political loyalty to Trump, which is not the best qualification for leading the CIA.

Pompeo immediately showed his true colors in the selection of his deputy, Gina Haspel, a key player in the CIA's policy of torture and abuse at secret prisons in East Europe and Southeast Asia. Pompeo had expressed regret at President Obama's declaration of an end to torture and, like Trump, favored restoring the sadistic practices. Haspel, for her part, was known at CIA headquarters as "Bloody Gina" for her promotion of torture and extraordinary renditions. There were films of the torture and abuse, and it was Haspel who sent the order to destroy them.

At CIA, Pompeo challenged intelligence assessments that concluded Iran was observing the Iran nuclear accord, which stopped it's nuclear weapons program. Pompeo distorted the intelligence community's assessment of Russian interference in the presidential election of 2016, arguing the assessment concluded Russian actions had no impact on the election itself. The intelligence

---

[27] Baker and Haberman, "Unwelcome Attention for Man," p. 19.

community was not tasked to pass judgment on the impact of Russian hacking into the computers of the Democratic National Committee. (Previous CIA directors who served on Capitol Hill—Porter Goss and George Tenet—also politicized intelligence to support presidents.)

In addition to appointing a deputy identified with torture and abuse, Pompeo challenged the diversity reforms that were a special project of his immediate predecessor, John Brennan. In the summer of 2017, the parents of Matthew Shepard who had been a victim of anti-gay violence were invited to speak to a CIA audience on diversity and LGBTQ rights. At the 11th hour, Pompeo cancelled the talk, questioning whether it would have any value to the CIA mission. Pompeo, an evangelical Christian, has never made a secret of his opposition to same-sex marriage and, as a congressman, sponsored legislation to weaken the rights of gay couples. Sources in the intelligence community noted that Pompeo attended weekly Bible studies in the CIA headquarters building, and referred to Christianity repeatedly in his remarks to CIA personnel.[28] Pompeo wanted to start a chaplaincy at the CIA similar to the institution in the military. There was no reason to expect that Pompeo was willing to tell truth to power, a major responsibility for the CIA director.

The appointment of former senator Dan Coats as the Director of National Intelligence brought into the decision-making circle another player without a background in strategic intelligence. Like all of Trump's appointments, Coats was selected primarily because of his neoconservative views in the domestic arena. Coats is a pro-life evangelical, who opposes both abortion and gay marriage. In the 1990s, he helped draft the cynical "Don't Ask; Don't Tell" policy that the Clinton administration supported to appease the Pentagon.

---

[28] Jenna McLaughlin, "More White, More Male, More Jesus: CIA Employees Fear Pompeo is Quietly Killing the Agency's Diversity Machine," *ForeignPolicy, com*, September 8, 2017, p. 4.

The only important "civilian" voice in the national security arena initially was Rex Tillerson, former chief of Exxon-Mobile, who was totally lacking in experience with geopolitical matters that confronted the United States. His confirmation testimony was laughable for its irrelevance and superficiality; his first trip abroad brought guffaws from his diplomatic counterparts in Germany; his State Department soon became an invisible member of the national security policy process. Of the top 24 positions on the department's hierarchy, only four had been filled when he was finally forced out in March 2018.

With general officers in charge of the Pentagon and the National Security Council as well as Chief of Staff to the President, the fact that the steward of the Department of State was a neophyte created a problem. Once the preeminent voice of U.S. foreign policy, the State Department stopped giving the regular press briefings that had been customary for the past 70 years. It was silent as the president shunned diplomatic agreements, such as the Paris Accord and the Iran nuclear agreement, and abandoned conventional U.S. foreign policy, including the two-state solution for Israel and Palestine. Instead of relying on his Secretary of State, Trump assigned a major role for Israeli-Palestinian talks to his inexperienced son-in-law, Jared Kushner.

Not since the McCarthy era of the 1950s had morale at the Department of State been so low as when Tillerson supported a reduction in the budget of nearly 30 percent as well as an elimination of more than 2,000 jobs. Tillerson personally blocked promotions for senior officers at the department, knowing that the "up or out" process of the department would hasten the departure of key officials. Like Trump, Tillerson had no understanding of the role of diplomacy in rebuilding the West European democracies, and managing the dissolution of the Soviet Union in 1991 and the reunification of Germany.

The work of diplomacy requires rigorous and intense negotiation for which an inexperienced president, a stable of general officers, and a neophyte secretary of state were not prepared. Tillerson never consulted previous secretaries of state prior to his confirmation hearings, and upon confirmation proceeded to hollow out the State Department. Senior assistant secretaries and ambassadors were purged and many were not replaced.

Nixon and Trump shared an animosity toward the Department of State that was evident in the appointment of ambassadors to serve the president. For Nixon, it was a class issue with his resentment of elite Ivy League professionals who traditionally occupy key positions at the Department of State. Nixon prided himself on naming ambassadors who were wealthy businessman and even labor leaders, whom he referred to as the "deese" and "dose" guys.[29] He believed that career diplomats tended to be timid bureaucrats, afraid to take bold stands. He dismissed them as a "bunch of eunuchs."

No administration in U.S. history has introduced so many unsavory characters to high-level positions in the government as the Trump administration. Trump promised to "hire the best people" and to "drain the swamp" in order to excite his following; he brought an incredible array of men and women without qualifications to create a swamp like no other. The assistant to the secretary of energy, Sam Bowdidge, was the manager of a Meineke Car Care Branch in New Hampshire, until he lost that job after referring to Muslims as "maggots." Assistants at the Department of Agriculture included Christopher Hagan, a "cabana attendant" at a Westchester Country Club, where his resume noted that he "identified and addressed customer's needs in a timely and orderly manner," and Nicholas Brusky, who drove a truck.[30] (Trump's domestic appointments will be fully evaluated in Chapter 6: "Trump's War on Governance.")

---

[29] Farrell, "Richard Nixon," p. 545.

[30] I am indebted to Dana Milbank for much of this information from his column in the *Washington Post* on November 2, 2017, "Trump's 'extreme vetting' applies to immigrants but not his appointments," p. 2.

One of the more bizarre appointments was Sam Clovis, a former Trump campaign aide, who was named science advisor to the Department of Agriculture despite having no relevant credentials. Clovis got caught up in special counsel Mueller's Russia probe because he supervised campaign foreign policy adviser, George Papadopoulos, who struck a plea deal on charges he lied to FBI investigators about his communications with Russian contacts.[31] Clovis bowed out on November 2, 2017, telling the president that the "political climate inside Washington made it impossible for me to receive balanced and fair consideration."[32] In actual fact, the nomination was in serious jeopardy because he lacked the agriculture or science credentials required for the position of undersecretary for research, education and economics. Clovis was one more example of a climate change skeptic being offered the position of chief scientist.

Clovis, a former talk radio host in Iowa, was also known for his inflammatory comments on race, women, the LGBT community, and Democrats. Clovis used his radio program to call former Attorney General Eric Holder a "racist black," and referred to former president Obama as a "narcissistic liar given a free pass because he is black." The fact that Clovis encouraged Papadopoulos to pursue meetings with Kremlin-linked contacts made confirmation problematic.

Trump's militarization of national security policy deepened the divide between the military and civilian worlds. Recent administrations, including those of Clinton, Bush, and Obama, catered to the military, and appointed too many general and flag officers to positions that should have been in the hands of civilians. Clinton deferred to the military in declaring the cynical policy of "don't

---

[31] The imbroglio between the White House and the FBI over the use of an informant in the Trump campaign in 2016 involved not only information gathered against Clovis and Papadopoulos for the contacts with Russian officials, but also Carter Paige. The three men are part of the investigation of Special Counsel Mueller regarding possible collusion between the Trump campaign and the Russian government.

[32] Andrew Restuccia, Josh Dawsey, and Helena Bottemiller Evich, "Trump USDA pick, linked to Russia probe, withdraws from consideration," *Politico*, November 2, 2017.

ask, don't tell;" Bush increased military power and influence with two wars in the Middle East and Southwest Asia; and Obama retained Bush's Secretary of Defense, Robert Gates, in order not to create concerns within the Pentagon regarding military reform. But Trump went overboard in deference to the military, ignoring the Founding Fathers' emphasis on civilian control of the military as well as the Constitutional emphasis on civilian decision making in the use of force and national security policy. Trump's first defense budgets created record spending for the Pentagon.

The militarization of policy under President Trump not only placed too much power in national security affairs to general officers, but anointed generals whose experience and background revolves around only one issue: the global war on terror. McMaster's Chief of Staff was three-star general, Keith Kellogg; both earned their high ranks fighting terrorism together in Iraq and Afghanistan. A prominent military analyst noted that most observers believe their familiarity "with the terrible cost of war" would make them "unlikely to support the military interventions that had marred the terms of the four previous presidents."[33] Unfortunately, we are witnessing the opposite as the generals favor greater military power in Iraq, Syria, and Afghanistan to support Trump's promise to "start winning wars again."

In 1997, then Secretary of Defense William Cohen, a Republican serving in a Democratic administration, warned about a "chasm developing between the military and civilian worlds where the military doesn't understand why criticism (of the military) is so quick and unrelenting." Others have noted a "gap" in values between the armed forces and civilian society, which could threaten civil-military cooperation as well as the military's loyalty to civilian authority. Liberals praise senior military officers who state they will not carry out illegal orders, but do we

---

[33] See Mark Perry, *The Pentagon's Wars: The Military's Undeclared War Against America's Presidents*, New York: Basic Books, 2018.

want a society where military officers determine the legality of presidential orders?

There is no more important task in political governance than ensuring that civilian control of the military is not compromised, and that the military remains subordinate to political authority. The Trump administration has fostered an imbalance in civilian-military influence that is more threatening to U.S. security than the military challenges in Iraq, Syria, and Afghanistan.

The die was cast four decades ago when President Nixon ended the draft and created a volunteer military. The Reagan administration endorsed the Goldwater-Nichols Act in 1986, which created regional commanders-in-chief (CINCs) with expanded military influence in geopolitical matters throughout the Third World that was once the province of the Department of State. CINCs became more influential than U.S. ambassadors and assistant secretaries of state.

The Goldwater-Nichols Act created a powerful chairman of the Joint Chiefs of Staff, and during the Desert Storm War in 1991 the Chairman often ignored the Secretary of Defense and personally briefed the president on war plans. The Act passed the Senate without opposition. The Department of State has never been weaker in the modern era, and the dominance of the Department of Defense over State has never been greater. Losing wars in Iraq and Afghanistan led to unnecessary increases in defense spending that required reduced domestic spending. Vice President Dick Cheney wanted a more powerful military (and even a war) to create a more powerful presidency. There is reason to believe that Stephen Bannon and Stephen Miller, who wrote Trump's passionately nationalistic inauguration speech, used the same playbook.

During the campaign, Donald Trump was critical of the military and promised to remove many general officers if elected. Conversely, too many politicians and pundits believe that the generals would act as "adults" and would moderate Trump's authoritarian tendencies, but the generals advanced their own agendas regarding the use of military force, expansion of the military budget, upgrading nuclear forces and creating a Space Command. Trump has created a national security phalanx that militarizes decision making and politicizes the military. The deployment of military forces to the border with Mexico before the mid-term elections of 2018 marked a new low.

— 2 —

DONALD TRUMP'S WAR ON DIPLOMACY

"President Trump grew frustrated with lawmakers in the Oval Office when they discussed protecting immigrants from Haiti, El Salvador, and African countries as part of a bipartisan immigration deal. 'Why are we having all these people from shithole countries come here?' Trump said. Trump then suggested that the United States should instead bring more people from countries such as Norway."

—*Washington Post*, January 12, 2018

"To refuse the obligations of international leadership for the sake of some half-baked, spurious nationalism cooked up by people who would rather find scapegoats than solve problems is unpatriotic."

—Senator John McCain, *The Restless Wave: Good Times, Just Causes, Great Fights, and Other Appreciations*, 2018

"What worries me most…is the fact that the rules based international order is being challenged" not by the "usual suspects, but by its main architect and guarantor, the United States."

—European Council President Donald Tusk, June 8, 2018 at the Group of Seven Summit in Quebec, Canada

Diplomacy is the art of conducting negotiations in the realm of international relations. It is the first tool of statecraft, designed to create opportunities for advancing policy interests with friends and foes. The Trump administration is unusual because there is no one in the White House on the national security team who appreciates the importance of diplomacy, let alone the conceptualization and implementation of diplomatic practice.

The decline of the Department of State in the Trump administration created an additional obstacle for the role of diplomacy. Moreover, the tension between the president and his first secretary of state was intense and counter-productive; the inexperience and obsequiousness of the second secretary of state created problems as well.

It is not unusual for presidents and secretaries of state to differ on policy and process. One of our very first secretaries of state, Thomas Jefferson, had major differences with President George Washington, and resigned from his office in 1793. Washington did not want to alienate the English government, and Jefferson's pro-France sympathies were intense. Jefferson's successor, Edmund Randolph, turned out to be a stronger Francophile than Jefferson, and was accused of treason because of his close ties to the French Ambassador to the United States. Randolph's relations with President Washington were even worse than Jefferson's, and he resigned in 1795 when Washington signed the Jay Treaty with England that gave pride of place to London on the U.S. diplomatic agenda.

Secretary of State William Jennings Bryan argued with President Woodrow Wilson and gave up his seal of office in 1915 without trying to explain himself. "I go out into the dark," Bryan said, for the "president has all the prestige and power on his side."[34] He knew that it would be futile to challenge the president of the United States. Like Randolph, he retired in bitterness and died in obscurity.

President John F. Kennedy was dissatisfied with the stewardship of his secretary of state, Dean Rusk. Prior to the Cuban missile crisis in 1962, Kennedy instructed Rusk to remove the Jupiter missile squadron in Turkey, which consisted of 15 intermediate-range missiles. With the deployment of Polaris

---

[34] Robert H. Ferrell, *American Diplomacy: A History*, New York: W. W. Norton and Company, 1969, p. 88.

strategic submarines to the Mediterranean in the early 1960s, the deployment of the liquid-fueled, "soft"-sited Jupiters had become obsolescent. Secretary of State Rusk approached the Turkish government in the spring of 1962, but the Turks opposed removal of the missiles.

Kennedy ordered Rusk to ignore the Turks and remove the missiles without their approval. He was mortified to learn that Rusk never carried out the order, which became particularly vexing when the Soviets justified having missiles in Cuba on the basis of U.S. missiles in Turkey on the Soviet border. The United States ultimately agreed secretly to remove the missiles some months after the removal of Soviet missiles and TU-28 bombers from Cuba.

In the wake of the missile crisis, Kennedy and Rusk crossed swords again over a key diplomatic issue. The president had ordered his advisors never to claim victory over the Kremlin as a result of Moscow capitulation to U.S. demands. It was Rusk, our senior diplomat, who publicly remarked, "we were eyeball to eyeball, and Moscow blinked."

Trump's innate nationalism and xenophobia prevent the conduct of diplomacy in a traditional or rational way. These traits were displayed in Trump's targeting of President Obama's legacy. In addition to pulling out of the Paris climate accord and decertifying the Iran nuclear accord, Trump denigrated the normalization of relations with Cuba, which took two years of secret diplomacy. Trump has even threatened to leave the NATO alliance that was established seven decades ago, and has no understanding of arms control and disarmament, a part of presidential agendas since President Dwight D. Eisenhower introduced the open skies initiative in the 1950s. In abrogating the Intermediate-range Nuclear Forces Treaty, he walked away from the first disarmament accord to abolish an entire class of nuclear weapons. This is the first administration since the 1950s to lack an arms control agenda or fail to demonstrate interest in disarmament.

31 | AMERICAN CARNAGE

Trump's authoritarian style complicates his handling of international issues. In June and July 2017, for example, Trump caused a crisis with our European allies, including a diplomatic imbroglio with our closest ally, and mishandled a summit meeting with Russian President Putin.

In an unprecedented display of arrogance and boorishness, Trump blew up the Group of Seven summit in Canada on June 9 and 10, 2018. He repudiated an agreement he had made with allied leaders only hours earlier, and insulted his Canadian host, Prime Minister Justin Trudeau. In a trio of *ad hominem* attacks, Trump referred to Trudeau as "weak and dishonest;" Larry Kudlow, Trump's senior economic adviser, accused Trudeau of "stabbing us in the back;" and—worst of all—Peter Navarro, Trump's top trade adviser, said "there's a special place in hell" for Trudeau.[35]

Trump's conduct was shocking but not surprising. Since assuming the presidency, he has turned his back on the international order and treated traditional allies with contempt. Trump was cool toward German Chancellor Angela Merkel from the start. Merkel, who grew up in East Germany under Soviet occupation, was particularly incensed by Trump's accusation that "Germany…is captive to Russia because it's getting so much of its energy from Russia."[36]

Trump castigated British Prime Minister Theresa May who was irate over the President's exploitation of anti-Muslim propaganda from a fascist group in Britain. He treated French President Emmanuel Macron dismissively and trumpeted Macron's low approval ratings at home. Macron struck back by rejecting the president's "America First" agenda, exposing Trump as a leader of a country that is looking out only for itself.

---

[35] Dan Bilefsky and Catherine Porter, "Canadians Rally Behind Trudeau After Scorn From Trump and His Team," *The New York Times*, June 11, 2018, p. 5.

[36] Ruby Mellen, "Trump's Global Year in Perspective," *The Washington Post*, January 1, 2019, p. 6.

After his first face-to-face meeting with Putin at an economic summit in Germany, Trump accepted the Russian leader's denial of any role in manipulating the presidential campaign of 2016, thus separating himself from the assessment of the U.S. intelligence community. Putin told Trump that, if Russia interfered in the election, "we wouldn't have gotten caught because we're professionals."[37] Trump remarked that was a good point because the Russians "are some of the best in the world" at hacking. Trump then created greater concerns with the two-hour meeting by taking his interpreter's notes and instructing her not to brief anyone. Not even Trump's national security team has a genuine understanding of the exchange between the two men.

Trade disputes are part and parcel of the Trump administration. He has started trade wars with our closest allies, and threatened sanctions against European countries that trade with Iran. In August 2018, he boldly announced changes to the North Atlantic Free Trade Agreement (NAFTA), which was second only to "the wall" as a campaign issue for Trump. But the new agreement with Mexico could lead to lower productivity, higher prices for consumers, and a less competitive automobile industry in North America, which will have difficulty competing with European and Asian car producers. The new NAFTA is a defeat for the rules and regulations of the World Trade Organization, which relies on goodwill and not Trump-style bullying.

The Trump administration has demonstrated no interest in using political and economic diplomacy to create opportunities for advancing bilateral and multilateral relations. A diplomatic approach toward our European and Asian allies, who traditionally give a new U.S. president the benefit of the doubt, would have created opportunities for closer relations. Similarly, in the case of China, a broad diplomatic approach would have created openings for improved relations

---

[37] Peter Baker, "Trump and Putin: Five Meetings Infused with Mystery," The New York Times, January 16, 2019, p. 6.

on the peninsula between North and South Korea as well as less tension between China and Japan. Instead, we faced a trade and tariff war with China, and worsened relations with Asian allies such as Japan and South Korea. Trump's hard line toward Europe is opening diplomatic opportunities for Russia; the hard line in Asia is giving greater opportunity to China.

The U.S. pressure for greater European defense spending is a specious issue. The combined defense budget of NATO nations has grown by nearly $15 billion in the past several years, with the increases beginning in President Obama's second term. Every NATO country but one is increasing its defense spending, and all but two are sending troops to NATO overseas missions. At least sixteen nations are on track to spend 2 percent of their gross domestic product on defense by 2024, the target set by the Obama administration in 2014. The European NATO nations, moreover, spend more than $300 billion on defense, which is eight times Russian defense spending. The real issue is why does the United States spend so much on defense, not whether the European nations spend enough.

The Trump administration is making no effort to capitalize on its leverage with Russia, which would require diplomatic skills. Trump has the advantage politically of a strong American economy, while Putin faces a worsening economic situation that requires easing of Western sanctions. U.S. and European sanctions on Russia in the wake of Moscow's seizure of Crimea in 2014 has prevented any real growth in the Russian economy. The oil boom that boosted Putin's popularity in the wake of Boris Yeltsin's leadership is over, and the cost of living for most Russians has become increasingly burdensome. In July 2018, the Russian Duma had to raise value-added taxes and the pension age to increase revenues. As a result, Putin is the demandeur for sanctions relief and direct foreign investment, but this opportunity has been ignored.

The president's awkward and authoritarian style was displayed in the on-again/off-again summit meeting with North Korean leader Kim Jong Un that took place on June 12, 2018. On one level, there was evidence of incompetence and mismanagement of foreign policy as Trump became the "wild card" in the negotiations between Washington and Pyongyang. Kim Jong Un emerged as a reasonable conciliator in discussions over the fate of the Korean peninsula. The administration was divided over the wisdom of holding high-level talks with the Korean leader, but Trump's national security team was particularly perplexed by the twists and turns of Trump's utterances. And when Trump decided on a conciliatory approach toward Kim Jong Un, he was countered by Secretary of State Pompeo's bombastic remarks. As a result, the North Korean leader has ignored the secretary of state, and focused his efforts on the president.

The Singapore summit produced a vague communique that referred to the "denuclearization of the Korean peninsula" with no timetable, no specifics, and no reference to verification. In fact, Trump said "We don't have to verify, because I have one of the great memories of all time. So I don't have to, okay?"[38] The only specific concession was from the United States, which announced a pause in military exercises with South Korea, a huge surprise to the Joint Chiefs of Staff and the U.S. commanders in South Korea as well as to the South Korean leadership. Trump called the joint statement "comprehensive," but the document was mere political theatre and revealed no detailed discussions or agreements between the two sides.

The denuclearization of the Korean peninsula is a long way off, and it is difficult to imagine a serious disarmament treaty without verification. In view of the secret mobile deployment of North Korean nuclear weaponry, similar to Chinese deployments, there is no possibility that the U.S. intelligence community could provide military planners with definitive information on North Korea's nuclear inventory. U.S. intelligence does not know the actual number of North

---

[38] Philip Rucker, "Getting a good picture?: Trump, the producer in chief," *The Washington Post*, June 13, 2018, p. 9.

Korean nuclear weapons, let alone their location and disposition. The mobility of these weapons creates additional confusion and uncertainty.

In addition to Trump's unruly behavior, his national security team is the least qualified to conduct diplomacy in the post-war era, if not in the history of the United States. The appointment of so many general officers at the start reflected Trump's lack of interest in the role of diplomacy. The President's most unsuitable appointment was Rex Tillerson, the CEO of ExxonMobil, as secretary of state. There has never been a more acrimonious and dysfunctional relationship between a U.S. president and a secretary of state than the one between Trump and Tillerson. Their "wars" were constant.

Tillerson had been introduced to Trump by Robert Gates and Condoleeza Rice, former national security officials in the administration of President George W. Bush. Gates and Rice have a consulting firm; Tillerson and Exxon-Mobil were their clients, so they knew their man had no background in international relations and diplomacy. Nor did he have experience in dealing with the Washington decision making community. Their rationale for advocating Tillerson was to garner more influence and business for their firm.

The poor relations between Trump and Tillerson as well as the irrelevance of the Department of State made it certain that U.S. policy toward North Korea would be problematic from the start. Trump's war of epithets with Kim Jong Un found Tillerson to be an observer. Every time Tillerson called for talks to deal with North Korea's nuclear weapons program, Trump told the Secretary of State he was wasting his time. The verbal taunts between "Little Rocket Man" and "Big Rocket Man" over their nuclear buttons were unprecedented in the nuclear age.

When Tillerson said on December 12, 2017 that he favored talks "without preconditions," the White House and the National Security Council went ballistic.[39] National Security Adviser McMaster sided with the president. Exactly seven months later, however, Trump and Kim Jong Un held their first summit meeting in Singapore, indicating that Tillerson's favored approach could be made to work.

The one area of cooperation between the president and his first secretary of state was their combined efforts to weaken the role of the Department of State and the Foreign Service. The call to reduce the department's budget by 30 percent and the lost of two thousand career diplomats would cripple the global reach of the Department of State. While the military budget continues to expand, reaching Trump's goal of more than $700 billion, the investment in diplomacy is threatened. The war on diplomacy led to significant resignations from the Foreign Service as well as a sharp decline in those people willing to take the rigorous examination to enter the Foreign Service.

Even before his confirmation was complete, Tillerson forced out six of the top career diplomats, including Patrick Kennedy who had been appointed to his position by President George W. Bush. Kristie Kennedy, the department's counselor and one of just five career ambassadors, was fired as well. None of these individuals was given a reason for the action, although several had been reprimanded for answering queries from Trump's pick for Ambassador to the United Nations, Nikki Haley. Haley had been rumored as a successor to Tillerson; as a result, there was bad blood between them.

In a Town Hall talk to 300 Foreign Service Officers and State Department officials in December 2017, Tillerson conceded that he had never met, let alone had a discussion, with a U.S. diplomat.[40] Few laughed when Tillerson jocularly noted that he had not known a single person in the department when Trump

---

[39] Mark Landler, "White House Corrects Tillerson on North Korea Talks," *The New York Times*, December 14, 2017, p. 10.

[40] Gardiner Harris, "No Embassy Move Soon, Tillerson Says," *The New York Times*, December 13, 2017, p. 18.

tapped him to run it. He added that "more importantly, I didn't know anything about your culture, didn't know what motivates you, didn't know anything about your work, or how you get your work done."[41] He then blithely referred to his plans to reorganize the department, referring to 300 ideas, 150 "identifiable projects," 16 "keystone projects" and the introduction of "tiger teams" to handle implementation.

Tillerson was the very embodiment of the second aspect of the Peter Principle that finds those elevated to positions for which they are not qualified turning the job into the only thing with which they are familiar. In the case of Tillerson, he used his CEO training to turn to efficiency-driven management consultants, which had nothing to do with his role as the nation's steward for foreign policy.

Tillerson stated that the heel-dragging on personnel appointments was due to the need to conduct reorganization, but the woman he named to study and implement the reorganization, Mary Elizabeth Maliz, resigned in November 2017 after several months on the job. She stated that she could not capture the secretary's attention and was being undermined by her deputy Christine Ciccone, who managed staffing for Tillerson and whose father was a lawyer with the Republican National Committee. Maliz understood that reorganization was a smokescreen for drastic personnel cuts. Tillerson knew neither woman before they arrived; they were picked by the White House and not the Department.

Six months after Tillerson's confirmation, there were still more than 70 unfilled ambassadorships, along with scores of other vacant senior postings. When Tillerson called for diplomacy to resolve the U.S.-North Korea conundrum, he was dismissed by Trump; he had no role in the delicate Israeli-Palestinian peace talks that were dominated by three Zionists: Trump adviser and

---

[41] Harris, "No Embassy Move Soon."

son-in-law Jared Kushner; Ambassador to Israel David Friedman; and Trump confidant Jason Greenblatt. He failed in his efforts to keep Trump from leaving the Paris climate accord, and decertifying the Iran nuclear accord.

Tillerson's botched reorganization plans and his support for Trump's plan for huge cuts in the Foreign Service assured tensions between the new secretary of state and his diplomatic cadre. Senior members of the Foreign Service were offered $25,000 buyouts at the end of 2017, a year marked by the lowest number of new entering officers in recent memory. In Tillerson's first year, the number of career ambassadors and career ministers—the highest ranks in the Foreign Service, equivalent to four- and three-star generals—were cut in half from 39 to 19. Minister-counselors, with two-star equivalent rank, were cut from 411 to 369, a 10% reduction.[42] Tillerson only filled ten of the top 44 political positions in the department, nominating no one to fill the vacant positions before he was replaced by CIA Director Pompeo in March 2018.

The vacancies at the senior level at the State Department were particularly harmful, and pointed to implementation of Stephen Bannon's plan to "deconstruct the administration state." Despite the war in Syria and increasing tensions between Saudi Arabia and Iran, Tillerson had no assistant secretary of state for the Middle East. Zimbabwe was undergoing a succession crisis, but there was no assistant secretary for Africa and no ambassador to South Africa, a country also dealing with succession issues. Many of the top experts on Africa and Latin America were fired or sidelined; one side effect was to cut deeply into the number of female officers at an institution that suffered from a diversity problem.

Nearly one year into Pompeo's stewardship and there were still no ambassadors in strategically important nations, including Saudi Arabia, Turkey, Jordan, Egypt, Qatar, Pakistan, and Australia. Thirty-eight additional countries

---

[42] Gardiner Harris, "Disquiet Increases at State Dept. While Tillerson Thins the Ranks," The New York Times, December 11, 2017, p. 1.

had no U.S. ambassador, and key regional bureaus such as East Asia and the Pacific as well as South and Central Asia had no directors at the assistant secretary level, which makes it difficult to discuss policy at a strategic level. Only one of the State Department's six under secretary positions had a Senate-confirmed appointee.

No administration in U.S. history has been slower in nominating appointees and getting them confirmed. A further problem is the mediocrity of those nominated, such as Doug Manchester to be ambassador to the Bahamas. In 2017, Manchester described the Bahamas as a protectorate of the United States, which came as a shock to the Bahamians who have historical ties to Britain.[43] The nominee for Morocco, David T. Fischer, a Michigan car dealer, failed to mention his involvement in a lawsuit in the confirmation process. Even James Carafano, a fellow at the Heritage Foundation and a member of Trump's transition team, called the problem of vacancies a "self-inflicted wound."

The United States finally named an ambassador to Germany in May 2018, and it proved to be a disaster. Ambassador Richard Grenell, an acolyte of Stephen Bannon, upset the Berlin government on his first day on the job, urging German companies to "wind down operations immediately" with Iran because President Trump had decided to unilaterally withdraw from the nuclear accord. Grenell, a former Fox News contributor, boasted about the wave of conservatism in Europe, which he wanted to "empower."[44] He expressed special admiration for Austrian Chancellor Sebastian Kurz, an extremist who heads a far-right coalition in Austria. Breaking with protocol, the ambassador invited Kurz to lunch during his visit to Berlin in May 2018.

---

[43] Gardiner Harris, "Administration Revives Use of Special Envoys," *The New York Times*, August 21, 2018, p 14.

[44] *The New York Times*, editorial, "Mr. Trump's Man in Berlin," May 11, 2018, p. 22.

The situation in Asia was similar. Tillerson had no assistant secretary of state for Asia, and no ambassador to South Korea despite the crisis on the Korean peninsula. Tillerson tried to name a genuine expert on the Korean peninsula, Victor Cha, who had served in the Bush administration, but President Trump deep-sixed the nomination. Cha had received agreement from the South Korean government, but when he dismissed Trump's threat of a preemptive strike against North Korea, Trump pulled the rug out from under him.

By the time Tillerson was fired, there was no one in charge of arms control, human rights, trade policy, or the environment. Tillerson left without having an impact on any key policy debate. Fittingly, he was on a commode in Africa dealing with food poisoning when he received a Twitter message from the president in March 2018, announcing his replacement, CIA director Pompeo.

The sad state of morale at the Department of State was Tillerson's legacy. The personnel of the Department of State have not been this demoralized since the attacks in the 1950s from the late Senator Joseph McCarthy (R-WI). A sense of intimidation obviously exists within the Department of State as its lobbying organization, the American Foreign Service Association, remained quiet throughout. Foreign Service Officers created a lottery to predict Tillerson's departure, referred to as "Rexit," with most entries saying that the secretary would be home for Christmas 2017. Well, he was home for Easter 2018.

Months before Pompeo was named secretary of state, the rumor mill was rife with stories that he or U.N. Ambassador Haley would replace Tillerson. Tillerson's diplomatic ignorance was matched by Ambassador Haley, whose appointment registered one more setback to U.S. diplomacy. She had no diplomatic or international experience, and she soon made this obvious with her irresponsible tirades. In her very first public statement as ambassador, Haley chilled her international counterparts with an extraordinary salvo: "For those who don't have our backs, we're taking names," which she repurposed with the hashtag: #Taking Names. She made bellicose remarks regarding Iran and North

Korea, and warned Syria that the United States was "locked and loaded" before the actual cruise missile attack in March 2018.

Haley and Pompeo were ideological hardliners and Trump loyalists, but rivals for face time in the White House. Haley's sudden decision to resign her UN post at the end of 2018 probably reflected her defeat in the contest with Pompeo for Trump's approval. It was difficult to imagine things getting any worse at the Department of State, but Pompeo's swagger has threatened to make it so.

Pompeo inherited a hollowed out Department of State lacking 13 assistant secretaries of state; 6 deputy and undersecretaries; and nearly 40 ambassadors. As a result of Tillerson's unpopularity in slashing funding and personnel levels, Pompeo faced a low bar in rebuilding morale. His support for lifting of the hiring freeze on family members of diplomats assigned abroad made a huge impact. Pompeo actually had no choice because the Congress's funding decisions in March, before Pompeo was on board, had ended this particular freeze.[45]

As bad as Tillerson's stewardship proved to be, naming Pomeo to succeed him created additional problems. Pompeo immediately rebranded the department as the "Department of Swagger," but there was no sign of a greater role for the institution in implementing foreign policy. Pompeo's experience for the job of running the CIA was limited; he had less credibility to be the nation's leading diplomat. Throughout his congressional career, Pompeo displayed support for military force and a contempt for diplomatic negotiation. He made false accusations about the links between American Muslims and terrorism, and made damning statements on the LGBT community that compromises any concern for advancing global human rights.

Pompeo, the most conservative secretary of state in recent U.S. history, was a former tea party congressman from Kansas. He has been a longtime beneficiary

---

[45] Gardiner Harris, "After Nudge, Pompeo Lifts Hiring Freeze At State Dept.," *The New York Times*, May 11, 2018, p. 14.

of the neoconservative Koch brothers (Charles G. and David H.), who reside in Pompeo's home district in Wichita. Like the Koch brothers, Pompeo, a denier of climate change, opposes the Paris climate agreement, and refuses to believe that human activities are responsible for the warming of the atmosphere. He took great satisfaction from the U.S. rejection of the Paris agreement, the only member of the UN to do so.

Pompeo's military background helps to explain his support for the use of military force. He graduated first in his class from West Point in 1986, and served as a tank commander in Germany from 1986 to 1991. When he left the military, he received venture funding from Koch Industries to buy an aircraft parts manufacturer. With the possible exception of General Alexander Haig, there has never been a secretary of state with more bombastic language or policy views. His bad temper in congressional testimony will complicate any effort to seek bipartisan solutions to foreign policy problems.

Pompeo is an aggressive "American Firster" in an administration running from international agreements and international comity. The international arena is facing the worst refugee crisis in modern history, with more than 60 million refugees, but the United States is the only member of the Security Council to withdraw from the UN Commission on Global Migration and Refugees. The refugee rights program coordinator at Human Rights Watch, Bill Frelick, termed the United States's withdrawal a "head-in-the-sand" denial of a basic reality of human history."[46] Tillerson previously weakened the Department's offices tasked with preventing violent conflict and mass atrocities, which benefits authoritarian regimes in Kenya, Burundi, Sri Lanka, and the Democratic Republic of Congo.

Pompeo and Haley had their differences but they shared hard-line position on migrants and refugees. Both believed that any agreement on migrants and

---

[46] Rick Gladstone, "U.S. Quits Talks on a U.N. Migration Pact, Saying It Infringes on Sovereignty," *The New York Times*, December 12, 2017, p. 14.

refugees would infringe on U.S. sovereignty. Haley, a child of Indian immigrants, argued that U.S. "decisions on immigration policies must always be made by Americans and Americans alone."[47] This is reminiscent of the debate on the formation of the UN when neoconservatives wanted no U.S. role in the United Nations, and a later debate that favored moving the UN out of the United States. The backwards step on immigration comes at a time when there are more than 60 million displaced persons around the world, the largest figure since the Second World War.

Haley's delivered her hard-line views in December 2017 on the eve of a UN conference on migration in Mexico, where the United States was supposed to be an active participant. There is a special urgency in this discussion because of the growing refugee crisis as a result of the wars in the Middle East, Africa, and parts of Asia. The chaos of cross-border migration has created a political backlash in Europe, where right-wing populist parties are increasing their influence in Germany, Austria, France, Poland, and Hungary. The callous disregard for victims of international conflict matches Trump's domestic programs that ignore the disadvantaged at home.

Pompeo's first major public speech as secretary of state took place on May 20, 2018 at the Heritage Foundation, the Washington mecca for neoconservatives, where he delivered a hard- line polemic on Iran with no hint of an opening for diplomacy. Pompeo threw down the gauntlet to Iran, calling on the Iranian people to overthrow its government. He insinuated support for the use of military force, warning that, if Iran restarted its nuclear program, the United States "will respond."[48] Pompeo consistently cited objectionable aspects of Iran's foreign policy that have nothing to do with the nuclear agreement. He never

---

[47] Gladstone, "U.S. Quits Talks on a U.N. Migration Pact," *The New York Times*, December 12, 2017, p. 14.

[48] Gardiner Harris, "In Hard-Line Speech, Pompeo Criticizes Iran's Behavior," The New York Times, May 21, 2018, p. 14.

acknowledged that Iran observed every aspect of the nuclear accord. As a congressman, Pompeo called for "2,000 sorties to destroy the Iranian nuclear capability."

As CIA director, Pompeo ignored the CIA charter that prohibits policy advocacy and made the case for regime change in Iran and North Korea. He went outside the lines of CIA's intelligence analysis on the Iran nuclear accord, and took advantage of every opportunity to denounce Iran as a "despotic theocracy" or a "pernicious empire that is expanding its power across the Middle East."[49] He did not directly challenge CIA's judgment that Iran was living up to the agreement's terms, but as secretary of state he will be able to do so. It is rare for Foreign Service Officers to challenge the authority of the secretary of state; not even senior leaders do so. Pompeo faced substantive limits imposed by National Intelligence Estimates at the CIA; he faces no political limits at Foggy Bottom.

In walking away from the Iran nuclear accord, Trump and Pompeo drove a wedge between the United States and its key European allies as well as with Russia and China. There was no better example in recent years of the importance of diplomacy than the Joint Comprehensive Plan of Action, better known as the Iran nuclear deal. The deal blocked every pathway for Iran to develop a nuclear weapon, thus reducing the risk of another U.S. confrontation in the Middle East. Diplomacy transformed a potentially violent situation into an arena for political compromise. The trajectory toward war that had been fueled by threats and sanctions was reversed.

The Iran agreement took years of negotiation and extraordinary diplomatic skills to accomplish; it is impossible to imagine comparable substantive agreements in the Trump era. Trump decertified an agreement that had Iran's compliance, according to the International Atomic Energy Agency, the nuclear

---

[49] Scott Shane, "Trump-Pleasing Hawk Goes From Spy to Diplomat," *The New York Times*, March 14, 2018, p. 12.

watchdog for the United Nations, as well as the endorsement of the U.S. intelligence community. In its second quarterly report since Trump announced in May 2018 that the United States was leaving the accord, the IAEA concluded that Iran was within treaty limits on uranium enrichment levels, enriched uranium stocks and other items.[50] The agency noted that it conducted the access inspections needed to verify Iran's compliance.

Iran shut down enrichment at the once-secret, heavily fortified, underground facility at Fordow, south of Tehran. Iran disabled and poured concrete into the core of its plutonium reactor, which foreclosed the route to plutonium and uranium-based nuclear weapons. This activity is subject to IAEA supervision and inspection; no obstacles block the inspectors, including at sites that previously had never been inspected. Iran's acceptance of limits on research and development are another obstacle to its engaging in covert activity. Iran's commitments cover the next 10 or 15 years, and Iran remains a member of the Non-Proliferation Treaty.

Thus, Trump and his "war cabinet" walked away from an intrusive disarmament agreement, unswayed by the intelligence community. If Trump produced the kind of agreement with North Korea that President Obama and Secretary of State Kerry obtained with Iran, Trump would be eligible for the Nobel peace prize he seeks. Even then Secretary of Defense Mattis and Chairman of the Joint Chiefs of Staff Joseph Dunford testified that remaining in the Iran deal was in our national security interest. The survival of the accord in view of Trump's reimposition of sanctions against Iran is now questionable, but the European nations are doing their best to keep it alive.

Another member of Trump's national security team would like the nuclear disarmament regime to collapse, possibly to justify the use of military force.

---

[50] "IAEA: Iran is abiding by nuclear restrictions," Reuters, August 31, 2018, p. 9.

National Security Adviser Bolton requested the Pentagon last year to provide options for the use of force against Iran. Then Secretary of Defense Mattis and other military leaders "adamantly opposed" the idea of attacking Iran, and even Pompeo, who had taken a hard line against Iran, has not endorsed military action. Since Bolton has virtually eliminated policy discussions at the National Security Council, his one-on-one relationship with Trump carries extra influence. Bolton's bombastic managerial style also reduces the possibility of discussing the risks of any escalation with Iran.

Pompeo is creating havoc on another diplomatic front by attacking our European allies and our important international commitments. In a speech in Brussels, Belgium in December 2018 that was widely criticized, Pompeo maligned the security architecture that the United States created to prevent confrontations after WWII.[51] He targeted the United Nations, the European Union, the Organization of American States, and the African Union, the very institutions charged with maintaining regional stability. The World Bank the International Monetary Fund, and the World Trade Organization, created to secure economic stability, were also maligned. There has never been a secretary of state so undiplomatic in an august international setting and so critical of the very institutions that U.S. presidents—Democrats and Republicans—created.

The Trump administration's release of its National Security Strategy on December 18, 2017 confirmed Trump's "America First" thinking. The strategy review is supposed to consider the country's "worldwide interests, goals, and objectives," and to cite the use of "political, economic, military elements of national power," but the current rendition is primarily a rhetorical statement that confirms the dearth of strategic thinking in Washington. The Cold War language

---

[51] Gardiner Harris, "Pompeo Questions the Value of International Groups Like U.N. and E.U.," *The New York Times*, December 4, 2018, p. 16.

is a reversal of statements produced by the Bush and Obama administrations over the past two decades.

The absence of strategic thought in the statement is consistent with Trump's "seat of the pants" thinking that marked his campaign rhetoric from 2015-2016. The document's justification of the withdrawal from the Trans-Pacific Partnership and the Paris climate accord; the abrogation of the Intermediate-range Nuclear Forces Treaty; the handling of the North Korean and Russian summits; and the recognition of Jerusalem as Israel's capital weakened U.S. diplomatic positions and reinforced the notion of "America First." These decisions were opaque; there was no evidence of National Security Council deliberations on any of them.

Unlike Tillerson, who seemed to recognize the importance of U.S. relations with NATO and key European partners, particularly France and Germany, Pompeo does not do so. Trump has no regard for international alliances, not even NATO, and his secretary of state does not want to lead the Western community. In a typical display of offensive bluster aimed at our European allies, Trump told an audience in Montana in July 2018 that "We're the schmucks that are paying for the whole thing. I'll tell NATO, 'you've got to start paying your bills'."[52] Secretary of State Dean Acheson was "present at the creation;" it is possible Pompeo will be "present at the destruction."

Previous U.S. strategy statements acknowledged the changing climate as a threat to national security, but Trump's team downplays the climate issue by making it a subordinate issue in a section on "energy dominance" that highlights U.S. leadership as "indispensable to countering an anti-growth energy agenda."[53] The National Security Strategy is at odds with the Pentagon and the intelligence

---

[52] "Why NATO Matters," editorial, *The New York Times*, July 9, 2018, p. 22.

[53] See "National Security Strategy," Department of Defense, Washington, D.C., December 2017.

community, which highlighted the threat of climate change for the past several years, citing the danger of refugee flows due to droughts, intensifying storms, and rising sea waters.

The description of China and Russia as "revisionist powers" contradicts Trump's ostensible efforts to improve relations with Putin and Xi Jinping. It marks a shift from previous statements that emphasized the importance of these countries as potential partners in dealing with problems in North Korea and Iran. The Bush and Obama administrations deemphasized the role of nuclear weapons and made a pitch for arms control, but the Trump document refers to nuclear weapons as the "foundation of our strategy to preserve peace and stability."

The erratic nature of U.S. policy under Trump is regularly on full display. In August 2018, Trump announced that he was willing to meet with Iran's leaders "anytime they want" without preconditions. Nevertheless, Pompeo listed three conditions for engagement, including an Iranian "commitment to make fundamental changes in how they treat own people."

Trump gloats about his "great meeting" with Putin, while his national security team lambastes Russian interference with the November 2018 midterm elections. His solicitous approach toward North Korea is countered by the intelligence community's emphasis on North Korea's continued activity in developing ballistic missiles. Trump's announcement of troop withdrawal from Syria and Afghanistan had no support from the national security team, and was immediately challenged.

U.S. allies have no sense of the direction that Washington will take on international issues in view of the dissonance between the president and his national security team. Our European allies are most uncomfortable about Trump's hostility toward NATO and the European Union, and do not find the reassurances of his national security team as sufficient. Conversely, autocratic leaders around the world, particularly in China, the Philippines, Russia, Saudi Arabia, and Turkey have manipulated Trump's narcissism and have found themselves on good terms with the American president. Trump gives special treatment to Chinese President Xi Jinping, Russian President Putin, Philippines President Rodrigo Duterte, and even North Korea's Kim Jong Un.

Israeli President Benjamin Netanyahu maneuvered Trump into recognizing Jerusalem as the Israeli capital without any *quid pro quo*. Seventy years of U.S. policy were reversed without discussion, putting the lie to Trump's professed interest in a two-state solution for Israel and Palestine. Trump's key negotiators, were known for their hostility to Arab causes and partiality to Israel. Trump's evangelical and Jewish backers in the United States were euphoric; an overwhelming majority of the UN Security Council and the General Assembly was appalled.

Trump's threatened cuts in aid to the Palestinian Authority led Israeli officials to press the American president not to do so. The Israelis are responsible for the primitive conditions that exist in the Gaza, and they implored the United States not to reduce its assistance because the "economic situation of the people of Gaza is very important from a security perspective," according to the former intelligence chief of the Israeli military, General Eli Ben-Meir.[54] The Israelis have turned Gaza into an "outdoor prison," so they need to keep the situation under control. An Israeli professor at the Hebrew University disingenuously referred to the aid cuts as "brutal pressure from the United States," that "would be catastrophic" for Israel. Israel's hypocrisy on this issue is illustrated by its charge that relief agencies perpetuate the refugee problem, while valuing the contributions to health care and food assistance their aid provides.

American credibility in the Middle East plummeted when Trump recognized Jerusalem as the capital of Israel, which was accompanied by threats to cut off military and economic assistance to those countries that failed to support our

---

[54] Loveday Morris and Ruth Eglash, "Trump is warned against cutting aid to Palestinians," *The Washington Post*, January 4, 2018, p. 8.

position in the UN General Assembly. The vote against recognition of Jerusalem was a harsh rebuke as most West and East European states either voted against the United States or abstained. The final vote was 128 to 9, with 35 abstentions, as the United States could not garner support beyond the island states in the Pacific Ocean.

Trump's obsessive concern for trade deficits threatens a tariff war that serves no one's interest. The president believes that "trade wars are good, and easy to win," and from day one in the White House he ordered that all intelligence items on foreign countries include specifics of trade deficits. Meanwhile, Trump's back-and-forth statements on tariffs carry greater penalties for allies than adversaries; his failure to anticipate the negative domestic consequences of retaliation was noteworthy.

Trump's appointment of his trade representative, Robert Lighthizer, and his trade adviser, Peter Navarro, to handle trade and tariff negotiations with China placed two more hardliners in a sensitive position. In doing so, Trump bypassed Secretary of the Treasury Mnuchin and Secretary of Commerce Wilber Ross, who urged the president to avoid a trade war with China. Another moderate on trade issues with China, former director of the National Economic Council Gary Cohn, had a shouting match with Lighthizer on these issues, which led Chief of Staff Kelly to pull the combatants out of the Oval Office in the fall of 2017.[55]

Trump's coercive diplomacy against China not only threatens a trade war, but compromises U.S.-Chinese cooperation on climate control, clean energy, and the environment, which require the participation of the world's two largest economies. Cooperation between Beijing and Washington is also required for arms control and disarmament as well as the non-proliferation of strategic weapons, particularly regarding North Korea's development of fissile materials

---

[55] Glenn Thrush, "Trade Assigns Trade Warrior, a China Skeptic, to Make Peace with Xi," *The New York Times*, January 2, 2019, p. 11.

and missiles. Like so much of Trump's foreign policy, his anger toward China is driven by his irrational anger over trade deficits.

During the annual meeting of the UN General Assembly, Trump dined with leaders of four Latin American countries, who were treated to a diatribe that included the need for a "big, beautiful wall," the danger of the North American Free Trade Agreement (NAFTA), and a "military option" against Venezuela.[56] The fact that the U.S. president was considering war with its third-largest oil supplier didn't create much of a ruckus in the United States, but the presidents of Argentina, Brazil, Columbia, and Panama were shocked. According to a former senior U.S. official, the Latin American presidents found Trump uninformed and dangerously unpredictable, concluding "This guy is insane."

President Trump's juvenile use of Twitter posts was counterproductive, drawing strong protests. It is impossible to assess the meaning and implications of his random and chaotic twitter posts. Is he letting off steam or reassuring his base that the president is on-the-job? Richard Haass, president of the Council on Foreign Relations, cited Trump's more belligerent tweets and said: "This is our commander in chief. Think about it."[57] The losers in this mindless display have been the credibility of the president, his administration, and the nation itself.

Imagine that you were a foreign policy adviser or an intelligence officer in another country, and your job was to analyze U.S. foreign policy statements for your principal officer. There is no way to gauge the meaning of Trump's tweets, but perhaps there is some solace for foreign policy analysts in the fact that Trump's bark is often far worse than his bite, and that his words are rarely followed by actions.

---

[56] Susan Glasser, "Donald Trump's Year of Living Dangerously," *Politico*, January 2, 2018, p. 1.

[57] Steven Erlanger, "Countries See Executive Disorder in Trump's Foreign Policy Tweets," *The New York Times*, January 8, 2018, p. 8.

Conversely, one might conclude that the president is barking mad, and totally oblivious to the damage he is doing to the presidency and the United States. My travels in Europe over the past several years have gleaned that the most common words that Europeans use to describe the U.S. president could be translated as "lunatic" and "laughingstock." Europeans disbelieve that the United States could elect anyone with the limits that Trump displays, and European diplomats cite the confusion that Trump has created. These diplomats have no idea about what is happening in Washington; than again, neither do Americans.

The Trump administration has placed a higher priority on military sales to clients, although the greatest beneficiaries of U.S. military aid (Israel, Egypt, Afghanistan, Iraq, Pakistan, and Turkey) provide little return on our investment. Pundits believe that U.S. military aid is a source of leverage, but it is not. The United States is constantly embarrassed by Israeli actions despite the huge amounts of military aid that Israel has received. Israel has overwhelming military dominance in the Middle East; it doesn't need aid.

Egypt has received more than $60 billion in military and economic aid over the past three decades with no sign that Egyptian policy was susceptible to U.S. influence. Cairo adheres to the peace treaty with Israel because it is in Egypt's interest to do so, not because of U.S. assistance. Pentagon officials believe that close ties between U.S. and Egyptian armed forces helped the Egyptian military council become a force for social cohesion rather than repression. A retired commandant of the U.S. Army War College, Major General Robert Scales, has argued that "they learn our way of war...and they learn our philosophies of civil-military relations." Not so.

The Egyptian military is the dominant political force in the country. It is the richest (and most corrupt) institution in the country, and hardly needs U.S. largesse. There is no external security threat to Egypt that requires the huge weapons platforms that it demands. U.S. policy should be based on getting Egypt to establish a coalition government and a consensus-based transition process.

Cutting military aid to Egypt would give the United States an opportunity to reduce military assistance to Israel as well, sending a signal to U.S. clients that military aid will not dominate U.S. foreign policy.

The most futile example of U.S. military aid is Pakistan. The Bush and Obama administrations sent billions of dollars in aid to Islamabad, but Pakistan never stopped its double-dealing on pledges to fight the Afghan Taliban. At the same time, the United States has never used its assistance to promote democracy in Pakistan. The U.S. military presence in Pakistan contributes to militant anti-Americanism.

Military assistance to Iraq and Afghanistan does not foster U.S. influence. No sooner had U.S. forces withdrawn from Iraq than the Obama administration announced multibillion-dollar arms sales to Iraq, including advanced fighter aircraft, tanks, and helicopters. This deal was announced as the Iraqi government consolidated its authority, created a one-party Shiite-dominated state, and abandoned the U.S.-backed power-sharing arrangement. Iraq has improved its bilateral relations with Iran, raising the prospect that U.S. forces in the Persian Gulf could encounter U.S. weaponry in foreign hands in a future conflict.

With the United States winding down its combat role in Afghanistan, the Kabul government is demanding $4 billion annually for its military forces over the next decade. Afghanistan is unable to use the assistance that it receives, and unable to create a military force to counter the Taliban. The surge in Afghan soldiers killing U.S. and European military personnel, and the increased corruption in Afghanistan that is fueled by U.S. dollars argue for withdrawal and not for additional assistance.

Turkey has received huge amounts of military assistance, but U.S.-Turkish relations have seldom been worse due to differences over Syria, particularly U.S. support for Syrian Kurds. The violence in Istanbul's Taksim Square could one day match the combustion in Cairo's Tahrir Square, as Prime Minister Erdogan—Turkey's most important leader since Ataturk—is not receptive to demands for pluralistic democracy. Erdogan meanwhile has improved bilateral relations with Russia and Iran.

The United States gives military assistance to numerous countries that do not need it or do not deserve it because of serious human rights violations. The recent sale of $30 billion in arms to Saudi Arabia was ill-timed because that aid will contribute to war crimes the Saudis are committing in Yemen. Indonesia, a human rights violator, receives $20 million annually in military aid. Eastern European countries need economic and political stability, not U.S. weaponry.

Trump even resorts to "alternative facts" in dealing with heads of state. In March 2018, discussing the trade deficit with Canadian Prime Minister Trudeau, Trump misstated the trade numbers and spoke of a nonexistent deficit. Trump conceded later that "I didn't even know....I had no idea."[58] In June 2018, he reminded Trudeau that Canada was responsible for burning down the White House during the war of 1812. It was Britain. Trudeau retaliated that as "Canadians, we're polite, we're reasonable, but we will not be pushed around."[59] Trump also attacked U.S. allies who were "ripping off the United States for decades and pillaging the U.S. workforce."

Trump continues to bleat disingenuously that he inherited the worst international situation of any modern American president, which was rhetorically forceful but factually wrong. That is not to say that the world is not embroiled in crisis, including nightmares in Syria and Yemen; and violent conflicts in Iraq, Afghanistan, Somalia, and Nigeria. But his international inheritance was far less challenging than his predecessor's, which included failed military adventures in Iraq and Afghanistan as well as a nuclear imbroglio with Iran.

---

[58] Josh Dawsey, Damian Paletta, and Erica Werner, "Trump boasts of made-up claim in Trudeau meeting," The Washington Post, March 17, 2018, p. 8.

[59] Mellen, "Trump's Global Year," p. 6.

55 | AMERICAN CARNAGE

There was no international issue too small for the Trump administration's display of authoritarian behavior. In July 2018, the international community was poised to pass a resolution to encourage breast-feeding, sponsored by the World Health Assembly, a UN affiliate. At the last minute, the United States tried to block the breast-feeding accord, and threatened Ecuador, which had planned to introduce the resolution, with trade sanctions and cuts in military aid. The United States suffered a double diplomatic defeat when the resolution passed easily with little change to the original language, having been introduced by Russia.

This petty display by the United States was a key example of Trump's support for corporate interests on public health and environmental issues, which will be discussed in Chapter Six. In this case, the Trump administration was trying to rescue the $70 billion baby food industry, which is dominated by a small group of American and European companies. The costs are enormous; a British medical journal, *The Lancet*, concluded in 2016 that universal breast-feeding would prevent 800,000 child deaths annually and save $300 billion in health care costs.[60]

There was no diplomatic failure greater than Trump's response to Saudi Arabia's sadistic killing of a Saudi journalist, Jamal Khashoggi, in the Saudi consulate in Istanbul, Turkey. Khashoggi, a dissident, who was residing in the United States and writing for the *Washington Post*, was killed on the orders of Crown Prince Mohammed bin Salman in October 2018. Trump, a close supporter of Saudi policy, immediately campaigned for the exoneration of bin Salman, although the Central Intelligence Agency had reported with "high confidence" that the Crown Prince gave the order to carry out the killing.

International relations are simple for Trump. Latin American immigrants are rapists and criminals; African countries are "shitholes;" and Muslims from various countries don't belong in the United States. Even legal immigration is restricted,

---

[60] Andrew Jacobs, "U.S. Delegation Disrupts Accord On Breast Milk," The New York Times, July 9, 2018, p. 7.

and children are separated from their parents at the border. No wonder European Council President Donald Tusk remarked that "with friends like that who needs enemies."[61] Overall, most of Trump's problems have been self-inflicted by a president lacking the temperament and experience to manage U.S. statecraft.

Mark Twain once remarked that "if the only tool in your toolbox is a hammer, than all problems look like nails." Well, the only tool in the Trump administration's toolbox is clearly a hammer and the plan du jour threatens force. In Trump's first two years, there has been no diplomatic creativity to rival President Obama's exchange of diplomatic relations with Cuba or the Iran nuclear accord. The summit with North Korea initially promised a major change in East Asia, but the two sides are back to the starting point after a year's worth of feckless maneuvers. The president and his "war cabinet" have stepped up air strikes in the Middle East, Southwest Asia, and North Africa, with an increasing number of civilian fatalities.

Ever since the Spanish-American War in 1898, the United States has been a global power at the center of most diplomatic and military challenges that have confronted the international community. Since the end of WWII, Democratic and Republican administrations led the way in arms control and disarmament talks; regional conflict resolution; and crisis management. In both hard power and soft power categories, the United States has been the most important independent variable in the international arena. This is no longer the case.

Tillerson, treated so shabbily by the president, got a measure of revenge on May 15, 2018, when he gave the commencement address at the Virginia Military Institute in Lexington. Without mentioning Trump by name, Tillerson warned that our democracy was threatened by a growing "crisis of ethics and integrity."[62]

---

[61] Susan Rice; "How Trump Helps Putin," *The New York Times*; June 9, 2018, p. 23.

[62] Gardiner Harris, "In Rebuke of Trump, Tillerson Says Lies are a Threat to Democracy." *The New York Times*, May 16, 2018, p. 12.

He charged that when "our leaders seek to conceal the truth, or we as people become accepting of alternative realities that are no longer grounded in facts, then we as American citizens are on a pathway to relinquishing our freedom." He stunned his audience with the warning that the crisis of integrity would place American democracy in its "twilight years," and encouraged graduates to "look for employers who have high standards for ethical conduct." If Tillerson had these views in 2017, then perhaps he would not have decimated the Foreign Service, the apex of the American diplomatic establishment.

The deterioration of the Foreign Service, the capstone of the American national security establishment, harms American international interests because it punishes the men and women who manage development and humanitarian aid to Third World trouble spots; coordinate counterterrorism and narcotics programs; and challenge unfair barriers to U.S. trade and investment. It will be difficult and expensive to rebuild the Foreign Service, another institution compromised by Trump's wars.

Thus far, Trump's initiatives vis-a-vis Iran, North Korea, and Russia have been self-aggrandizing efforts to promote his own image without regard for implications and outcomes. Trump's discussion of "denuclearization" regarding North Korea has not led to genuine disarmament measures, and has created genuine apprehension in Japan and South Korea, our most important Asian allies. Trump's meeting with Putin in Helsinki has created confusion regarding U.S. goals and objectives, and has upset our European allies. Trump's offer to meet with Iran's President Rouhani without preconditions has not only confused our friends in the Middle East, but his own national security team shows signs of being perplexed. It is impossible to define Trump's broader policies with these nations and, as a result, his initiatives have not created the opportunities that follow sound diplomacy.

Trump has even attacked the bedrock of American Grand Strategy for more than 100 years, the importance of "Europe First" to U.S. national security.

Democratic and Republican presidents, including Theodore and Franklin Roosevelt, Woodrow Wilson, and Ronald Reagan, knew the importance of forging alliances with European allies; supporting multilateral institutions such as the United Nations; and embracing arms control and disarmament. In substituting "America First," Trump has turned his back on traditional diplomatic policy; labeled the European Union as a "foe;" and befriended authoritarian leaders around the world, including President Putin and Crown Prince Mohammad bin Salman. Like American governance, the pillars of our national security policy will have to be rebuilt when the Trump era ends.

– 3 –

TRUMP'S WAR ON NATIONAL SECURITY POLICY

"North Korean Leader Kim Jong Un just stated that the 'Nuclear Button is on his desk at all times.' Will someone from his depleted and food starved regime please inform him that I too have a Nuclear Button, but it is a much bigger & more powerful one than his, and my Button works."

 –Donald J. Trump, Tweet, January 2, 2018

Kim Jong Un "wrote me beautiful letters. And they're great letters. We fell in love."

 –Donald J. Trump, September, 2018.

Donald Trump's campaign for the presidency in 2015-2016 criticized the presence of U.S. military forces in Afghanistan, Iraq, and Syria. But he used the first two years of his presidency to make bellicose threats concerning the Middle East, particularly the role of Iran and the presence of the Islamic State (or ISIS). He supported the Saudi-led war in Yemen, a humanitarian nightmare, and made no attempt to temper the militancy of Israeli President Bibi Netanyahu. Trump's call for an "Arab NATO," a security alliance among Egypt, Jordan, and the Gulf states, went nowhere, but indicated he viewed military power as the answer to the instability in the Middle East.

On December 19 and 20, 2018, however, Trump unilaterally altered U.S. policy in the Middle East and Southwest Asia with a roll of the geopolitical dice, announcing the withdrawal of 2,200 U.S. troops from Syria and ordering the

Pentagon to withdraw 7,000 troops from Afghanistan, which would halve the U.S. presence there. Although Trump had given indications over the past several years of his discomfort with the U.S. involvement in the region and his preference for devoting fewer resources and less time to the conflicts, the withdrawal notices created shock and anger throughout Washington as well as capitals in Europe and the affected regions.

As a result, Secretary of Defense James Mattis abruptly resigned in protest, the first secretary of defense in U.S. history to do so. (On January 2, 2019, Trump told a Cabinet meeting that he "fired" Mattis.[63]) Although Mattis wanted to devote more resources to the China threat in the Asian Pacific and the Russian challenge in Europe and the Middle East, Mattis' letter of resignation emphasized the U.S. military presence in Syria and Afghanistan was essential to the success of any diplomatic bargaining in the region. Brett McGurk, the special presidential envoy to the coalition fighting the Islamic State, also resigned in protest.

National Security Adviser Bolton and Secretary of State Pompeo agreed in principle with the substance of Mattis' letter, but their diplomatic silence indicated a desire to stay on the president's team. Bolton's predecessor, Lt. Gen. H. R. McMaster, also had made the case for maintaining forces in Syria. Bolton and Pompeo were not on the same page, however, as the national security adviser wanted to keep U.S. troops in Syria until Turkey guaranteed it would not attack the Syrian Kurds, which infuriated Turkish President Erdogan. The secretary of state emphasized the United States would withdraw only after the Islamic State's last pocket of territory had been defeated. These contradictions at the top level of the national security team reflect the incoherence of the administration's national security policy.

---

[63] Maggie Haberman, "Upset With Mattis, Trump Says Resignation was 'Essentially' a Firing," *The New York Times,* January 3, 2019, p. 13.

61 | AMERICAN CARNAGE

Unlike Bolton and Pompeo, Mattis had gone to the mat with the president on several issues, beginning with his restrained use of force in Syria in the wake of Syrian President Assad's chemical weapons attacks against civilians. Before becoming secretary of defense, Mattis referred to Trump's border wall as "simplistic" and "absurd." He dragged his heels on Trump's ban on transgenders serving in the military, the creation of a Space Force, and a costly military parade in Washington, D.C. Mattis also understood the importance of allied partners such as Britain, France, and Germany, and the need for strong ties to the democracies in NATO that supported the United States in the wake of the 9/11 terrorist attacks and are part of the "Defeat-ISIS coalition."[64] Professional military officers consider allied nations to be "force multipliers."

Mattis' deputy, Patrick Shanahan, was named acting defense secretary, marking a victory for the military-industrial complex. Shanahan's professional background is almost entirely with the Boeing Corporation where he was senior vice president for operations. At the Pentagon, Shanahan scuttled a pledge to destroy the military's stockpile of cluster munitions, a weapon banned by more than 100 countries, He is an enthusiastic supporter of the Space Force, which senior military officers oppose, and has expressed no support for the importance of allies and alliances to national security policy.

At the start of his second year in the White House, Trump created the "war cabinet" he favors. In March 2018, he appointed individuals whose backgrounds suggested support for torture and abuse; military force; and even the use of nuclear weapons. The problem is no longer one of too many generals because CIA director Haspel, Secretary of State Pompeo, and National Security Adviser Bolton are civilians with a militant approach. We learned about the danger of chicken hawks in the Bush administration, when George W. Bush, Dick Cheney,

---

[64] "Full Text Of Letter To Trump From Mattis," *The New York Times*, December 21, 2018, p. 10.

and David Addington lied about Iraq's military arsenal and supported secret prisons and torture in the war on terror. The authorization for the use of force against Iraq in March 2003 was based on falsified intelligence that received congressional approval. This failure of congressional oversight marked a setback to constitutional governance and the separation of powers.

In naming Pompeo and Bolton, Trump garnered supporters for the madman theory of international relations. Ironically, Daniel Ellsberg, who famously leaked the Pentagon Papers, introduced the madman theory in his lectures in 1959 to Henry Kissinger's Harvard seminar on the political use of irrational military threats. Ellsberg called the theory the "political uses of madness," believing that an extreme threat would be more credible if the person making the threat were perceived as not being fully rational. Ellsberg believed that irrational behavior could be a useful negotiating tool, although he couldn't imagine an American president acting irrationally.

Kissinger, who became Nixon's national security adviser ten years later, said that he "learned more from Dan Ellsberg than any other person about bargaining." And in his book "Nuclear Weapons and Foreign Policy," he advocated a "strategy of ambiguity" in any discussion of the use of tactical nuclear weapons. Nixon's madman theory was an extension of Kissinger's belief that power was not relevant unless one was willing to use it.

Nuclear weapons were not used in Vietnam, but the secret war in Cambodia and the unconscionable carpet bombing in Vietnam were desperate acts to convince Hanoi to make concessions to the United States. The tactics elicited no concessions from Hanoi nor did they curtail the operational abilities of North Vietnamese forces, but Kissinger loved "playing the bombardier" along with his military aide, General Alexander Haig. Kissinger enjoyed screening the raids and reading raw intelligence on the bombing. Nixon and Kissinger believed in the logic of escalation, although the results in Vietnam were futile.

During the campaign, Trump displayed madman tendencies. He vowed to "take out" the families of suspected terrorists and, as president, he asked "Why did you wait?" when observing footage of a drone crew holding fire until a target had moved away from a house with family members inside. Trump made radical changes to our lethal-force policies without informing Congress or the American people. He ended Obama's efforts to exercise greater control over the use of force, particularly to limit the risk to innocent civilians. Congress, which has relinquished its role in war powers, never demanded an explanation of Trump's changes.

Trump and Bolton have talked irresponsibly about nuclear weapons, and displayed an impulsiveness and explosiveness that points to megalomania. The thought of Trump and Bolton discussing the use of force as part of a "madman" policy is frightening. Trump told interviewers that there is no point in having nuclear weapons if we are not willing to use them. Bolton still defends the use of force in Iraq, and favors it in dealing with both Iran and North Korea. Their abrogation of the Intermediate-range Nuclear Forces Treaty could initiate a new nuclear arms race among the major powers.

Two former secretaries of state, Condi Rice and Rex Tillerson, refused to accept Bolton as a deputy secretary because of his extreme views and his brutal treatment of underlings. Bolton described his job of national security adviser as ensuring that the bureaucracy does not impede the decisions of the president. He ignores the primary task of the national security adviser to be an honest broker, bringing different views to the president. This has never been Bolton's *modus operandi*.

Bolton rarely convenes his cabinet colleagues, known as the principals committee, for policy discussions. The decisions regarding troop withdrawals from Syria and Afghanistan involved no discussion by the National Security Council, which should have prepared policy papers for dealing with Congress, our allies, and the press. Bolton hasn't appointed a deputy to manage the NSC, which is needed because of his busy overseas travel.

Mattis' resignation means that the generals whom Trump appointed initially and described as "handsomer than Tom Cruise" would not be around for the second half of the President's first term. Regarding Mattis, Trump asked his Cabinet principals on January 2, 2019, "What's he done for me? How has he done in Afghanistan? Not too good."[65] He added that he wasn't "happy" with what Mattis did in Afghanistan, and "I shouldn't be happy." A series of retired general officers rose to Mattis' defense and lambasted the president, which points to the beleaguered state of civilian-military relations in the United States.

It would take an extremely unusual general officer to handle one of the high ranking positions in the national security arena, but being subordinate to Trump was too much for Generals McMaster, Kelly, and Mattis. In June 2017, when Mattis hosted a meeting for the president in the Pentagon's "Tank," the secretary of defense tried to explain the importance of U.S military and economic alliances to our security. Trump replied: "This is exactly what I don't want."[66] Mattis likened the president's worldview to "traveling on a plane and putting on your oxygen mask before helping others."

General George C. Marshall who served as President Truman's Secretary of Defense and Secretary of State was certainly the gold standard for holding posts that should be in civilian hands. More recent examples have not fared so well. Admiral Stansfield Turner, director of CIA during the administration of President Carter, was an admirable and hard-working officer, but his lack of exposure to Washington politics made him vulnerable to the manipulations of national security adviser Zbigniew Brzezinski, who would not share power with the CIA

---

[65] Haberman, "Upset With Mattis," p 13.

[66] Henry Olson, "Trump is now forging foreign policy. Where will he take us?," *The Washington Post,* December 21, 2018, p. 21.

chief. General Colin Powell, George W. Bush's secretary of state, is admired by many, but it was telling that he looked away from military abuses as a junior officer in Vietnam in the 1960s, and supported an Iraqi war he opposed while serving as secretary of state. Vice President Dick Cheney engineered Powell's address to the United Nations in February 2003 to justify the invasion, and heavily influenced the specious text that the CIA prepared.

There are political and cultural differences that make a professional military background the wrong skill set for key national security positions. The all-volunteer military has drifted too far from the norms of American society; it is inordinately right-wing politically, and is much more religious—and fundamentalist—than America as a whole. The fact that the senior officer corps has been "Republicanized" is well established. Too many career military officers believe their moral code is superior to civilian norms, and there is constant criticism within senior military ranks about the moral health of civilian society.

Senior officers have opposed cultural change since World War II, opposing the service of African Americans, women, and homosexuals in their ranks. Secretary of Defense Robert Gates and the Pentagon's military leadership worked to undermine President Obama's call for an end to President Clinton's cynical policy of "don't ask, don't tell," which was a sellout to the Pentagon and compromised the place of gays in the military. President Obama had to deal with the insubordination of General Stanley McChrystal and his senior staff as well as those officers who lobbied on Capitol Hill to increase forces in Afghanistan when the White House was trying to withdraw from this quagmire.

Unfortunately, the service academies and the war colleges devote insufficient time to studying U.S. political culture or the traditions of civil-military relations. The commandant at the National War College in the late 1980s, in the wake of the Iran-Contra revelations, which found military officers ignoring their own code of conduct, even reduced the number of hours devoted to U.S. policy and politics—just when these hours should have been expanded. I was part of a faculty delegation arguing against these cuts, stressing that the curriculum should make sure that senior officers understood the U.S. society, particularly the rule of law.

In an exasperated moment, I told the commandant, Major General Walter Stadler, that we were trying to keep his soldiers out of jail. One of my faculty colleagues who was not part of the delegation, a navy captain, helped to stuff sensitive documents into Fawn Hall's bra in one of the more bizarre aspects of the Iran-Contra coverup in the 1980s. The indictment and sentencing of Lt. Gen. Michael Flynn was a stark reminder of the failure of general officers to recognize the political norms of democratic government. Stadler, moreover, tried to dissuade me from testifying to the Senate intelligence committee in 1991 after I had been subpoenaed, which is a federal crime.

There is no more important task in political governance than making sure that civilian control of the military is not compromised and that the military remains subordinate to political authority. The National Security Strategy that was released in December 2017 referred to "Competitive Diplomacy" and not cooperation under the heading of "Diplomacy and Statecraft," which reveals a dangerous mindset that works against conciliation and compromise. Secretary of State Pompeo refers to the Department of State as his "Department of Swagger."

NORTH KOREA

Of all the anxiety-producing scenarios that preoccupy us these days (e.g., Iran, Syria, Afghanistan, and worsening relations with Russia and China), nothing compares to Trump's nuclear brinksmanship with North Korea in his first year. Even in the worst years of the Cold War, we didn't have leaders with nuclear nicknames such as "Big Rocket Man" (President Trump) or "Little Rocket Man" (Kim Jung Un). Addressing the North Korean leader, President Trump boasted that his "nuclear button is much bigger and more powerful" than yours, and "my button works." The exchanges between the two leaders were juvenile and potentially deadly

The bellicose language ignored the fact there are more than tens of millions of Koreans living on either side of the demilitarized zone that separates the North and the South; any nuclear or even non-nuclear exchange between the United States and North Korea would threaten them. Yet, then national security adviser McMaster told PBS Newshour's Judy Woodruff that the United States will "respond with overwhelming force to North Korean aggression and improve options to compel denuclearization." When asked whether war on the Korean peninsula was becoming more likely, McMaster noted that the "president has asked us to continue to refine a military option, should we need to use it." Secretary of Defense Mattis and National Security Adviser Bolton supported the president's bellicose rhetoric on the Korean situation.

Only several weeks before President Trump was scheduled to meet with Kim Jong Un, Secretary of State Pompeo nominated the Commander of U.S. Forces in the Pacific, Admiral Harry B. Harris, Jr. to become U.S. ambassador to South Korea. This marked another step to militarize American foreign policy as a key ambassadorial appointment was given to the Pentagon. Since Pompeo favors regime change in North Korea and Bolton supports a preventive strike against North Korea, the appointment of an ambassador with hard-line views maintains the Trump administration's continued commitment to threats of force.

In 2016, the Obama administration placed a gag order on Admiral Harris because of his bellicose statements toward China at a time when President Obama was set to meet with Chinese leader Xi Jinping. A former State Department official, Danny Russel, noted that Harris was "fairly harsh" in private meetings and not only in public.[67] Harris must step outside of his military role in

---

[67] Nakamura and Hudson, "Admiral to get key role," p. 11.

order to function effectively and diplomatically as an ambassador. Pompeo's special envoy for North Korea, Stephen Biegun, an executive at the Ford Motor Company, has limited diplomatic experience, but Pompeo explained that Biegun's efforts with "foreign governments to advance Ford's goals all around the world" would serve U.S. interests in North Korea.[68]

In March 2018, only several days after the stunning announcement of President Trump's acceptance of an invitation to meet with Kim Jong Un, Admiral Harris testified before the Senate Armed Forces Committee, emphasizing the importance of a "maximum pressure campaign" against North Korea and, with regard to any disarmament deal, the importance of "distrust but verify."[69] Harris was critical of the notion of a limited or "bloody nose" strike at Pyongyang, arguing that only a full-fledged military assault would work; he referred to this as the "whole thing." Thus, Trump headed to a summit meeting with Kim with a trio of hawks from the National Security Council, the Department of State, and the U.S. embassy in Seoul.

One of my former students at the National War College, Admiral Mike Mullen, a former chairman of the Joint Chiefs of Staff, told ABC news on the last day of 2017 that the United States was "actually moving closer to nuclear war with North Korea than we've ever been."[70] He was pessimistic about the ability of the generals, the so-called adults in the room, to restrain such a "disruptive" and "unpredictable" president. When one of these adults, former Secretary of State Tillerson, tried to urge a diplomatic solution to the imbroglio, President Trump

---

[68] John Hudson, "Pompeo picks Ford Motor Col. executive to lead North Korea negotiations," *The Washington Post*, August 21, 2018, p. 8.

[69] David Nakamura and John Hudson, "Admiral to get key role in diplomacy," *The Washington Post*, May 3, 2018, p. 11.

[70] ABC News, December 31, 2017.

typically tweeted that "he's wasting his time trying to negotiate with Little Rocket Man. Save your energy, Rex, we'll do what has to be done."

The most bizarre aspect of U.S. contingency planning under the Trump administration was the public discussion of invading North Korea to seize its nuclear weapons in the event of a political collapse in Pyongyang that compromised the government. In December 2017, then Secretary of State Tillerson remarked at an international conference that the United States and China have had "conversations in the event that something happened internal to North Korea; it might be nothing that we from the outside initiate—if that unleashed some kind of instability, the most important thing to us would be securing those nuclear weapons they've already developed and ensuring that they—that nothing falls in the hands of people we would not want to have it."[71]

These comments were irresponsible. The Beijing government presumably was aghast that a senior U.S. official would refer to a secret U.S.-Chinese plan to invade a Beijing ally. In view of the secret underground deployment and development of nuclear weapons in North Korea, there is no certainty regarding the numbers or location of Pyongyang's nuclear inventory. The Defense Intelligence Agency, well known for its worst-case estimates of military threats, believes that North Korea has more than 50 nuclear weapons and/or devices. The Central Intelligence Agency's estimates range from 15 to 30. We simply lack reliable intelligence on North Korea, particularly its weaponry.

China's failure to comment on Tillerson's *faux pas* speaks to Beijing's sensitivity on this matter. Is it possible that Tillerson was ignorant of the Chinese response to U.S. forces on its border during the Korean War, which led to the unexpected Chinese entry into the war? It is conventional wisdom among military analysts in Washington that any aggressive U.S. moves in North Korea could lead

---

[71] David E. Sanger, "Tillerson Speaks on a Largely Secret North Korea Contingency Plan", The New York Times, December 18, 2017, p. 5.

to Chinese intervention. It is unlikely that China would tolerate a U.S. military presence north of the demilitarized zone for any reason. Was Tillerson unaware of the sensitivity of similar U.S. plans regarding Pakistani nuclear weapons, which led to tensions in U.S. relations with Pakistan and China?

The diplomatic tension over North Korea worsened a month later, when then CIA Director Pompeo remarked in January 2018 that Pyongyang is a "handful of months" away from having a nuclear weapon that could reach the United States.[72] In saying so, Pompeo implicitly challenged the president to make good on his red line that North Korea would never be able to develop a nuclear weapons that could reach United States. Trump says repeatedly that the era of "strategic patience" is over, and that traditional deterrence will not work, but there is no sign of strategic direction. Victor Cha, an experienced hand on Asian policy, was removed from consideration as ambassador to South Korea merely because he said that there was no such thing as a limited military option against North Korea, not even a strike to "bloody" Pyongyang's nose.

The United States can only hope that the North Koreans do not seize an American naval vessel (as they did in 1968); or shoot down an American reconnaissance plane (as they did in 1969); or sink a South Korean naval vessel (as they did in 2010). Such an event could lead to war. The presence of a volatile and bellicose figure in the White House magnifies the danger inherent in these scenarios. The one certainly is that North Korea would respond to any U.S. use of military force, and that China would not stay on the sidelines in the event of U.S. military operations on the peninsula. U.S. intelligence was wrong in the 1950s about China's likely involvement in the Korean War; there is far greater risk in being wrong today.

---

[72] Fareed Zakaria, "Crossing Trump's three red lines," *The Washington Post*, January 23, 2018, p. 18.

EXPANDING AND CONTRACTING THE WAR AGAINST AFGHANISTAN

Just as the discussion of withdrawal of forces from Syria created greater instability and chaos in the Middle East, the sudden announcement of a withdrawal of 7,000 U.S. troops from Afghanistan threatened sensitive negotiations regarding a role for the Taliban in an Afghan government. The Afghan withdrawal announcement took place only hours after Mattis announced his resignation, which shocked senior Afghan officials as well as Western diplomats in Kabul. The same day of the withdrawal announcement, the U.S. special representative for talks on Afghan reconciliation, Zalmay Khalizad, stressed to his Taliban counterparts that the United States was committed to Afghanistan. Khalizad was in the United Arab Emirates, which was sponsoring two days of talks between Washington and the Taliban. Trump's withdrawal plan is one more signal to U.S. allies (and adversaries) that Washington was abandoning strategic positions without any consultation with allies who have committed their own forces to support the United States. There are more than 16,000 NATO and allied troops in Afghanistan.

Throughout the campaign and his presidency, Trump consistently criticized Barack Obama for announcing plans for a drawdown in advance, thus compromising commitments based on conditions on the ground. Just as the Syrian withdrawal will open greater opportunities for non-Arab actors such as Russia, Iran, and Turkey, the Afghan withdrawal will make it easier for Pakistan to finally realize its goal of a friendly Taliban government in Kabul. Russia will take advantage of the Syrian opportunity; China will benefit from the Afghan opening.

The U.S. war in Afghanistan was doomed from the start because the Bush administration never took into account the opposition of Pakistan, particularly its intelligence services, to an Afghan government that wasn't dominated by the Taliban. Pakistan wants to secure its western border with Afghanistan so that it could concentrate on its insecure eastern border with India. The Bush administration was initially correct in deploying a small mobile force in the wake of the 9/11 attacks to rout al Qaeda from the country and to counter the Taliban government, but it was senseless to widen the deployment to more than 100,000 troops committed to "victory" in Afghanistan.

Billions of dollars of U.S. assistance over the past two decades created conditions for the corruption, violence, and instability that marks Afghanistan. There is no victory in sight for U.S. interests and no stability for any Afghan government that fails to include the Taliban as a coalition partner. As long as Pakistani intelligence agents and religious fanatics hold the upper hand in dealing with the Taliban, there is no chance for success. Afghanistan is known as the "graveyard of empires" for good reason. Directorate S of the Pakistani spy agency, the Inter-Services Intelligence (ISI), understands this problem and devotes significant resources to covert operations in support of the Taliban, Kashmiri guerrillas, and other violent Islamic radicals. Pakistan Foreign Minister Khawaja Asif supports "joint efforts against terrorism," but there is no evidence of a lesser Pakistani role in Afghanistan.[73]

In committing itself to large-scale force deployments, the United States made the same strategic mistakes that the Soviet Union made in Afghanistan from 1979 to 1989, attempting to create a strong central government in Kabul and ignoring the special interests of the ISI. It took a wise Soviet leader, Mikhail Gorbachev, to recognize the problem and withdraw all Soviet forces. The United States has lacked wise leadership since the initial success of its modest deployment of special forces from the Pentagon and the Central Intelligence Agency in October 2001.

U.S. forces have never been successful against an insurgency with a sanctuary on its border (see the United States or France in Vietnam), and Afghanistan will

---

[73] Pamela Constable, "Afghan officials allege Pakistani involvement in recent attacks," *The Washington Post*, January 17, 2018, p. 11.

not be the exception. Pakistan's response to Trump's red line regarding continued support to the Taliban has been to pursue closer relations with China and to increase violence in Afghanistan. The United States has no counter to an Islamabad government that can increase chaos in Afghanistan and create problems for U.S. forces.

SUPPORTING ISRAELI MILITARISM

President Trump's one-sided support for Israel created conditions for greater violence in the Middle East. Gaza remains an "outdoor prison," in the words of one British analyst, and Israel, which bombed Gaza in 2008, 2012, and 2014, faces no pressure from the Trump administration not to do so again. Donald Trump loves to apply the word "shithole" to the Third World, and Gaza is one place where he could apply it effectively. Trump's recognition of Jerusalem as the capital of Israel, abandoning 70 years of U.S. policy under Democrats and Republicans alike, destroyed the hopes of Palestinians and progressive Israelis for a two-state solution. Trump's actions undermined the credibility of the Palestinian Authority and the leadership of Mahmoud Abbas, and gave Israeli right-wing ideologues a huge victory without gaining anything in return.

The appointment of three Zionists—Jared Kushner, David Friedman, and Jason Greenblatt—to key negotiating positions between the Israelis and Palestinians was the first indication that Trump would support continued Jewish colonization of the West Bank. Trump's generals know that walking away from a two-state solution contributed to instability that threatens the security of U.S. forces in the region, but no one spoke out against the president's reckless rhetoric and one-sided policies.

Trump's recognition of Jerusalem as the capital of Israel ended any pretense that the United States was an honest broker in the region. His boast that he had taken Jerusalem "off the table" was a rebuff to moderate Palestinians seeking a diplomatic solution to the conflict. Secretaries Tillerson and Mattis tried to get Trump to reverse his initiative, but there was no stopping the chaotic impulses of the U.S. president. Abbas, who had been vilified by the U.S. president at their meeting in the summer of 2017, called the Jerusalem gambit the "slap of the century" and ruled out future U.S. mediation.

Vice President Pence, a prominent evangelical more supportive of Israel than the trio of Zionists, traveled to Israel in 2018 and increased tension in the region by using his Knesset speech to cite biblical references to Jewish ties to the Holy Land and to announce that the U.S. embassy would move to Jerusalem in 2019, sooner than expected. Pence made no attempt to meet with Palestinian officials, Israeli opposition members, or even Israeli-Arabs. Instead, he played a political and religious card by inviting West Bank settlers to his speech to the Parliament. Israeli-Arab members of the Parliament who held up signs saying, "Jerusalem is the capital of Palestine," were forcibly removed from the hall when Pence began speaking. On the eve of his departure for Israel, the U.S. government announced significant cuts in aid for health and education projects for Palestinian refugees, which Israeli national security officials realize will destabilize the region even further.

In August 2018, the Trump administration announced the United States would no longer contribute to the UN Relief and Works Agency (UNRWA), which was established in 1949 to assist more than 700,000 Palestinians who fled or were expelled from their homes during the Arab-Israeli War of 1948. The loss of financial support from the United States added to instability in the Middle East at a time of rising tensions between Israel and its neighbors. Jordan, the only stable neighbor on the Israeli border, will be hardest hit because it houses 2 million refugees who represent a fifth of the country's population.

The Trump administration has taken advantage of every opportunity to distance itself from the Palestinians. In 2018, the United States cut off $200 million in aid for the Palestinians in Lebanon and Jordan, and stopped its annual pledge of $25 million for Palestinians hospitalized in East Jerusalem. It also closed the office of the Palestine Liberation Organization in Washington, and the U.S. consulate in East Jerusalem that served the Palestinians. Meanwhile, Israel has added to settlements on the West Bank at a record pace.

THE SYRIAN QUAGMIRE

Syria barely exists as a nation-state, and it will not become stable anytime soon. The Trump administration has little insight into the complexities of the Middle East in general, and specifically Syria, where more than half of the population of 22 million is in refugee status. Several million refugees are outside the country and the remainder are displaced refugees who have had to flee their homes, if not their country. President Trump and his generals believe that Iran is the cause of the crisis, and are unwilling to concede (or unable to understand) that President Bush's ill-fated decision to invade Iraq in 2003 destabilized the entire region.

In April of 2017 and 2018, there was authoritative evidence of Syrian use of chemicals against civilians, which led President Trump to use military force. On both occasions, then Secretary of Defense Mattis took over the reins of decision making and made sure that U.S. power was used moderately, precisely, and proportionately. Trump's "war cabinet" will not have to deal with Mattis the next time around.

In April 2017, the United States fired fewer than 60 cruise missiles against one Syrian airfield, putting it out of commission for only a few days. In April 2018, when the president promised a large-scale attack with "nice, new, and 'smart'" weapons, it was Mattis who succeeded in getting active military support from two NATO allies, Britain and France; the attack struck only three chemical sites and involved fewer than 110 missiles over a two-minute period. Mattis made an unsuccessful effort to get the president to consult with Congress before attacking.

On these occasions, Mattis was the adult in the room. His role was significant because he challenged the desires of the president and ignored the new war cabinet that Trump had formed. There were no reported casualties or fatalities and no venting of chemical materials in April 2018, suggesting these facilities had been abandoned on the eve of an attack or were no longer in active production. Since chlorine, the chemical favored by the Assad regime, does not require sophisticated research or storage capacity, it is likely that Mattis chose symbolic targets that carried no risk to Russian or Iranian advisers on the ground in Syria. The Pentagon opposed action that threatened to widen the conflict.

President Trump maintained that he was "prepared to sustain this response until the Syrian regime stops its use of prohibited chemical agents." Mattis proclaimed, however, that the United States was "not out to expand this [confrontation]; we were very precise and proportionate." But Trump's sudden announcement in December 2018 of a U.S troop withdrawal from Syria created far more chaos than the limited use of military force against the Assad government.

Trump's decision led to serious wrangling within the national security team as well as diplomatic tensions with Israel and our European allies who favor a small U.S. military presence in Syria. Israeli President Netanyahu tried to get Trump to reverse his decision, and even Turkish President Erdogan indicated he thought a sudden withdrawal would create havoc. Having failed to convince Trump of the dangers of a withdrawal, the key advisors—National Security Adviser Bolton and Secretary of State Pompeo—created additional confusion in differing on our commitments in the region.

Any U.S. withdrawal puts at risk the 30,000-strong American-backed security force that is composed largely of Kurdish fighters as well as 50,000 Syrian refugees living under the direct protection of U.S. forces. Whenever Syrian President Assad has liberated an area in Syria, he has tortured and murdered civilians, particularly anyone who worked with the United States, such as the rescue workers known as the White Helmets. The Russians have aided these efforts. Israel immediately increased its military operations against Iran's presence in Syria to exploit the confusion Trump's announcement created.

A deteriorating Syrian situation increases the havoc in Lebanon and Jordan, home to several million Syrian refugees, a majority of them Sunni Muslims. Most of these refugees do not want to be there, and they are not welcomed by the Shia Muslims, Druze, and Christians who view the Syrians as vulnerable to Islamist radicalization. Meanwhile, Saudi Arabia has been manipulating events in Lebanon in order to challenge the power of Hezbollah, a state within the Lebanese state and an Iranian proxy, that backs President Assad. The rising tensions in Lebanon are part of the proxy wars being fought by Saudi Arabia and Iran throughout the region.

The Syrian situation is also threatening because of the presence of so many non-Arab actors, including Turks, Russians, Iranians, Israelis, and Kurds, let alone Americans, who are involved in a struggle without end. If the Syrians themselves had been allowed to pursue their civil war without foreign interference in the wake of the Arab Spring of 2011, President Assad probably would have lost Damascus. But the involvement of so many outside powers, each with its own agenda, has created a problem without an obvious solution. Russia, Turkey, and Iran are the winners of Trump's withdrawal announcement; the Israelis and the Kurds are the losers.

Meanwhile, the Saudi-Iranian struggle for influence has spread elsewhere with more casualties. Yemen—a humanitarian nightmare—has been decimated by the war, and Lebanon could be the next victim. The Saudis are flying fighter aircraft purchased from the United States and refueled by U.S. tanker aircraft. So the United States has abetted Yemen's slide into chaos. Unlike the Obama administration, which reduced weapons sales to countries such as Bahrain, Nigeria, and Saudi Arabia that violated civil and human rights, the Trump administration has removed these constraints.

For 50 years, the United States was the most prominent outside player in the Middle East, but that is no longer true as the Trump administration has no strategic, diplomatic, or even political role it wants to play in the region. There is no plan, and certainly no Trump doctrine. The strong encouragement of Saudi adventurism will create problems for the United States in dealing with with both Shia and Sunni Muslims in the region. For the first time in recent history, the struggle between Sunni and Shia has taken on a military cast, one of the many costs of the Bush administration's ill-designed adventure into Iraq. Any U.S. withdrawal that increases the influence of Russia, Turkey, and Iran will make the security situation in Syria more dire.

EXPANDED NUCLEAR FORCE

When former Secretary of State Tillerson referred to President Trump as a "fucking moron,"he was responding to the president's case for expanding nuclear forces and justifying the use of nuclear force. The Pentagon got the message, however, and the draft U.S. nuclear strategy that was forwarded to the president in January 2018 endorsed the use of nuclear weapons even against non-nuclear attacks against the United States, including cyberattacks. This recommendation is similar to what Secretary of Defense Dick Cheney approved in 1991 for the administration of George H.W. Bush, which was prematurely leaked to the *Los Angeles Times*. National Security Adviser General Brent Scowcroft and influential Senators used the leak to kill Cheney's draft.

Trump's nuclear strategy reverses the Obama Administration's efforts to reduce the size and scope of the U.S. arsenal and minimize the role of nuclear weapons in defense planning. Mattis boasted the changes reflected a need to "look reality in the eye" and "see the world as it is, not as we wish it to be."[74] Trump raised the specter of the North Korean threat to justify a greater U.S. nuclear capability, and Mattis supported it by arguing that the "great power competition—not terrorism—is now the primary focus of U.S. national security."[75]

President Obama, the winner of a Nobel Peace Prize in 2009, believed that the United States had a moral obligation to lead the effort to rid the world of nuclear weapons. Conversely, Trump's national security team has created a geopolitical fiction to justify the production of new nuclear weapons. This serves to heighten the possibility of their use through miscalculation or, even worse, calculation. The overkill capability of U.S. and Russian nuclear forces is probably the greatest example of irresponsible leadership in the post-war world, and Trump's enhancements could reignite the arms race and increase the chances of nuclear war.

Before Trump was inaugurated, Obama reluctantly agreed to a large and expensive upgrade of U.S nuclear forces in order to gain Senate confirmation of his arms control treaty with Russia in 2010. The cost of this modernization will be more than $1.5 trillion over the next thirty years. As a result, the Navy is designing a new fleet of a dozen ballistic missile submarines, and the Air Force is discussing a new long-range strategic bomber, the B-21 Raider, as well as a new long-range cruise missile. The Air Force seeks replacements for existing land-based intercontinental ballistic missiles, and the Department of Energy is modifying and extending the life of nuclear bombs and warheads.

Trump's nuclear posture review argues for modified nuclear warheads of lower yield as well as a new, nuclear-armed, sea-launched cruise missile. None of

---

[74] Paul Sonne, "U.S. nuclear shift: Better arsenal, not smaller one," *The Washington Post*, February 2, 2018, p. 15.

[75] David Sanger, "U.S. Chases Russia into a New Arms Race," *The New York Times*, January 21, 2018, p. 16.

these systems is necessary in view of the huge U.S. nuclear inventory, and any of them would increase the risk of resorting to so-called "limited" nuclear strikes, as if this were a realistic prospect. The notion of limited nuclear war is the most dangerous oxymoron of this era. The call to reintroduce a nuclear submarine-launched cruise missile reverses the decision of President George H. W. Bush to stop deploying such weapons, and Obama's order to remove such weapons from the nuclear arsenal.

The worst aspect of the mindless spending on defense is the Pentagon's investment in missile defense, including a $6.5 billion contract with Boeing in February 2018. The sole-source contract is to complete the "accelerated delivery of a new missile field with 20 additional silos" at Fort Greeley, Alaska, as well as 20 additional ground-based interceptor missiles.[76] The total cost of the contract will exceed $12 billion through 2023 for a flawed system that has never distinguished a genuine warhead from a decoy. The United States has been throwing good money after bad for six decades in pursuit of a phantom defense against ballistic missiles; this is part of the Star Wars illusion of U.S. defense planners.[77]

In January 2019, the Pentagon announced an expansion of U.S. missile defense to shield U.S. allies from regional threats and to destroy missiles from space. This would involve investment in technologies that were abandoned after the collapse of the Soviet Union in 1991. Similar to President Reagan's "Star Wars" initiative, the plan would develop high-energy lasers to destroy missiles after their launch or so-called "boost phase."[78] In the 1980s, the Congress

---

[76] Christian Davenport and Aaron Gregg, "U.S. missile contracts balloon as North Korea threat grows," *The Washington Post*, February 2, 2018, p. 17.

[77] See Craig Eisendrath, Melvin Goodman, and Gerald Marsh, "The Phantom Defense: America's Pursuit of the Star Wars Illusion," London: Praeger Publishers, 2001.

[78] Paul Sonne, "A missile plan akin to Reagan's 'Star Wars'," The Washington Post, January 17, 2019, p. 18.

opposed Reagan's "Star Wars' notions because of their high cost and questionable effectiveness, but today's Congress is far more supportive of the Pentagon. Presumably national security adviser Bolton is advocating the new plan, which would be consistent with his views as George Bush's adviser in 2002, when the United States abrogated the Anti-Ballistic Missile Treaty.

The Pentagon is justifying new weapons on the basis of new threats from a "resurgent" Russia and China, and creating "tailored" options to enhance deterrence. In fact, these nuclear systems will merely increase the overkill capability that already exists in the U.S. inventory. Even liberal media support "limited nuclear options that are more credible and should be pursued."[79] Trump's abrogation of the Intermediate-range Nuclear Forces Treaty in November 2018 threatens a new arms race in the European theatre as well as Asia.

The idea of limited nuclear war made no sense during the Cold War in the 1950s, when such theorists as Henry Kissinger made their names by promoting the concept. It makes even less sense today when we possess a massive destructive nuclear force that includes various types of gravity bombs as well as air-launched cruise missiles with lower yield options. Air Force General John Hyten, the commander of the strategic command, finds that he is "very comfortable today with the flexibility of our response options." It is appalling that we are talking about the idea of limited nuclear warfare, a dangerous concept that left the U.S. lexicon when the United States and the Soviet Union got serious about arms control and disarmament in the 1960s.

The uneven and unpredictable course of the Trump administration has led to the legitimate pillorying of the president and his national security characters. The criticism has come from all quarters, including journalists on the right such as George Will and Michael Gerson, both card-carrying Republicans; academics

---

[79] "An unnecessary nuclear detour," *The Washington Post*, January 11, 2018, p. 22 (editorial).

such as Professor Tom Nichols from the Naval War College; and historians such as Max Boot. According to these critics, the "root cause of America's troubles...is the lack of any kind of a coherent grand strategy." That seems to be the least of the problems in view of Trump's "American First" strategy that has isolated the United States in an international community it once dominated.

The situation is serious and, for the first time in the history of the nuclear age, U.S. generals are stating publicly that they would not carry out an illegal order regarding the use of nuclear weapons. At a conference in Canada in November 2017, General Hyten remarked that he would "resist an illegal order from President Trump." There is no certainly, however, that a general officer would resist an order from the President, who is accompanied at all hours by an Air Force officer with a mundane briefcase that carries the nuclear button.

The worrisome aspect of the Nuclear Posture Review is the fact that the most irrational president in the history of the Republic is residing in the White House. We have had bad presidents in our history, but the bar has never been this low. Trump's volatility and unpredictability, his paranoia and lack of impulse control, make him temperamentally unsuited to be the commander-in-chief. At the outset of his presidency, George Washington observed that the president cannot "demean himself in his public character" and must act "in such a manner as to maintain the dignity of the office." Trump has never displayed the poise and civility required for the President of the United States.

Too many pundits believe that Donald Trump is more farce than tragedy, despite the sufficient evidence of the irresponsibility and unpredictability of the commander-in-chief. The fact that he has surrounded himself with a war cabinet that opposes arms control and has a limited understanding of the geopolitical arena is cause for concern. Vice President Cheney convinced President Bush that he could enhance his powers by becoming a wartime president. Could an authoritarian president surrounded by a "war cabinet" and supported by a political base that thrives on chauvinistic fulminations enhance his position by resorting to force.

In addition to reviving the idea of limited nuclear war, Trump directed the Pentagon to create a sixth branch of the armed forces dedicated to protecting American interests in space. In March 2018, Trump told a Marine audience that "Space is a war-fighting domain, just like the land, air and sea."[80] His references to space as a "war-fighting domain" could spur a dangerous arms race in space and make war-fighting there more likely. Trump finds it insufficient to threaten war on earth against Iran, North Korea, and even Venezuela, so a Space Force reviving the illusions of President Ronald Reagan's Star Wars was seductive.

In fact, the Outer Space Treaty of 1967, signed by more than 100 nations including the United States, declared space a "province of mankind" and not to be militarized by nations. The United States and the Soviet Union took the lead in formulating a treaty to ban placing nuclear and other weapons of mass destruction in space. For the past decade, China and Russia have tried to get the United States to join a follow-on treaty to ban the placement of weapons in space, but Washington has demurred. There is no nation on earth more dependent on the resources of space than the United States, so militarization would find the United States a major loser. There is no reason on earth to use space for anything more than scientific exploration.

Trump's impulsive and bellicose manner has led a few congressional voices to search for limits on the presidential power to use military force, which the Founding Fathers placed in the hands of the Congress. Article one of the Constitution gives the power "To declare War" to the Congress as well as the power "To provide for organizing, arming, and disciplining, the Militia." But our Global War on Terror is being fought in at least 14 countries around the world as

---

[80] Peter Wismer, "Space is not the place for war," The Washington Post, June 19, 2018, p. 17.

Congress has given Presidents Bush, Obama, and Trump a blank check to wage war.

In a bipartisan effort, Senators Tim Kaine (D-VA) and Bob Corker (R-TN) introduced a new military authorization to repeal the open-ended 2001 authorization after the 9/11 attacks and the outdated 2002 authorization to justify the Iraq War. According to their measure, Congress would vote to "approve continued military actions for four years against al Qaeda, the Islamic State, the Taliban and designated combatants who are engaged in hostilities against the United States or our battlefield partners."[81] Kaine believes this would "establish an expedited procedure to revise, repeal or extend military action against these terrorist groups every four years."

But the Kaine-Corker initiative would approve military action against six groups that were not included in the 2001 authorization: the Islamic State, al Qaeda in the Arabian Peninsula, al Shabab in East Africa, al Qaeda in Syria, al Qaeda in the Islamic Maghreb, and the Haqqani network in Afghanistan and Pakistan. In doing so, force would be authorized in additional countries such as Syria, Yemen, Somalia, and Libya. A further danger is that the Kaine-Corker bill would effectively repeal the War Powers Act of 1973, which mandated that, if a president sent troops into "hostilities," they could only stay 60 to 90 days unless Congress approved the deployment or extended the time period. As long as the United States considers Iran and North Korea as state sponsors of terrorism, the initiative would permit the Trump administration or its successor to justify a "bloody nose," in the words of national security adviser Bolton, against those nations as well.

The only congressional effort to push back against Trump's militarism took place in the Senate in December 2018, when a resolution was unanimously passed

---

[81] Tim Kaine, "Limit Trump's ability to wage war," *The Washington Post*, April 30, 2018, p. 17.

to censor the Saudi killing of dissident Saudi journalist Jamal Khashoggi and a majority called for an end to the U.S. support of the Saudi-led war in Yemen. The resolution provides firm support for CIA assessments that concluded Crown Prince bin Salman ordered and monitored the killing of Khashoggi. The House of Representatives would not vote on either measure, but that should change with Democrats assuming the majority in the House. The Congress then might be able to sanction Saudi Arabia and limit weapons transfers to the Kingdom.

Trump is all about pomp and circumstance. So it was no surprise that the president, overwhelmed by a French military parade in Paris on Bastille Day, July 14, 2017, told his closest associates that he wanted a similar parade on an American holiday on Pennsylvania Avenue, the site of not only the White House but the Trump International Hotel. On January 18, 2018, Trump held a secret meeting in the Pentagon's Tank, which is typically reserved for top secret discussions, with the Secretary of Defense and the Chairman of the Joint Chiefs of Staff.[82] An abstract idea about a parade soon became a directive to military leaders from a president who received deferments from the Vietnam War because of bone spurs.

Military parades are a standard feature in authoritarian states such as Russia or Third World states such as Cuba, but not in the United States. As a former soldier, I can vouch for the fact that parades are a waste of time and totally disliked by the military. Parades take up too much time; cost too much; and provide no return or reward whatsoever. The cost will be in the tens of millions of dollars, and that is before the repairs that will be necessitated by 70-ton battlefield tanks chewing up the macadam on Pennsylvania Avenue.

Fortunately, the Pentagon dragged its feet on the idea of parading in Washington, and Trump's extravaganza has been put off. True to form, Trump

---

[82] Greg Jaffe and Philip Rucker, "Plans for U.S. military parade take step ahead," *The Washington Post,* February 7, 2018, p. 1.

tweeted that local Washington officials were to blame for inflating the price of the parade "so ridiculously high that I cancelled it."[83] And in an effort to make the best of a bad situation, he added that "Now we can buy some more jet fighters."

But to an authoritarian leader such as Donald Trump, parades are one more way—a somewhat neofascist way—to call attention to the military role of the president and brandish the toys at his disposal. In an interview with *The Washington Post* before the inauguration, Trump warned that the "military may come marching down Pennsylvania Avenue. I mean, we're going to be showing our military."[84] With the United States dropping bombs in seven countries without a declaration of war, a show of force at home would be redundant.

Our democracy depends on citizens having trust in the sense and sensibility of our leaders. In a world that appears to be spinning out of control, it is not possible to have faith in the decision making of our current leadership. At the point of its dissolution in 1991, the people of the Soviet Union found its leaders were no longer credible. The increased cynicism of Americans toward their leaders weakens the underpinnings of our democracy.

According to Alexandra Stubin, the American ideal at home and abroad has been sullied. For the first time in recent U.S. history, we have a president known abroad as a racist and a demagogue who fails to represent U.S. values. Trump has demonstrated that he is more comfortable dealing with authoritarians and autocrats around the world than with traditional democratic allies. The fact that Trump lacks impulse control and that his actions beg serious questions regarding his fitness for office point to an existential threat at home. There is the possibility that we are one narcissistic rage from greater use of military force.

---

[83] Eileen Sullivan, Helene Cooper and Michael D. Shear, "Plan for Military Parade Fizzles In a Chorus of Recriminations," *The New York Times*, August 18, 2018, p. 1.

[84] Jaffe and Rucker, "Plans for U.S. military parade," p. 6.

– 4 –

DONALD TRUMP'S WAR ON INTELLIGENCE

"When the full extent of your venality, moral turpitude, and political corruption becomes known, you will take your rightful place as a disgraced demagogue in the dustbin of history."

> –former CIA director John Brennan following Donald Trump's firing of FBI Deputy Director Andrew McCabe a day before McCabe's retirement.

"If this government ever became a tyranny, the technological capacity that the intelligence community has given the government could enable it to impose total tyranny, and there would be no way to fight back, because the most careful effort to combine together in resistance to the government, no matter how privately it was done, is within the reach of the government to know."

> –Senator Frank Church, Chairman of the Senate Investigation of the Central Intelligence Agency, 1976.

In August 2018, President Trump followed through on threats to remove the security clearance of former CIA director John Brennan, who led the Agency from March 2013 to January 2017. Brennan was one of Trump's severest critics, denouncing his performance at the summit meeting with Russian President Putin as "treasonous" and casting doubt on the President's fitness for office. The President of the United States can reward and revoke security clearances, but there is no precedent for the action against Brennan that was taken without any suggestion that Brennan was guilty of a security breach. There was also no precedent for a president trying to intimidate and politicize the entire intelligence community.

The intelligence community was designed to provide assessments to serve the White House and the national security team. The U.S. intelligence apparatus is the largest and most expensive in the world, and it works in the shadows to collect intelligence and conduct clandestine activities and covert action. No intelligence agency wants to see its efforts publicized, which is why it was so unusual for the president-elect of the United States to cast aspersions on the community, particularly the Central Intelligence Agency, before his inauguration.

Trump's war on intelligence is comprehensive, involving every aspect of intelligence leadership and policy. This is a major part of Trump's war against fact finders, including scientists, the press, the judiciary and the Federal Bureau of Investigation—as well as the intelligence community for which fact finding is central. Trump's incantations of "fake news" have compromised the credibility of the media. His efforts to discredit the intelligence community have harmed the reputation of key institutions, particularly the FBI, challenging its ability to do its job.

Secret intelligence institutions are not compatible with the democratic process so there has always been tension between an open democratic society and a closed secret community. President Harry S. Truman encountered opposition when he created the CIA in 1947, and the crimes of the CIA, the FBI, and the National Security Agency during the Vietnam War, which included illegal surveillance of Americans, mail openings, and wiretaps, led to opposition from liberals and conservatives. More recently, the NSA's massive surveillance campaign, the CIA's program of torture and abuse, and the FBI's use of "national security letters" to collect confidential information on American citizens without a warrant have outraged civil libertarians.

Truman created the CIA to collect and analyze intelligence, not to become another "cloak and dagger agency." Truman opposed the covert actions of

Presidents Eisenhower and Kennedy. Trump, however, is not targeting the cloak and dagger operations; he is targeting intelligence analysis that does not conform to his personal views. He rejects the validity of the Iran nuclear accord and Iran's observance of it as well as the fact that Russia interfered in the 2016 presidential election, which the intelligence community confirmed. Trump neither accepts the responsibility of Crown Prince bin Salman for the killing of a dissident journalist nor the fact that North Korea has continued its nuclear weapons programs.

No presidential administration in recent history started with more disarray than Trump's, and the uneasy relationship between the president and the intelligence community was a major element in the chaos. Trump entered the White House with no background, no experience, no understanding, and no obvious curiosity about international relations. As a result, the major elements of his stewardship, such as personnel, policy, politics, and process, were marked by uncertainty and confusion. The selection of the national security team, the least qualified of the post-war era, raised immediate concerns about Trump's judgment. Trump's authoritarian style during the presidential campaign attracted an authoritarian following, so it was no surprise that he selected an authoritarian national security team dominated by general officers and a West Point graduate. Trump ignored the Founding Fathers' commitment to civilian control of the military.

President Nixon shared his negative views on the CIA with very few advisors, but Trump publicly displayed his opposition before his inauguration. As a candidate, he made it clear that he wouldn't sit for daily top-secret briefings. As a president, he hasn't. No sooner had Trump been elected president that he labeled Director of National Intelligence James Clapper and CIA Director Brennan "political hacks." Lieutenant General Flynn, a bitter enemy of Clapper, became national security adviser. Clapper had engineered Flynn's firing as Director of the Defense Intelligence Agency and his early retirement from the Army.

Trump and Flynn were ideological soul mates, particularly in opposing the CIA. Flynn was a close ally of General Stanley McChrystal, who was forced to retire because of his attacks on leading members of the Obama administration, including Vice President Joe Biden. Flynn, who professed to worshipping the "god of beer," was once asked, "How the hell did you ever get your security clearance?" "I lied," replied Flynn.[85] McChrystal tried to temper Flynn's attacks on Hillary Clinton during the presidential campaign, but without success.

The Trump administration has demonstrated little interest in truth and one of his top advisors, Kellyanne Conway, introduced the concept of "alternative facts." It will take courage at CIA and oversight in Congress to ensure that the world of intelligence doesn't join the Orwellian world of alternate facts (i.e., "pants-on-fire" lies). There is a heavy burden on the CIA to inform the president about foreign developments that affect Trump's personal views, and will have to choose its words carefully on issues dealing with Iran, Russia and North Korea or risk his ire. The intelligence community's global threat briefing to Congress in January 2019 indicated that the leaders of the community were willing to tell truth to the power on Capitol Hill, if not to the White House.

Many bizarre events marked the first two years of the Trump administration, starting with his first full day as president when he traveled to CIA headquarters. Several weeks before his inauguration, Trump compared the CIA to the Gestapo in Germany's Third Reich, and lambasted CIA Director Brennan. On his Twitter account, he called the agency's assessments "ridiculous" and politically motivated. Trump views the CIA as part of the so-called "deep state." His repeated references to the CIA's intelligence failure regarding Iraqi weapons of mass destruction was designed to justify his criticism of the Agency and to compromise its credibility.

---

[85] James Bamford, "Anti-Intelligence: What Happens When the President Goes to War with His Own Spies?," *The New Republic*, April 2018, p. 17.

Trump's self-aggrandizing and egomaniacal performance at CIA Headquarters ignored his previous criticisms, but marked a new low in presidential efforts to politicize the key civilian agency in the intelligence community. He brought many supporters from the White House with him, and they occupied seats in the front rows where they cheered the president's remarks. Trump faced two groups of agency personnel. The main section consisted of agency staffers who provided cheers for the President's embarrassing political statements, particularly his efforts to intimidate the press. The heaviest applause followed Trump's accusation that journalists were "among the most dishonest people on earth." A separate section consisted of senior agency officials, including clandestine operatives, who stood throughout but remained stoic and offered no support.

Trump's visit to the CIA was brief—less than fifteen minutes. Standing in front of the Memorial Wall in the lobby of the headquarters building, Trump made no mention of the meaning of the 112 stars on the wall, representing CIA officers who paid the ultimate sacrifice in the line of duty. Trump also stood near the biblical inscription at the entrance to the Langley headquarters: "The Truth Will Set You Free." Trump, who is obviously self-conscious about his girth, never took off his overcoat as he reminded his audience of his own "intelligence," and repeated the pathetic lies about the size of his inaugural crowd.

Trump launched into the perfunctory praise that he typically gives to his audiences ("very, very special people"), especially to the ones that he previously vilified. Forgetting that he said he would not need regular intelligence briefings, Trump told his audience that "I respect you, there's nobody I respect more." And having no idea of the problem of the politicization of intelligence for Presidents

Ronald Reagan and George W. Bush, Trump treated the intelligence officers as political supporters who would soon tire of the backing that he offered them.[86]

With typical bellicosity, Trump reminded his audience that the United States should have kept the Iraqi oil fields that it occupied during the 2003 invasion, and reminded them "maybe we'll have another chance." It is often impossible to interpret what Trump's remarks mean, even what Trump intends to mean. Surely he was pandering to the intelligence officers when he concluded by saying that "we have to start winning again," a phrase that he uses in discussing foreign policy and comparing himself to his predecessor, Barack Obama, who he dismissed as a "loser."

The President was accompanied to CIA headquarters by Rep. Mike Pompeo, his choice to succeed Brennan. The appointment of Pompeo was not meant to appeal to senior CIA leadership. Trump employed this tactic elsewhere, naming stewards at the Departments of State, Justice, Energy as well as the Environmental Protection Agency, who were immediately unpopular with the senior leadership. With the exception of Rick Perry at Energy, none of these stewards crossed the half-way point of Trump's first term in office.

Pompeo was still awaiting confirmation and appeared embarrassed by the president's unseemly performance. Trump linked Pompeo to two retired general officers (Mattis at Department of Defense and Kelly at Department of Homeland Security), who had recently been confirmed. He noted that the military provided great support in the campaign and was confident that the intelligence community had done the same since the military and intelligence communities were on his "wave length." Secretary of Defense Mattis' resignation letter two years later indicated they weren't.

---

[86] *Washington Post*, January 22, 2017, p. 1.

In anticipating total support from the intelligence community for his policies, President Trump betrayed no understanding of the natural and necessary tension between policymakers and intelligence officials. This tension has been evident in virtually all U.S. administrations, and on two prominent occasions it involved the tailoring of intelligence. In the 1980s, CIA director William Casey and his deputy, Robert Gates, provided phony intelligence to the White House to justify hostile relations with the Soviet Union and unprecedented increases in defense spending in peacetime. In the run-up to the Iraq War 30 years later, CIA director George Tenet and his deputy, John McLaughlin, said it would be a "slam dunk" to provide intelligence to justify the use of force against Iraq. The handful of intelligence analysts who tried to block politicization on these occasions were moved aside or simply ignored. I happened to be one of them.

Trump's anger with the intelligence community and the CIA centered on an inter-agency intelligence assessment on January 6, 2017 that concluded Russian President Putin had sanctioned intervention in the presidential election. This assessment put the intelligence community in Trump's gunsights. A year later, Robert Mueller's special investigation confirmed the conclusions of the intelligence community when it indicted 13 Russian citizens as well as several Russian companies for interfering with the U.S. election. The fact that this issue was Trump's first encounter with the intelligence community worsened the tension between the commander-in-chief and his intelligence chiefs at CIA, NSA, and the FBI.

The CIA and the NSA, moreover, supplied sensitive documents to the investigations of the Special Counsel and the congressional intelligence committees, which stuck in the craw of the president. The mounting evidence of Russian intervention and the secret contacts between key members of the Trump campaign staff and Russian operatives caused the thin-skinned president to intensify his criticism of the intelligence community and Attorney General

Sessions, who recused himself from the investigations at the Department of Justice and failed to provide legal and political cover for the president.

In July 2018, the Senate intelligence committee, chaired by Senator Richard Burr (R-NC), corroborated the 2017 assessment of the intelligence community, calling it a "sound intelligence product."[87] The Senate report was a significant contrast to the report of the House intelligence committee, which criticized the intelligence assessment in March 2018 and tried to exonerate the Trump presidential campaign. Meanwhile, Putin repeatedly denied Russian intervention, and President Trump—unlike his intelligence tsar Dan Coats—sided with the Russian.

Trump's anger with the intelligence chiefs who prepared the January 2017 assessment and their continued criticism of his presidency led him to consider revoking their security clearances. Nothing can stop a president from awarding or revoking a security clearance, but never before have intelligence officials lost security clearances because of their political views. Former CIA director Brennan, former intelligence tsar Clapper, and former FBI chief Comey were frequent targets for Trump in the first 18 months of his presidency, including unfounded charges that they leaked classified information to the press and undermined his presidency. Brennan's views were particularly noxious to the president who was accused of a "treasonous" performance in the Helsinki summit with Putin that warranted impeachment.[88]

Actually, the statements of both Trump and Brennan went too far, incorporating indiscriminate allegations that marked McCarthyism in the 1950s. Senator Joseph McCarthy was fond of the word "treason," and it was used against

---

[87] "What Russia did in 2016," editorial, *The Washington Post*, July 9, 2018, p. 14.

[88] Shane Harris, Jon Wagner and Felicia Sonmez, "President threatens security privileges," *The Washington Post*, July 24, 2018, p. 4.

J. Robert Oppenheimer, the physicist who helped develop the atomic bomb, during the Red Scare to revoke his security clearance.

Early on, Trump demonstrated he had no understanding of the sensitivity of intelligence materials, particularly those items obtained from foreign liaison, when he shared a sensitive report from Israeli intelligence with Russian officials. In a bizarre meeting in the Oval Office on May 10, 2017, Trump displayed the report to Russia's Foreign Minister Sergey Lavrov and Ambassador Sergey Kislyak. This shocked key intelligence officials who leaked the story. Trump saw no contradiction in vilifying intelligence officers and then boasting to the Russians about the excellent intelligence he receives from them.

This embarrassing episode indicated there were no guardrails or impulse controls on this president, and it led to serious discussions within the intelligence community about sharing sensitive materials with the White House, particularly a White House where so many key officials were operating without full security clearances. CIA intelligence briefers were particularly hesitant to brief the president orally on issues dealing with Putin because of Trump's disbelief that Russian interference in the 2016 election contributed to his victory. In April 2018, President Trump fired his second national security adviser, Lt. Gen. H. R. McMaster, several days after the general finally acknowledged the fact of Russian interference.

Similarly, Trump fired FBI Director Comey, when Comey refused to accede to a declaration of personal loyalty to the president and persisted in the investigation of Russian hacking during the campaign. As far back as the summer of 2017, Trump wanted his White House counsel Don McGahn to fire Special Counsel Mueller, and before that he tried to get the FBI to stop an investigation of National Security Adviser Flynn who lied to Vice President Pence about his dealings with the Russians. Deputy Attorney General Sally Yates was fired soon after she informed the White House that Russian intelligence may have compromised Flynn.

Comey and Yates were targeted not only for their intelligence and integrity, but particularly for their credibility as truth-tellers. Truth-telling is particularly odious to Donald Trump. Yates stood up to the president on May 8, 2017 with riveting testimony in her Georgian lilt, and surfaced warnings to the White House several months earlier regarding the potentially criminal conduct of Flynn, the former national security adviser, who was forced to resign.

Yates spent more than two decades as a federal prosecutor in Georgia before being named a U.S. Attorney and then Deputy Attorney General. She spent 27 years at the Department of Justice, but her refusal to defend an executive order banning travelers from seven Muslim countries clearly put President Trump over the edge. Until then, no one had reason to doubt Yates's bipartisan credentials; she had served as an intern to Senator Sam Nunn, a Democrat from Georgia, and had been hired as an Assistant U.S. Attorney by a Republican, Bob Barr, a conservative critic of President Bill Clinton.

No one has provided a better description of Sally Yates' role as a truth-teller to the Senate Judiciary Committee than Yates herself. In a graduation speech to the Harvard Law School class of 2017, Yates noted that her opposition to the travel ban was a surprising but crucial moment where "law and conscience intersected."[89] Yates added that the "defining moments in our lives don't come with advance warning" or "with the luxury of time to go inside yourself for some serious introspection." This is typically the *modus operandi* of a whistleblower.

The threatening investigations of Special Counsel Mueller meant that the president had less reason to hector the CIA and more incentive for targeting the FBI, which he described as an organization in "tatters." What Trump failed to understand is that he will have to make decisions at some point based on

---

[89] Anemona Hartocollis, "Yates Tells Law School Students Why She Defied Trump," The New York Times, May 25, 2017, p. 18.

information from the intelligence community and will have to go to the public to defend policies or actions based on FBI and CIA information.

The Senate's confirmation of Trump's directors for the CIA—Pompeo and Haspel—was particularly troubling. Pompeo was one of the greatest Trump loyalists in the House of Representatives when he was appointed CIA director, not the best attribute for an intelligence director. He is the first person in U.S. history to occupy the positions of both Director of CIA and Secretary of State. There has never been a director or a secretary who worked harder to curry favor from the president of the United States and to trumpet his policies. Haspel was a central figure in one of the worst CIA programs in history, including torture and abuse, secret prisons, and extraordinary renditions.

Previous directors from the Congress—Porter Goss and Tenet—were too willing to provide their masters with the intelligence they were seeking, which marked the moral bankruptcy at the CIA. Tenet and his deputy, John McLaughlin, helped prepare the phony speech that Secretary of State Powell delivered to the United Nations in February 2003, and falsely described a "sinister nexus" between Iraq and al Qaeda prior to the 9/11 attacks. It was Tenet who told President Bush in December 2002 that it would be a "slam dunk" to provide intelligence to justify war against Iraq, and McLaughlin who gave the "slam dunk" briefing.

The short tenure of Representative Goss was also problematic. Goss surrounded himself with members of his congressional staff who conducted a witch hunt of CIA officials unwilling to conduct the dirty business of politicization. Goss's last official act in this regard was orchestrating a leak investigation within the CIA to find the source for the *Washington Post*'s Pulitzer-prize winning articles on CIA's secret prisons in Eastern Europe and the unconscionable rendition of an innocent German citizen. The investigation was designed to compromise the work of the Office of the Inspector General, which had produced sensitive reports critical of CIA actions.

Before his confirmation, Pompeo issued polemics that opposed agreed intelligence assessments from the community, particularly regarding the Iran nuclear deal for which the CIA provided essential intelligence support and verification. He was a strong opponent of Senator Dianne Feinstein's devastating report on CIA torture and abuse, and favored the return of waterboarding. When confronted with pictures of hunger strikers at Guantanamo, he facetiously remarked that it "looked like they had put on weight." Pompeo also favored a return to unrestricted massive surveillance as well as the death sentence for Edward Snowden, who exposed the illegal surveillance.

As director, Pompeo downplayed CIA's analysis of Russian meddling in the election. His Islamophobia, particularly the exaggeration of the threat from Iran, patronized President Trump, but it was at odds with intelligence evidence. Pompeo joined Trump in dismissing climate science as a fraud. He would not be a moderate counterweight to an impulsive and irrational president.

A Trump loyalist in the Congress, Pompeo immediately became the greatest loyalist in the Cabinet. He persistently told skeptical audiences that the president is an "enthusiastic consumer of intelligence" and particularly loves the "killer graphics" that he is given on a daily basis.[90] When Pompeo described the president's relationship with the intelligence community as "fantastic" at a talk to the Center for Strategic and International Studies in Washington, there was laughter in the audience. "Don't laugh," Pompeo responded, "I mean that."

When Pompeo made his first major decision at CIA in February 2017, the appointment of a deputy, he pandered to President Trump's support for torture and abuse by naming Gina Haspel. Ignoring the Senate Intelligence Committee's authoritative study of the illegality and immorality of CIA's torture and abuse, Pompeo appointed Haspel who was deeply involved in the torture program from

---

[90] Nafeesa Syeed, "Trump's Morphed From Spy Agency Critic to Fan, CIA's Pompeo Says," bloomberg.com, April 14 2017.

the beginning and drafted the order to destroy the 92 torture tapes that documented sadistic CIA activities at secret prisons, the so-called "black sites," where Abu Zubaida and Abd al-Rahim al-Nishiri were waterboarded.

Pompeo was so popular with the president that in March 2018 he was named Secretary of State to replace Tillerson, and Haspel was nominated to be Director of the CIA. With these two personnel moves as well as naming Bolton as Trump's third national security adviser, the president had a national security team that favored military force and the reinstitution of torture. A "war cabinet" was in place as two so-called "adults in the room," McMaster and Tillerson, were removed from the National Security Council and the Department of State, respectively.

After a difficult confirmation process due to her role in torture and the destruction of the torture tapes, Haspel was confirmed by the Senate on May 17, 2018, receiving a record breaking 45 negative votes. Her weak performance at her confirmation hearings was troublesome.

Haspel joined the CIA in the late 1980s as I was preparing to resign because of the politicization of intelligence. Our paths never would have crossed because she was a career officer in the directorate of operations, and my 24-year career was spent in the directorate of intelligence. She was initially assigned to the Central European Division, and spent long stretches overseas, including Europe and Central Asia. The mainstream media blandly described her as a "seasoned intelligence veteran;" her support for torture and abuse earned her the nickname "bloody Gina" to CIA insiders.

In 2011, when CIA director Leon Panetta wanted to name Haspel to become deputy director of operations, the number three position at the Agency, Senator Feinstein blocked the move. Feinstein, the former chair of the Senate Intelligence Committee, led the investigation of the CIA's sadistic torture program, which determined that CIA leaders lied to the White House about the extent and results of so-called enhanced interrogation techniques. The late Senator John McCain (R-AZ) was among the first to demand that Haspel publicly explain her role in the program. McCain, having spent five and a half years undergoing torture in North Vietnamese prisons, was the nation's iconic witness to the immorality and ineffectiveness of torture.

Haspel was a deputy and protege of Jose Rodriguez, the CIA's notorious former Deputy Director for Operations and former Director of the Counterterrorism Center. If the torture program had a godfather, it was Rodriguez. Haspel was a devoted acolyte. The CIA made at least 92 video tapes of its enhanced interrogation techniques and, in 2005, when Rodriguez decided to destroy these tapes, Haspel prepared the cable to do so. According to former CIA officers, she was an advocate for torture, and for destroying the tapes.[91] The Department of Justice investigated the entire episode, but no one was charged with obstruction of justice even though the White House and a federal judge had ordered that the tapes be protected.

Prior to the confirmation hearings in May 2018, former CIA directors and deputy directors, including former Deputy Director Mike Morell, declassified information and memoranda for the Senate intelligence committee to vouch for Haspel's qualifications. The CIA did the same for Bob Gates during his controversial nomination hearings in September 1991, violating the CIA charter against politicizing intelligence information for congressional committees. For Haspel, the CIA declassified and released a memorandum from Morell that cleared her of wrongdoing in drafting an order to destroy videotaped evidence of sadistic interrogation techniques. The memorandum was the result of a disciplinary review in 2011 in which Morell "found no fault with the performance of Ms. Haspel" because she drafted the cable "on the direct orders" of her

---

[91] *The New York Times,* March 14, 2018, p. 12.

superior.[92] Morell ignored the Nuremberg principles that recommend punishment for officials who carry out illegal orders.

The CIA's "selective" response to the demands of members of the Senate intelligence committee on Haspel's professional experience was initially counterproductive. Senator Feinstein said it was "completely unacceptable for the CIA to declassify only material that's favorable" to Haspel, while stonewalling efforts to declassify all documents relating to her involvement in the torture program. Morell's memorandum said nothing about her leadership of a prison where extensive waterboarding took place. In late April 2018, more than 100 retired general and admirals took the unusual step of circulating a statement opposing Haspel's confirmation because of her extensive role in CIA's torture program.

Although Rodriquez and Haspel were major players in the most shameful period in the history of the CIA, Rodriguez was given a minor administrative reprimand and Haspel got off scot-free. Haspel and Rodriguez told numerous senators that the tapes had to be destroyed to protect the identity of the CIA agents depicted in them. This was a lie. The agents and contractors who took part in the sadistic techniques were hooded, which is typical of torturers throughout history, and could not be identified. Rodriguez received only a reprimand because Morell determined Rodriguez acted in the interest of CIA agents and believed his actions were legal. Rodriguez's actions were in fact unconscionable as were Haspel's and Morell's in view of sadistic practices that went beyond what was authorized by the so-called torture memoranda of the Department of Justice. The torture began, moreover, before the memoranda were written.

Two memoirs by former CIA officials challenged Haspel's testimony regarding her role in torture and abuse and the destruction of the torture tapes.

---

[92] Karoun Demirjian, "CIA declassifies, releases memo exonerating director nominee," *The Washington Post,* April 22, 2018, p. 2.

In John Rizzo's memoir "Company Man," the former Acting General Counsel of the CIA wrote that he was stunned to learn about the destruction of the tapes because the decision was under senior-level review. He wrote that he "never thought that destruction was a realistic possibility" because "too many people adamantly opposed the idea."[93] Rodriguez, Haspel's boss, told an interviewer on May 9, 2018 that he told her, his chief of staff, that he planned to take the matter of the destruction of the tapes in his own hands and that she offered no objection.[94] At the hearings in May 2018, Haspel denied such a conversation took place.

One thing is clear. Haspel was heavily involved in the decision making to destroy the tapes and in drafting the cable ordering the destruction. Although Haspel testified that she believed Rodriguez would consult with the CIA director before ordering the destruction of the tapes, there is no indication that she got a definitive answer from Rodriguez or even asked if he had consulted the director. This is an excellent example of willful ignorance.

Moreover, Porter Goss, the CIA director, as well as the director of national intelligence and two White House counsels were opposed to destroying the tapes. Rodriguez ignored their opposition, and Haspel supported her boss.

Haspel's role in the implementation of the torture program and the destruction of the torture tapes led to overwhelming Democratic opposition to her confirmation. Her active involvement in the program was discussed only in the closed sessions of the Senate intelligence committee. Unfortunately, the CIA's Publications Review Board would not allow my discussion of Haspel's active role that was fully described in the *New York Times* and the *Washington Post*.

---

[93] John Rizzo, *Company Man*, New York: Simon and Schuster, 2015

[94] "Pro Publica," May 9, 2018.

The CIA considers this information to be classified although it is widely known throughout the United States and the international community.

In confirming Haspel, the Senate failed to appreciate the cynicism that consumes a government agency when an individual such as Haspel, a torturer whose methods exceeded the requirements of the torture memoranda, becomes the head of that agency. A similar episode took place in the early 1990s, when Bob Gates, who orchestrated the efforts to politicize intelligence in the CIA, was returned as its director in late 1991 following his nomination by President George H. W. Bush, a former CIA director himself. A decade later, two individuals who were linked to Gates—CIA Director Tenet and Deputy Director McLaughlin—politicized intelligence to take the country to war against Iraq. Tenet was staff director of the Senate intelligence committee that confirmed Gates, and McLaughlin was a Gates acolyte throughout his CIA career.

True to his word, Trump refused regular intelligence briefings that have been part of the presidential working day for the past six decades in the form of the President's Daily Brief (PDB). During the transition, he declined the daily intelligence briefings that every president-elect has received since the creation of the CIA in 1947. And only several days before his inauguration, he conceded in an interview with Axios that, if he were to receive briefings, "I like bullets or I like as little as possible. I don't need, you know, 200-page reports on something that can be handled on a page." Even before he was inaugurated, Trump told Fox News that "You know, I'm, like, a smart person. I don't have to be told the same thing and the same words every single day for the next eight years. It could be eight years—but for eight years. I don't need that."[95]

There have been presidential administrations (Ronald Reagan, George W. Bush) that have politicized intelligence, and there have been CIA leaders (Casey

---

[95] "Fox News Sunday," December 17, 2016.

and Gates as well as Tenet and McLaughlin) who abetted these efforts. In doing so, these intelligence officials created integrity and credibility problems for the CIA, which are once again at hand. The combination of a rule-breaking president (Trump) and a loyal and subservient CIA director is a formula for substituting partisan myth for realistic analysis.

Trump is not a reader of intelligence, although few presidents have been serious readers of intelligence products such as the President's Daily Brief. Presidents Kennedy, Carter, and Clinton were the exceptions to the rule in avidly reading intelligence documents. Carter was particularly unusual because he provided copious feedback on the PDB, and his Director of Central Intelligence—Rear Admiral Stansfield Turner—was careful to pass on the president's remarks.

There were presidents who liked oral briefings, such as Ford and Reagan. George H. W. Bush, the only president who also served as CIA director, took a special interest in his briefings. Trump is a special challenge because he gets his "intelligence" from Fox News, not from the intelligence community. His intelligence briefings took place later in the morning than was usual, and they soon became quite short and infrequent. The coincidental timing of briefings and presidential tweets from the Oval Office demonstrated that Trump's attention span was limited.

The PDB was started in the administration of John F. Kennedy when National Security Advisor McGeorge Bundy convinced the president that he needed regular intelligence briefings in the wake of the Bay of Pigs fiasco. The product for the briefing was called the President's Intelligence Checklist (PICL), which soon earned the sobriquet of the Pickle. When I joined the CIA's Office of Current Intelligence in 1966, the office was known as the "pickle factory," since its officers provided the editors and writers for the PICL.

The PICL became the PDB in the administration of Lyndon B. Johnson, and regardless of the nomenclature the document was the premier intelligence product of the intelligence community. The document was seen by very few people within the administration, rarely more than 10 or 12, and it contained the most sensitive intelligence known to the community. Satellite photography, intercepted communications and signals, sensitive Department of State cables, and clandestine reports were the stock in trade. As a junior analyst, there was an adrenaline rush in writing for the President and the senior members of the Cabinet and the White House staff.

In view of Trump's limited curiosity and acumen, it was no surprise that the president had no interest in receiving written documents such as the PDB. Trump continued to receive oral briefings that were based on the PDB, but even these briefings were not given regularly. A kind White House staffer acknowledged that Trump is "not a voracious reader."[96] According to my sources, President Trump's attention span is shorter than a television commercial. Pompeo conceded this point by noting analysts were particularly good at preparing "killer graphics."[97]

Former CIA director Panetta knew it was wrong for the president to deprive himself of the "important context and nuance" that the PDB affords. But Panetta went too far when he asserted that the chances for bad decision making will increase without access to this written product. My own experience based on serving six presidents is that decisions are rarely influenced by relevant intelligence, but are the end result of strongly held beliefs of the president and his closest advisers. If the administrations of Kennedy and Johnson had read CIA intelligence on Vietnam in the 1960s, they may not have pursued the unwinnable conflict.

---

[96] Patrick Badden Keefe, "McMaster and Commander: Can a national-security adviser retain his integrity if the President has none?" *The New Yorker*, April 30, 2018, p. 36.

[97] Carol D. Leonnig, Shane Harris, and Greg Jaffe, "President opts out of daily written intelligence report," *The Washington Post*, February 10, 2018, p. 14.

Trump lacks the context on sensitive geopolitical and military issues that is needed to understand the PDB or the complexities of most international issues. He complained his briefers were "talking down to him," which presumably took place when intelligence briefers tried to fill in the considerable gaps in Trump's knowledge.[98] The National Security Advisor is also responsible for filling in those gaps as the most accessible and powerful member of the national security team. McMaster was a survivor in the job, lasting more than a year, and he soon developed grave qualms about the president's intellect.

McMaster's successor, John Bolton, has been groveling to the president since his first day on the job, and there is no expectation that his supine posture will change. Unlike McMaster, Bolton does not even sit through the intelligence briefings that Trump receives irregularly. Bolton has his own problems with the assessments of the intelligence community, and prefers to use his place in the West Wing to whisper in the ear of the president with his own intelligence assessments when they are together. Fred Fleitz, a former intelligence officer for Bolton in the NSC, acknowledged that Bolton "basically is giving him vast amounts of intelligence throughout the day. I think he's getting most of it from what Bolton is able to recount for him."[99]

The only president whose disparagement of the CIA matched that of Trump was Richard Nixon, whose attitude, according to then CIA Director Richard Helms, was that "the only bright, really intelligent fellow in town was himself. He was constantly disparaging everybody else about their abilities."[100] If Nixon had had his druthers he would have conducted a "house-cleaning" at the CIA, which he described as a "muscle-bound bureaucracy" with a "paralyzed brain" and

---

[98] Leonnig, Harris and Jaffe, "President ops out of daily written intelligence report," p. 14.

[99] Greg Miller, "President's mistrust of spy agencies expands," *The Washington Post*, December 12, 2018, p. 17.

[100] John A. Farrell, "Richard Nixon: The Life," New York: Doubleday, 2017, p. 512.

having "personnel, just like the personnel at State," who were "primarily Ivy League and Georgetown." Nixon ordered chief of staff Haldeman to study "how many people in CIA could be removed."[101] Trump was no less paranoid, although he probably never gives much thought to the diminished Ivy League and Georgetown set that intimidated Nixon.

Nixon's obsession with the CIA stemmed from his losing campaign to John F. Kennedy in 1960, when he blamed the intelligence agency for allowing the controversy over the nonexistent missile gap to help the Democratic contender. CIA Director Helms believed the CIA's "standing with Nixon was never very good" and that "from the first day he came to office, the Agency had an uphill battle" with him.[102] Nixon finally removed Helms as Director because of his unwillingness to cooperate in the Watergate coverup and his pessimistic intelligence estimates on the Vietnam War.

Trump's criticism of the intelligence community is not only destructive of these key institutions, but it is self-destructive as well. Most decisions in the national security arena would benefit from insight from the intelligence community. Arms control and disarmament decisions require an intensive CIA role in the field of verification and monitoring of treaty commitments. If Trump followed up on his threats against North Korea or Iran, he would need intelligence to justify military action.

The Trump administration's efforts to ban travel from seven Muslim countries led to the first test between the White House and the intelligence community. A Federal three-judge panel indicated that the travel ban did not bolster national security in the United States, and the intelligence community found "no evidence" that anyone from the seven countries had committed

---

[101] Farrell, "Richard Nixon," p. 512.

[102] Farrell, "Richard Nixon," p. 630.

terrorism in the United States. Former intelligence tsar Clapper stated there was no intelligence to justify a ban.

Nevertheless, White House lawyer Rudy Giuliani was tasked with making the ban politically palatable. He was charged with "putting a commission together to show the right way to do it legally," and Attorney General Sessions had to document a case acceptable to the Court. The Supreme Court predictably deferred to the President on immigration, citing national security reasons. The Court ignored relevant intelligence information for its decision, which points to politicization at the highest level of the judicial system.

Trump's efforts to politicize the intelligence community reached its apogee in the summer of 2018, when he revoked Brennan's security clearance on August 15, 2018. There was a collective response from numerous intelligence chiefs who had served both Republican and Democratic administrations, including Judge William Webster and Leon Panetta. Their statement called Trump's actions "inappropriate and deeply regrettable" and charged that the president was trying to "stifle free speech."

Brennan's right of free speech had not been compromised, but there is a greater risk that current leaders of the intelligence community, particularly CIA director Haspel, will be less willing to tell truth to power when it involves an angry and vengeful reader of the President's Daily Brief such as Donald Trump. The fact that Brennan's clearances were revoked without any bureaucratic or legal process is also troubling.

Brennan probably went too far in putting on the gloves with the president, who has cited such criticism as examples of the "deep state" in action. Brennan compared Trump to convicted felon Bernie Madoff, which Trump's supporters cited as indicative of a "deep state" in the intelligence community. Brennan, after all, has his own tarnished record to defend, and should never have been appointed to be the CIA director in the first place. In any event, the brawl between the White

House and the CIA is not contributing to stabilizing U.S. national security policy that has been adrift under the Trump presidency.

As a key member of the executive staff of the CIA under director Tenet, Brennan was a key supporter of the unconscionable policies of torture and abuse; secret prisons; and extraordinary renditions. As a chief of staff and deputy executive director, Brennan took part in the cover-up of a CIA drug interdiction program in Peru that led to the death of an American missionary and her daughter. Finally, as President Obama's CIA director, Brennan ordered the hacking of Senate intelligence committee investigators in order to remove important documents from the congressional investigation, which was a violation of the separation of powers. Brennan said publicly that it was "beyond the scope of reason" to believe the CIA would undertake such activities, but it was Brennan who ordered CIA lawyers to conduct the hacking. There were no consequences, no accountability for Brennan's actions.

In the final analysis, the only protection against politicization is not in the system or process of intelligence, but in the courage and integrity of intelligence analysts themselves. The appointment of weak directors of the CIA (Pompeo and Haspel) points to an absence of a moral compass at the top of the intelligence ladder. Haspel demonstrated the absence of a moral compass at her confirmation hearings and, with the appointment of a loyal "war cabinet," there is no assurance that key decision makers will stand up against politicization of intelligence. Pompeo and Haspel were confirmed in part because a handful of Democratic Senators from Red States, facing tough reelection chances in November 2018, were afraid to join the overwhelming number of Democrats who opposed both nominations.

There are reports that intelligence agencies are reluctant to share sensitive information from foreign sources that contain criticism of the president as well as key advisors such as son-in-law Jared Kushner. One of the best sources of information on foreign perceptions of U.S. foreign policy is communications intelligence gathered by the National Security Agency. If intelligence analysts practice self-censorship because of President Trump's sensitivities, the national security team will lack a key element in assessing the implications of U.S. policy.

Weak leadership at the CIA will worsen the problem of recent intelligence failures that have caught U.S. leaders off guard. Haspel's experience is limited to operations, and her shaky confirmation performance before the Senate intelligence committee did not demonstrate an agile or energetic intellect. In the past ten years alone, Washington's national security decision makers have not received premonitory intelligence regarding the Arab spring and the Syrian rebellion; the Russian interventions in Crimea, Eastern Ukraine, and Syria; the pace of the nuclear program in North Korea; and the diplomatic thrust from Kim Jong Un for summitry with the United States and South Korea.

There is one silver lining in the dark intelligence cloud, however, and it was the performance of CIA Director Haspel in the wake of the Saudi killing of the dissident journalist Jamal Khashoggi. Although Trump, Mattis, and Pompeo denied any "direct reporting" linking the Crown Prince to the killing, Haspel made a strong case for his involvement to the president and the secretary of state as well as to congressional leaders.[103] Even a sycophantic senator such as Lindsey Graham (R/SC) emerged from Haspel's briefing to say the case against the Crown Prince was overwhelming.

Unfortunately, Trump ignored the authoritative intelligence. He insisted on sticking by the Saudis as a supportive ally against Iran. His administration has tightened relations with Israel and Saudi Arabia, who share a condemnation for Iran and its leaders. In doing so, Trump and Pompeo have underestimated the instability caused by the U.S. invasion of Iraq in 2003; the aggressive nature of the Israeli government; and the militant leadership in Saudi Arabia that has

---

[103] Greg Miller, "President's mistrust of spy agencies expands," *The Washington Post*, December 12, 2018, p. 17.

overplayed its hand in Yemen, Qatar, and Syria. Secretary of Defense Mattis described Iran as the "single most enduring threat to stability and peace in the Middle East." Secretary of State Pompeo echoed the view of Saudi Arabia's Foreign Minister Adel al-Jubeir that "Iran is on a rampage." The United States has never accepted that its military interventions in Afghanistan in 2001 and Iraq in 2003, which removed Iran's enemies to the east and west—the Taliban and Saddam Hussein, respectively—opened up opportunities for Iran in the region.

U.S. policy and intelligence are in fact falling behind the rapidly changing scene and the turmoil in the Middle East that has provided openings for Russia, Turkey, and Iran. Trump, Pompeo, and former UN Ambassador Haley used worst case views to challenge the Iranian nuclear accord and have exaggerated the success of Tehran's efforts to spread the Islamic Revolution throughout the region. National security adviser Bolton has a long record of politicizing intelligence to support his policy views and recommendations.

Iran's willingness to enter a diplomatic accord to control its nuclear program demonstrated the pragmatic nature of its leaders, and the ability of moderates to outflank extremists within the leadership, but the United States is not taking advantage of these opportunities. Trump's discarding of the Iran nuclear agreement, which U.S. intelligence vouched for, created greater instability throughout the Middle East and worsened the position of the moderates in Iran.

It is difficult to imagine Pompeo, Haspel, or Bolton having a beneficial influence over the thinking of the president or to even contribute to the substance of Trump's policies. He is no thinker, let alone a strategic thinker. There is no Trump doctrine or strategy to guide American policy abroad, and his war on intelligence will limit substantive discussions of his foreign policies. His thoughts emanate from the White House in 280-character sound bites that demonstrate no awareness of the consequences of his statements, let alone an appreciation for unintended consequences. Trump regularly ignored his communications directors (there were three of them in his first seven months); his chiefs of staff (there were two of them in the first six months); and his lawyers (far too many to track), who tried to silence his tweets or at least soften his edges.

In view of the conflict that the Trump administration is facing in the Middle East, North Africa, and Southwest Asia as well as the potential for conflict in North Korea and Iran, the importance of objective and balanced intelligence has never been greater. By maligning the intelligence community, particular the CIA and the FBI, President Trump has not made Americans safer, and has compromised the possibility for a thoughtful debate on U.S. actions abroad. President Harry S. Truman created a Central Intelligence Agency to provide information for decision making at the highest levels of government; President Trump has weakened and demoralized the intelligence institutions. The rebuilding process will be difficult and prolonged.

– 5 –

TRUMP'S WAR ON GOVERNANCE

"The one that matters is me. I'm the only one that matters because when it comes to it, that's what the policy is going to be."

—President Donald Trump, January 2017

"You know, the saddest thing is that because I'm the president of the United States, I'm not supposed to be involved with the Justice Department. I am not supposed to be involved with the FBI. I'm not supposed to be doing the kind of things that I would love to be doing. And I'm very frustrated by it."

—President Donald Trump, November 2017

"I have the absolute right to do what I want with the Department of Justice."

—President Donald Trump, January 2018

As a 42-year federal "lifer" (U.S. Army, Central Intelligence Agency, Department of State, and Department of Defense), I find Trump's war on governance an outrage. The President has created chaos throughout the government, weakening the professional civil service, a key to good governance, and this predates the government shutdown that began in December 2018. Public servants throughout the government are demoralized by Trump's attacks and the shutdown. What is it like to be in the FBI, which the president has described as "in tatters?" Or the national security bureaucracy, which he labels a sinister "deep state?" Applications to the Foreign Service have fallen by half, which speaks directly to the problem for the Department of State. Government scientists are being kicked to the side of the road.

Governance is the political process that involves the rules, norms, and actions of the federal bureaucracy. Western democracies have developed rules and norms essential to good government and to accountability for government. For the past two years, we have seen a steady degradation of these rules and norms, which has led to legislative and bureaucratic dysfunction.

Trump's war against governance began with his inauguration on January 21, 2017, when he dispensed with the customary niceties of the day and introduced the idea of an "American Carnage" that only he could repair. When former President George W. Bush left the inauguration platform, he was heard to utter, "That was some weird shit." The speech was Trump's battle plan, his declaration of war, in front of five former presidents who were accused of selling out the nation to special interests. There had never been such a dystopian inaugural speech in our history.

No institution of governance escaped Trump's wrath, including the Congress, the judiciary, and the intelligence community. During his campaign, Trump mocked members of both political parties, and gave them juvenile nicknames that would be fitting on a playground. Trump's war on truth is aimed at all fact-gatherers, regardless of government department or agency. The attacks on public service and the federal budget included freezing the hiring of nonmilitary federal employees, defunding international organizations that support abortions, and suspending immigration from Muslim countries in the Middle East. The attack on the media targets the most important non-governmental guardrail for governmental accountability.

The quickest path for implementing Stephen Bannon's "deconstruction of the administrative state" is to stop hiring key staffers and drive away those in place. The Office of Personnel Management records that in the first six months of the Trump administration 71,000 career employees quit or retired, compared with

40,000 in the first six months of the Obama administration.[104] The total turnover for White House appointees is unprecedented, reaching more than 80 percent in the first two years. The only survivors among the top twelve positions in the White House are the cabinet secretary Bill McGinley and the chairman of the Council of Economic Advisers Kevin Hassett.

In two years, the Trump administration has fostered the greatest instability and unreliability in the federal government in modern American history. In addition to a huge number of vacancies, the overall turnover rate in the Trump administration is unprecedented, reaching 34 percent in the second year of his administration. This triples the comparable number for the Obama administration, and doubles the number for the Reagan administration, which held the modern record until Trump arrived. One cannot begin to imagine the level of anxiety and chaos within the various bureaucratic institutions.

At the half-way mark of Trump's first term, there have been three press secretaries, two chiefs of staff, three national security advisors, and three deputy national security advisers. Communications are a particular problem for Trump, so it is no surprise that there have been six communications directors in addition to Trump himself, who essentially serves as his own communications director. The Secretary of Health and Human Services was gone in the first year; the director of the Environmental Protection Agency was gone in the second year; and most members of Trump's legal team, including the White House counsel, Donald F. McGahn II, went through the revolving door exit in the second year as well. When Secretary of the Interior Ryan Zinki resigned in December 2018, he was the fourth Cabinet secretary to resign under an ethics cloud in less than two years.

---

[104] Fred Hiatt, "We have a treasure," *The Washington Post*, January 7, 2018, p. 21.

Having served in the CIA under a corrupt director and deputy director in the 1980s, I can testify that it takes very little time and effort to harm a bureaucracy, and there is no assurance that it can be rebuilt. The CIA has never fully recovered from the politicization of intelligence in the 1980s, which was followed by the falsification of intelligence to justify the invasion of Iraq in 2003. When you lose senior people with institutional memory, their experience is lost as well as their mentoring for junior staffers. The Departments of State and Justice as well as the Environmental Protection Agency and the Consumer Financial Protection Bureau will need many years to recover from Donald Trump.

Numerous executive branch positions remain vacant, particularly key positions dealing with science and technology. President Trump needed 19 months to appoint a science adviser, one of the most important positions in the executive branch, and he wasn't confirmed for another five months. In the process, the Trump White House cast aside well-established scientific findings on global warming and climate change.

Prior to the elections in November 2018, the Congress—particularly the House of Representatives—demonstrated no interest in accountability or oversight for the bureaucratic chaos. President Obama's weakening of the institution of the Inspector General delivered a huge body blow to democratic governance, but that was modest compared to Trump's attacks. Ironically, the attack on the regulations concerning air and water introduced by the Obama administration was stepped up in the summer of 2018, a year marked by historic heat waves, wildfires, droughts, and greater Arctic ice melt.

Some of Trump's claims regarding his administration have been beyond ludicrous. Trump has falsely claimed to sign more legislation than any first-year president, when in fact he has signed less than most. He falsely claimed record crowds for his inauguration and then vilified the National Park Service for displaying photography that exposed the absurdity of his claim. Trump proclaimed that his first State of the Union speech attracted record listeners at home and abroad—not so. During the campaign, he questioned the authenticity of a recording that found him bragging about "grabbing…pussy," even though he had already apologized for the remarks heard around the world and dismissed by the First Lady as "boy talk." He accused NBC newsman Lester Holt of doctoring the tape that recorded Trump's admission that he fired FBI director Comey because of the Russian "witch hunt." In a move that was "Kremlinesque," a tape was altered in November 2018 to justify the revocation of a reporter's White House press credentials.

Trump's fascination with ovations, particularly standing ovations, is reminiscent of Joseph Stalin's fascination with "stormy and thunderous applause." Applause became panic-driven in the Soviet Union, and now Trump has accused Democrats of treason for not applauding his State of the Union in January 2018. Trump held a secret meeting with his military chiefs at the Pentagon in January to arrange a military parade on Pennsylvania Avenue.

Trump knew that an effective way to "deconstruct the administrative state" was to appoint stewards to undo the underlying mission of their departments and conduct a thorough housecleaning. In his 19 months at EPA, Scott Pruitt weakened every major piece of clean air and clean water legislation introduced over the past several decades. Former Secretary of State Tillerson, one of the so-called "adults in the room," drastically reduced the role of the Foreign Service as well as diplomacy itself, and caused a major crisis of morale at a once illustrious institution. Alex Azar at the Department of Health and Human Services, which is supposed to tackle the problem of overpriced prescription drugs, once ran a division of a drug company known for doubling the price of insulin. The mission of HHS has been compromised.

Then, there were the know-nothings. Kirstjen Nielsen at the Department of Homeland Secretary defended the president's travel ban and said she didn't know Norway was a predominantly white country. Betsy DeVos at the Department of Education demonstrated she knew nothing about public education. Ben Carson at the Department of Housing and Urban Development and Rick Perry at the Department of Energy were uninformed and worked to undermine the missions of their agencies.

A shameless pick was Steven Mnuchin at the Department of the Treasury, which had been led over the years by some of the most sterling practitioners in U.S. history, starting of course with George Washington's selection of Alexander Hamilton. Former Secretary of Defense Mattis was probably the only exception to Trump's list of bureaucratic mediocrities, but he offered no challenge to Trump's travel ban or the stationing of troops on the border with Mexico to protect our national security from an "armada" of asylum-seeking Central Americans.

In addition to their lack of experience, Trump's appointees have lacked integrity, misusing public funds. The leader was Pruitt, the former head of the EPA who registered hundreds of thousands of dollars in transportation costs in his first year, which did not include the travel expenditures for his personal security detail and aides who accompanied him. Pruitt's staff claimed that he needed to fly first-class because of the number of threats he had received as well as the "security protocols that require him to be near the front of the plane."[105] The taxpayers forked over thousands of dollars for a trip to Australia that never took place, and for domestic trips to industry groups supporting Pruitt's efforts to end environmental regulations.

There were other expenses that taxpayers had to bear. Pruitt's concern for security led to the construction of a soundproof phone booth in his office for a tidy sum of $43,000.[106] The phone booth was used on only one occasion. Pruitt

---

[105] Brady Dennis and Juliet Eilperin, "Pruitt ran up nearly $68,000 in recent trips," The Washington Post, March 21, 2018, p 12.

[106] Juliet Eilperin and Brady Dennis, "Trump Cabinet members are accused of living large at taxpayer expense," The Washington Post, March 15, 2018, p. 6.

ordered a staffer to shop for a used mattress from the Trump Hotel chain, which even the president found bizarre. Pruitt was forced to resign but remained under investigation by the EPA's Inspector General, the House Committee on Oversight and Government Reform, and the Government Accountability Office. The charges range from exorbitant expenditures on travel and security as well as conflict of interest issues and the legality of dismissing scientists from EPA advisory boards. Even the White House investigated Pruitt for "overall ethics and management decisions."[107] Finally, on July 5, 2018, the Trump administration had to drain—at least partially—the swamp it created, forcing Pruitt to resign.

Pruitt's successor, Andrew Wheeler, will do more harm to the mission of the EPA and will avoid the excesses of his predecessor. Wheeler "trained" for his current post as a lobbyist for the very interests that created so many problems for the EPA. These interests include electric utilities, uranium producers, and coal magnates. Wheeler's former lobbying firm earned several million dollars representing one of the coal barons. His most recent activity as a lobbyist for the coal industry was fighting the Department of the Interior's efforts to restrict coal companies from dumping waste into streams. Wheeler also has been involved in successful efforts to kill congressional plans to curtail carbon emissions. Another fox will be guarding the chickens.

Many others remain in the swamp. Secretary Carson ordered a $31,561 dining table for his executive suite in Housing and Urban Development, but he claimed that his wife was to blame. The order was eventually cancelled when the press called attention to Carson's profligacy, and he was summoned to the White House to answer for embarrassing the President. In addition to Carson, there were trips to the White House woodshed for Pruitt, David Shulkin of the Veterans Administration, and Secretary of the Interior Zinke. The first Secretary of Health

---

[107] "Pruitt under investigation," Chart, *The Washington Post*, April 11, 2018, p. 9.

and Human Services Thomas Price lost his job in September 2017 for misusing travel funds. The former head of the Centers for Disease Control and Prevention, Brenda Fitzgerald, was fired for suspicious stock trades; the head of the Department of Commerce, Wilbur Ross, is being investigated for the same reason.

The Trump administration's attack on governance targeted groups that protect the most vulnerable and powerless members of our society such as the Presidential Advisory Council on HIV/AIDS created by President Clinton in 1995 to advise on policy. The Council's members are appointed to four-year terms by the Secretary of Health and Human Services in consultation with the White House. Members are not paid, and their membership has included doctors, industrialists, and prominent people living with HIV. Their expertise is one of the reasons for the success in turning the HIV infection from a death sentence into a manageable illness.

A half-dozen members of the Council resigned in June 2017 because of Price's stance on health policy. One of them, Scott A. Schoettes, the HIV project director at Lambda Legal, a leading LGBT rights organization, accused the Trump administration of pushing legislation that will "harm people living with HIV and halt or reverse important gains made in the fight against this disease."[108] Several months later, the Trump administration dismissed the remaining members of the Council, some of whom were serving four-year terms that began in 2016. Patrick Sullivan, an epidemiologist at Emory University who was dismissed, has testified to the importance of having diverse outlooks on the Council.[109] Trump also left vacant the White House post of Director of National

---

[108] Matt Stevens and Daniel Victor, "Remaining Members of AIDS Council Fired," *The New York Times*, December 23, 2017, p. 18.

[109] Ben Guarino, "Holdovers on Trump's AIDS council are ousted," *The Washington Post*, December 30, 2017, p. 3.

AIDS policy, created by President Clinton in 1993 to provide strategic leadership in the campaign against HIV/AIDS.

The Trump administration has no plan for dealing with the HIV/AIDS epidemic and no interest in consulting with experts in the field, let alone pulsing the community voice for policymaking. Trump was particularly critical of the National Institutions of Health and the Center for Disease Control and Prevention during the campaign, and picked his first Secretary of Health and Human Services because of his opposition to Obamacare. Trump's position on controlling infectious disease is part and parcel of his stance on immigration—do not let the disease into the country in the first place.

One of the more Orwellian aspects of the Trump administration has been the censoring of certain words and phrases in government departments and agencies, particularly at HHS. Officials at the CDC were given a list of seven words and phrases that could not be used in budget documents. These words and phrases included "entitlement," "diversity," "vulnerable," "evidence-based," "science-based," "fetus," and "transgender." "Climate change" is particularly taboo. HHS officials were instructed to use the term "Obamacare," and never refer to the Affordable Care Act or ACA, in an effort to stigmatize the program.

Former HHS Secretary Price, like Trump, fixated on killing ACA. In short order, Price compromised the ACA by eliminating the individual mandate that penalizes Americans who didn't buy health insurance, which the Supreme Court upheld in 2017. Trump also permitted states to impose work requirements and other penalties on holders of Medicaid, which pushed millions of low-income Americans in the poorest states out of the program. In June 2018, the Trump administration told a federal court that it would no longer defend crucial provisions of the ACA that protect consumers with pre-existing conditions, one of the most important provisions of the act.[110] Azar is quietly following Price's play book.

Another target was Planned Parenthood, which provides funding to women for a variety of services other than abortion such as prenatal care and screenings for disease. Planned Parenthood serves low-income women who have few readily available alternatives to its services. President Reagan catered to the antiabortion movement in the 1980s, when he barred federal spending to advise patients about pregnancy termination, a ruling upheld by the Supreme Court in 1991.

The Department of State was ordered to stop using the term "sex education," and to substitute "sexual risk avoidance," which some puritanical bureaucrat presumably introduced. This ban was part of the Trump administration's campaign on Capitol Hill to stress abstinence-only practices until marriage as the primary form of sex education. Was President Trump aware of the personal irony of all this? Censorship at the Department of State will mean that money will not be spent overseas on abortions and maternal health, according to the vice president and director of global health and HIV policy at the Kaiser Family Foundation.[111]

The HHS press briefing to announce these changes was given anonymously, with the briefer acknowledging that specific agencies were not being named because language changes were on "close hold."[112] Particularly offensive was the ban on the word "transgender" in view of the high percentage of HIV infections among transgender women, the highest of any gender group. Censorship at the HHS agencies is particularly offensive because their programs must be science-

---

[110] Robert Pear, "Justice Dept. Acts Against Protections for People with Pre-Existing Conditions," *The New York Times*, June 8, 2018, p. 13.

[111] Sun and Eilperin, "Words banned at HHS agencies," p. 16.

[112] Lena H. Sun and Juliet Eilperin, "Words banned at HHS agencies include 'diversity' and 'vulnerable,'" *The Washington Post*, December 17, 2017, p. 16.

based or evidence-based as part of a larger search for truth. As a former surgeon general, Dr. Vivek Murphy, noted, "When science is censored the truth is censored."[113]

In addition to censoring language, the Trump administration has censored press coverage. In May 2018, the EPA barred reporters from three news organizations—CNN, AP, and the authoritative energy and environmental publication *E&E*—from attending a meeting on water contamination. The meeting included more than 200 representatives of regulatory and industry groups.[114] In 2017, the White House barred reporters from CNN, *The New York Times*, Politico, and the *Los Angeles Times* from a meeting with then press secretary Sean Spicer, who restricted attendance to conservative outlets.

Trump's dislike of foreign aid and his campaign against scientific research has led to deep cuts in medical work overseas, such as fighting disease, that will hurt the health of Americans. The new Ebola outbreak in the Congo this year is not a faraway problem; it could find its way to the United States. But the Trump administration had no science adviser for the first year and a half, and National Security Adviser Bolton reorganized the National Security Council to ignore pandemic threats. If the United States can't identify and fight outbreaks of infections abroad, it will be more costly and time consuming to fight these infections at home.

Much of the political debate in the Trump era has turned on appeals to emotion and fear through the use of polarizing rhetoric and fabrications. The best example of this is the heated debate over immigration marked by President Trump's vulgar language. Before his ugly reference to "shithole" countries, which

---

[113] Sheila Kaplan and Donald G. McNeil Jr., "Uproar Grows Over a Reported Word Ban at the Centers for Disease Control," *The New York Times*, December 19, 2017, p. 15.

[114] Paul Farhi, "EPA denies access to summit for reporters from 3 news groups," *The Washington Post*, May 23, 2018, p. 9.

exposed Trump's racism, the president made numerous references to so-called higher types and lower types that were reminiscent of the debate over immigration nearly 100 years ago. During the 1920's immigration debate, there were attacks on cheap immigrant labor and depressed wages as well as blatantly racist rhetoric designed to protect the "Nordic" race from "replacement types." Trump asked: Why should the United States take in immigrants from "shithole countries" in Africa over people from places like Norway?[115]

Ever since 1965, when the Congress repealed the per-country quotas and created a system that emphasized new immigrants' family ties and their skills, there have been "know-nothings" and nativists who have tried to restrict immigration to white Europeans. Trump has waged war against undocumented immigrants by sponsoring a border wall, abolishing sanctuary cities, and deporting illegals who are "killing American citizens." Trump's rudeness toward German Chancellor Merkel during a state visit in 2017 was his way of protesting her efforts to allow Muslim refugees to enter Germany in the wake of the chaos in the Middle East and Africa.

Trump's base encouraged his war for our borders as the beginning of a "new world order," and applauded his appointment of general officers to national security positions in order to save Western civilization from the "barbaric elements in both the radical left and Islam."[116] Neoconservatives remind us of the importance of having fought World War II far from our shores, which allowed us to "emerge relatively unscathed." Trump wants to keep the "Islamofascists" far from our shores so that the next war is fought elsewhere. The support for a military campaign in faraway places such as Syria, Afghanistan, and Somalia is motivated by such thinking.

---

[115] Vivian Lee, "Trump's Jabs Echo Attitudes From the '20s," *The New York Times*, January 11, 2018, p. 1.

[116] Michael Savage, "Trump's War: His Battle for America," New York: Hachette Book Group, 2017, p. 69.

125 | AMERICAN CARNAGE

There was never a reason to believe that Trump would be compassionate toward the 800,000 Dreamers who are hostage to his overall plan to "safeguard" our borders. Prior to his inauguration, Trump asked the Department for Homeland Security for "copies of every executive order and directive sent to immigration agents since Obama took office in 2009."[117] Trump stressed that Obama's "bleeding-heart liberal sensibilities," which he compared to Merkel's, were undermining U.S. borders. White House advisors Bannon and Miller provided the rhetorical fuel for Trump's fires, and the appointment of Marine General John Kelly, who once led the Southern Command, signaled that immigrants would face difficult times. The Trump administration's raid on more than 90 convenience stores in a dozen states in January 2018 symbolized a new aggressiveness for the U.S. Immigration and Customs Enforcement (ICE).

In a typically mean-spirited maneuver, the Trump administration rescinded an Obama-era policy that ordered immigration officials to release pregnant women from federal custody. His administration even opposed an appeals court's decision to stop the shackling of incarcerated pregnant women during child birth. The Obama administration instructed ICE to focus on detaining and deporting criminals, and provided some protection to undocumented immigrants. Philip Miller, the deputy executive associate director of ICE, announced in March 2018 that "We're no longer exempting any individual from being subject to the law."[118] ICE has separated parents from their children after illegal border crossings, and federal officials have made it harder for immigrants to get asylum hearings before a judge. The Trump administration's aggressive attack on illegal immigration led to a 40 percent increase in immigration arrests and a 35 percent increase in deportations in Trump's first year as president.

---

[117] Debra Heine, "Trump Posed to Build Wall and Undo Obama's Executive Actions on Immigration," PJ Media, January 3 2017.

[118] Maria Sacchetti, "U.S. ends policy for pregnant detainees," The Washington Post, March 30, 2018, p. 16.

Trump, who campaigned aggressively against Obama's protections for undocumented immigrants, suffered a major reversal in March 2018, when a federal judge cited Trump's "racially charged language" in preserving a program that protects hundreds of thousands of young undocumented immigrants from deportation. Judge Nicholas G. Garaufis of the Federal District Court in Brooklyn gave a huge boost to President Obama's DACA program (Deferred Action for Childhood Arrivals), which continues to draw heated congressional debate. Judge Garaufis pointed to Trump's numerous "racial slurs" and "epithets" as a candidate and as president, arguing that his efforts to end DACA violated the equal protection clause of the Constitution.[119] The judge cited Trump's description of Mexican immigrants as "rapists" and "criminals" as well as his attacks on an American-born jurist of Mexican descent. He also noted Trump's references to Latino immigrants as "animals" and "bad hombres."

The National Immigration Law Center and attorneys general of sixteen states sued the United States to prevent the Trump administration from ending DACA. Their statement on September 5, 2017 called Trump's decision a "morally bankrupt choice," and opposed policymakers trying to "erect barriers that block youth from contributing their best to this country, which is their home."[120] Thus far, two federal courts are in agreement on this issue, and even the Supreme Court has permitted DACA to remain in place while the legal process continues. Meanwhile, Judge Garaufis wrote that his "court does not see why it must or should bury its head in the sand when faced with overt expressions of prejudice."

---

[119] Alan Feuer, "Judge Cites Trump's 'Racial Slurs' in Denying Move to End DACA Suit," *The New York Times*, March 30, 2018, p. 18.

[120] William Boardman, "President's Blatant Bigotry May Save DREAMERS in Federal Court," *Reader Supported News*, April 3, 2018, p. 1.

Trump argued that immigrants bring crime into the cities, and that sanctuary cities are nothing more than "safe havens for terrible people."[121] There is strong evidence that cities with significant immigrant populations have lower incidences of crimes and violence than cities with fewer immigrants. Various studies indicate that immigration tends to reduce crime because of greater economic and cultural revitalization or that there is simply no relationship between the two factors. Nevertheless, the Trump administration has based its border enforcement strategy and its travel bans on the mythology of linking crime to immigration.

The Department of Justice even conceded that its report linking terrorism in the United States and immigration was replete with errors and deficiencies, but refused to retract or even correct the document. Trump requested the report to support his executive order in March 2017 to ban travel from seven Muslim-majority countries. It is unusual for any department of government to acknowledge flawed reporting, but even more unusual to do nothing about it. The counsel for Protect Democracy, Ben Berwick, opined that this practice "erodes trust in government. It erodes democracy."[122]

On Easter Sunday in April 2018, Trump issued a series of tweets that accused liberals and Democrats of blocking Border Patrol Agents from doing their jobs. He blamed Mexico for "doing very little, if not NOTHING, at stopping people from flowing...into the U.S."[123] Trump then repeated his message from September 2017 for ending DACA and challenged lawmakers to come up with a legislative solution for 'Dreamers." Yet when Democrats brought forth a

---

[121] Anna Flagg, "The Myth of the Criminal Immigrant," *The New York Times*, March 30, 2018, p. 12

[122] Ellen Nakashima, "Justice Dept. admits error but won't fix report tying terrorism, immigration," *The Washington Post*, January 4, 2019, p. 11.

[123] geobeats.com, "Trump Lashes Out Over Border Security, Immigration on TWITTER: 'NO MORE DACA DEAL," April 1, 2018.

compromise on immigration legislation that would have provided funds for Trump's wall, the President rejected it.

Former Attorney General Sessions reversed some of Obama's key steps to reform the criminal justice system, including investigations of police abuse and commutations for low-level drug offenders who have spent decades behind bars. As a senator, Sessions was one of the leading opponents of justice reform, and as Attorney General one of his first acts was to challenge the Sentencing Reform and Corrections Act and to resume the use of private, for-profit prisons. Sessions pandered to Trump in linking immigration to crime, and in charging incorrectly that undocumented immigrants commit more crimes than U.S. citizens.

No aspect of governance is overlooked in Trump's campaign to "drain the swamp" and to carry out Bannon's "deconstruction of the administrative state." Secretary of the Interior Zinke worked overtime to reduce the size and impact of good governance. Zinke reassigned 35 top department employees in June 2017, retaliating for their failure to support his policies. Zinke was on record as saying that "30 percent of the crew is not loyal to the flag," explaining an unprecedented purge.[124] He reassigned the National Park Service's most senior officials, reflecting President Trump's anger at the failure of the Park Service to corroborate his false claims regarding record crowds at his inauguration.

Zinke's ethical lapses caught up with him in December 2018, when he resigned in the wake of multiple probes of his real estate deals and his conduct in office. Allegations of unethical behavior surrounded his tenure soon after he took control of the Interior Department, and by the time of his resignation there were at least twelve investigations opened against him. The most serious charge covered a land deal between the chairman of Halliburton, the nation's largest oil services company, and Zinke who was responsible for regulating the oil industry

---

[124] Joel Achenbach, Dino Grandoni and Juliet Eilperin, "Proposed shake-up at Park Service could make senior leaders hit the road," *The Washington Post*, April 28, 2018, p. 3.

on public land. In less than two years as steward for the Department of Interior, Zinki garnered a record number of ethics investigations; one of them was sent to the Department of Justice's public integrity section.

The Justice Department's investigation could determine a criminal violation because it involves a land deal in Zinke's home state of Montana and a casino project by Native Americans in Connecticut. These cases were referred to Justice because the inspector general's office of the Interior Department believed Zinke lied to them.

In February 2019, Trump announced that David Bernhardt, Zinke's deputy chief, would be nominated to head the Department of the Interior. While Zinke was the public face of the rollbacks for protecting public lands, it was Bernhardt who opened millions of acres of land and water to oil, gas and coal companies. Bernhardt developed a plan for opening the U.S. coastline to offshore drilling. Environmentalists view Bernhardt as the "most dangerous man in America for endangered species and public lands."

Trump's war on governance immediately targeted the Consumer Financial Protection Bureau (CFPB), the brainchild of Senator Elizabeth Warren (D/MA), dubbed "Pocahantas" by a president who loves to dismiss his political opponents with labels. Mick Mulvaney, serving as acting chief of staff to the president as well as the head of the White House budget office, was named the Interim Director of the CFPB in the wake of the sacking of Richard Cordrey, a favorite of Senator Warren's.[125] Mulvaney's gutting of consumer financial protection is part of the war on the poor, the most vulnerable victims of financial exploitation. This is another example of how low income whites who voted for Trump are becoming his primary victims.

---

[125] Mulvaney told a group of South Carolina banking executives in May 2018 that, as a congressman from South Carolina, he never met with out-of-town lobbyists unless they had given him campaign donations. "If you were a lobbyist who never gave us money, I didn't talk to you. If you were a lobbyist who gave us money. I might talk to you." See Renae Merle, "Mulvaney points to a 'hierarchy' for lobbyists," *Washington Post*, May 2, 2018 p. 3.

In June 2018, Mulvaney appointed his deputy at the Office of Management and Budget, Kathy Kraninger, to be the new director at the Bureau. Kraninger has no experience in financial services and consumer affairs; she was appointed so that Mulvaney could maintain control of the Bureau. Her appointment continues Trump's war against Senator Warren and the CFPB.

College students have become major victims of the management changes at the CFPB. When the CFPB began in 2011, one of its first tasks was to target the for-profit education industry, which was lying about job-placement rates and leaving its graduates with large debts from predatory lenders. Education Secretary DeVos and Mulvaney are collaborating to undermine investigations of the for-profit schools by reassigning investigators charged with exposing corruption. In 2018, major investigations were halted at several institutions as Republican leaders in the Congress cooperated with the Department of Education and the CFPB. In her testimony to Congress, DeVos claimed there were no problems in the industry.

A greater problem for students is the debt on student loans that has doubled over the past decade. On August 27, 2018, the CFPB's ombudsman for student loans, Seth Frotman, suddenly resigned, accusing the bureau's political appointees of "undercutting enforcement of the law" and ending oversight of the student loan industry.[126] Ever since Mulvaney's appointment to CFPB as acting director, the bureau has either stopped or downsized investigations into misbehavior in the financial sector, ranging from payday loans to discriminatory lending policies. The Obama administration pursued banks that were charging excessive fees to college students with credit and debit cards; the Trump administration walked back these regulatory practices.

---

[126] Helaine Olen, "The scandalous handling of student loans," *The Washington Post*, August 29, 2018, p. 15.

131 | AMERICAN CARNAGE

Secretary of Education DeVos created additional havoc in the first two years of her stewardship, reversing regulations of the Obama administration to rein in predatory practices of for-profit colleges. These colleges, central to the DeVos family fortune, have been exploiting low-income students and American taxpayers who pay the bill for defaulted student loans. Trump's own "university" paid $25 million to settle fraud claims.

Nearly all fraud claims filed by students with the Department of Education concern for-profit educational institutions. Two of the largest for-profit institutions, ITT Technical Institute and Corinthian Colleges, have collapsed under the weight of various legal claims and government inquiries, but DeVos is trying to stem the tide. Her department has been staffed for the most part with aides connected to for-profit schools.

Secretary DeVos created new rules at the Department of Education on campus sexual misconduct to bolster the rights of students accused of assault, harassment, and rape, and to reduce liability for institutions of higher learning. These steps reversed regulations established during the Obama administration. Senator Patty Murray (D-WA) referred to DeVos' steps as "shameful and appalling…making it harder for students to seek justice if they've been sexually assaulted on campus."[127]

In addition to attacking public policy and public servants, Trump took an axe to departmental budgets of important domestic agencies. Overall, Trump's budget for 2019 was one of the meanest in the post-World War Two era, although the Republican-led Congress restored nearly all of the domestic cuts. In order to increase the defense budget to a record-level of $716 billion, the Trump administration made major cuts in the budgets for the Department of State, the

---

[127] Laura Meckler, Valerie Strauss, and Nick Anderson, "Greater rights considered for students accused of sex assault," *The Washington Post*, August 30, 2018, p. 8.

Environmental Protection Agency, Medicare and Medicaid, and the Department of Education. (The proposed budget for 2020 was even meaner.)

The proposed 13 percent increase in defense spending meant huge windfalls for major defense industries. Lockheed Martin, the manufacturer of the enormously expensive F-35 Joint Strike Fighter, has averaged nearly $40 billion in federal sales over the past decade, which is close to the budget of the Department of State and nearly twice as much as the budget for NASA. The five biggest defense contractors (Lockheed Martin, Boeing, General Dynamics, Raytheon, and Northrup Grumman) had total sales of nearly $110 billion to the U.S. government in 2017, which represents more money from the federal government than the next 30 non-defense companies combined.[128] The defense budget exceeds $1 trillion when the budgets for the Veterans Administration, the Department of Energy, and the intelligence community are included.

When Secretary of Defense Mattis was a Marine Corps general several years ago, he told Congress, "If you don't fully fund the State Department, then I need to buy more ammunition." Well, the cuts in the budget for the Department of State equalled the increased funding for a Department of Defense that is buying more missiles and munitions. The increased funding for defense for 2019, which exceeds $51 billion, matches the entire Russian defense budget.

The proposed cuts in Medicare were particularly comprehensive, involving $48 billion over ten years for teaching hospitals and graduate medical education; $69.5 billion over ten years for "uncompensated care" at hospitals; and $95 billion over ten years for nursing homes and home health agencies. During the campaign, Trump made a special point of saying that he would not cut Medicare, Medicaid, and other programs that benefit poor and middle-class families. Once in the White House, Trump moved quickly to compromise the Affordable Care Act in

---

[128] Christian Davenport and Aaron Gregg, "Lockheed gets more taxpayer money than some agencies," *The Washington Post*, February 18, 2018, p. 1.

every possible way. The compromise to Medicare and Medicaid is presumably the next target.

There is no better example of Trump's hypocrisy than his response to the horrific massacre at the Marjory Stoneman Douglas High School in Parkland, Florida on Valentine's Day in 2018. His rote address to the nation emphasized the need to "secure our schools and tackle the difficult issue of mental health." But his budget addressed the issue of mental health by cutting the Medicaid budget by $250 billion over the coming decade. Medicaid pays for more than 25 percent of the nation's mental health care.

The United States has one of the worst transportation systems in the industrial world, and the Trump budget would keep it that way. Grants to Amtrak were cut in half, and the Army Corps of Engineers, which manages public infrastructure programs, were designated for cuts of more than 20 percent.[129] Again, this is from a president who campaigned on the promise of building "gleaming new roads, bridges, highways, railways and waterways all across our land."

The proposed budget for 2019 called for deep cuts in public arts and media funding. Funding for the National Endowment for the Arts and the National Endowment for the Humanities was reduced by almost 80 percent, which would have eliminated these two important cultural institutions. Modest grants from these institutions have funded the work of such writers as Raymond Carver, Ernest J. Gaines, and Philip Levine who is know as the "Walt Whitman of the industrial heartland." If it were up to Trump, the Corporation for Public Broadcasting, responsible for the Public Broadcasting System, would see its budget go from $445 million to $15 million; the Institute of Museum and Library Services would be eliminated. The Trump administration awarded no prizes in

---

[129] Julie Hirschfeld Davis, "Trump's Budget Favors Military, Inflating Deficit," *The New York Times*, February 13, 2018, p. 12.

the arts field in its first two years, another unprecedented and dubious achievement.

Any department that has anything to do with limiting immigration will receive significant increases, particularly the Department of Homeland Security, which will be able to hire 2,000 new Immigration and Customs Enforcement and 750 Border Patrol agents. There was an additional $1.6 billion to build 65 miles of Trump's favorite wall in Texas. At the same time, Trump's White House and the Department of Homeland Security prevented any compromise to resolve the fate of the Dreamers, the 800,000 immigrants brought here illegally as children. Trump ultimately killed the bill that provided money for his wall because it would have saved the Dreamers. Trump declared the government shutdown in December 2018 to coerce the Congress in passing funds for his border wall.

Fortunately, Congress rejected much of Trump's "vision" for cutting back on governance. The Congress ignored many efforts to cut domestic programs or simply blocked his budgetary goals. Trump got his large increase in defense spending, but he didn't get his deep cuts to foreign aid; the Department of State; and various domestic programs dealing with education, the environment, clean energy, and biomedical research. His massive cuts in federal arts programs were rejected. The Institute of Museum and Library Services and the Children's Health Insurance Program were saved.

Even Trump's "big, beautiful wall" took a heavy hit. The $1.6 billion for border security was primarily given to new technology and repairs to existing barriers. The $641 billion for about 33 miles of fencing was previously authorized by the 2006 Secure Fence Act.[130] But a concrete wall was specifically prohibited; instead, there was financing for new aircraft, sensors and surveillance technology.

---

[130] Julie Hirschfield Davis, "A Republican Budget, but Not Exactly What the President Asked For," *The New York Times*, March 23, 2018, p. 20.

Instead of 10,000 additional Immigration and Customs Enforcement officers, the congressional budget capped the number of addition ICE offices at 65.

Secretary of Education DeVos wanted to decrease the education budget; in fact, education received an additional $3.9 billion in spending. Her pet project, private school vouchers, were specifically barred, and Congress increased the budget for two K-12 programs that DeVos wanted to eliminate, including an after-school program for 1.8 million low-income students as well as funding for mental health services and violence-prevention measures.

Former EPA Administrator Pruitt wanted a 30 percent cut in his budget; instead, Congress kept the $8.1 budget from the previous year, which is still a lower funding level than President Ronald Reagan's last year in the White House. Congress blocked Pruitt's efforts to defund the EPA's Office of the Inspector General, which was investigating his extensive first-class travel and security expenses. The Inspector General kept his previous budget of $41.5 million. Congress also blocked the huge reduction that Pruitt wanted in staffing, which he referred to euphemistically as "work-force reshaping."

Instead of deep cuts to the Department of Energy's development of clean energy technologies, the Congress substantially increased funding. Trump wanted to cut the department's Office of Energy Efficiency and Renewable Energy by nearly 70 percent; Congress increased funding by nearly 15 percent. There were also double-digit increases for programs for basic science, nuclear power, advanced manufacturing and fossil fuels that Trump tried to cut or eliminate.

There were across-the-board rejections of Trump's plans for deep cuts in social programs. Secretary of Housing and Urban Development Carson wanted to cut $6 billion from the HUD budget; he got an increase of $4.7 billion. Trump and Carson wanted to cut or kill community development block grants and funding for affordable housing; instead, Congress allocated a 42 percent increase in funding for the nation's crumbling public housing infrastructure and the department's core rental assistance program.

Carson, however, managed to harm HUD, stopping the Obama-era rules to ensure that communities end long-standing patterns of segregation. Carson, who grew up in public housing, has been a long-time critic of government efforts to remedy social and economic inequality. As a result, he refused to pursue landlords charged with discriminatory policies, and banks and real estate companies that ignored systemic racial discrimination. Due to the diminished commitment to its fair-housing mission, HUD has become dysfunctional with "people leaving and no one trying to stanch the bleeding," according to one official.[131] HUD thus joins the long list of departments that will have to be rebuilt when the Trump era ends.

Trump wanted to cut the Department of State's budget by 30 percent; instead, there was a modest cut and Trump was denied his efforts to kill George W. Bush's program to address H.I.V. in Africa. Trump's proposal to cut $7.5 billion from the budget of the National Institutes of Health was rejected; instead, there was an increase of $3 billion. Congress rejected efforts to eliminate funding for the Low Income Home Energy Assistance Program, adding $250 million to last year's budget of $3.6 billion.

Congress blocked Trump's culture war by providing an additional $153 million in funding for both the National Endowment for the Arts and the National Endowment for the Humanities. This represented an increase of $3 million for each agency over last year's budget. Trump's efforts to eliminate environmental programs also failed, including $300 million for cleaning up toxic sediment from the Great Lakes, and $73 million to restore the Chesapeake Bay.

The war over the Veterans Administration is typical of the ideological battles within the Administration. Trump's conservative supporters were never happy

---

[131] Tracy Jan, "HUD cuts anti-bias efforts in housing," *The Washington Post*, January 2, 2019, p. 4.

with the renomination of David Shulkin as the VA secretary because he was appointed originally by President Obama. So the report from the agency's Inspector General detailing Shulkin's misuse of travel funds on a trip to Europe that included the improper acceptance of tickets to the tennis tournament at Wimbledon set off a fire storm. Shulkin had been targeted by Trump's ideologues because he was standing in the way of their goal of privatizing health care for veterans.

The backstory is illustrative. Shulkin, unlike most of Trump's cabinet appointees, is a political moderate and an experienced hospital executive, popular on Capitol Hill. Shulkin and the congressional veteran's committees collaborated on several popular bipartisan legislative initiatives to improve the beleaguered health-care system for veterans. The Republican chairman of the Senate's Veterans Affairs Committee, Johnny Isakson of Georgia, was a particularly strong supporter. At a signing ceremony for one of these bills in June 2017, President Trump even noted that his Secretary didn't have to worry about hearing the president's old reality-show catch phrase, "You're fired."[132]

But this is where the Koch brothers and their front group, Concerned Veterans for America, entered the story. The Koch brothers oppose any public, fully integrated health system, whether it is Medicare or a system for veterans. Their campaign against Shulkin included the use of some of his deputies to lobby congress against the VA Administrator. Shulkin, facing a mutiny within his own department, reportedly placed armed guards outside his executive suite in the VA building; this would be dismissed as a surreal anecdote in any administration other than Trump's.[133]

---

[132] Maggie Haberman and Nicholas Fandos, "Veterans Affairs Secretary May Be Next One Ousted." *The New York Times,* March 14, 2018, p. 12.

[133] Michael Corcoran, "Koch-Supported Coup at the VA? The Veterans Health Administration Risks Being Dismantled," *Truthout,* March 20, 2018.

My discussions with members of such veterans groups as Vets for Common Sense in Florida and Vets for Peace in the State of Washington indicate that the Koch brothers are funding ideologues who would like to bulldoze the VA system and simply privatize the system. There are many veterans who believe that Shulkin went too far in taking privatization steps to appease his critics, walking away from his confirmation guaranty that privatization "will not happen on my watch." However, he apparently did not do enough to appease Trump's troglodytes.

The Koch brothers campaign against Shulkin is part of the larger battle against "socialized medicine" (Medicare and Medicaid) that they have waged for decades. The problems within VA have made the agency an easy target, and the problems in the British medical system have been cited to attack the VA. Meanwhile, there is increasing interest for a single-payer system, which was advocated by Senator Bernie Sanders in the 2016 presidential campaign. This will be a long-term battle with the Koch brothers prepared to throw hundreds of millions of dollars in the direction of privatization.

The George W. Bush Administration boosted privatization of the military and intelligence communities, and the Trump administration is picking up where Bush left off by privatizing domestic services as well. DeVos and Carson are outsourcing many of the services of their departments. Carson, a retired neurosurgeon who grew up in public housing in Detroit, and OMB Director Mulvaney have proposed legislation that would triple rents on the poorest tenants in federally subsidized housing. The plan would affect over 700,000 families over the next several years, and would increase rents for elderly and disabled people. This is a part of Trump's larger assault on the social safety net, exactly what his campaign said he would never do.

Mulvaney has targeted the social safety net programs of the Departments of Education and Labor by proposing their merger as well as a reshuffling of other domestic agencies to make it easier to cut various benefit programs. Mulvaney and his conservative allies are particularly eager to cut or revamp the Supplemental Nutrition Assistance Program (SNAP) as well as programs that provide direct-cash assistance to low-income citizens for food. More than 42 million Americans receive support from SNAP. Mulvaney favored a 30 percent cut in the budget for SNAP. Trump believes that he is the Republican reincarnation of President Theodore Roosevelt, but Roosevelt believed that "this country will not be a good place for any of us to live in if it is not a reasonably good place for all of us to live."

Even Senate Republicans moved to stop Mulvaney's heartless maneuvers against the food assistance program as well as his efforts to end the Community Development Block Grant Program by restoring his budget cuts. A bipartisan effort in the Senate certainly will block any efforts to merge the Education and Labor Departments as well as his efforts to kill rural and veterans' housing programs. Now that he is acting chief of staff and must work with Congress, Mulvaney will have to think twice about taking on bipartisan majorities in the House and Senate.

The most loathsome aspect of Trump's war on the budget and governance is his virtual war on children. In addition to the separation and detention of families on the border with Mexico, the Trump administration is trying to impose work requirements for a series of federal welfare and health benefits such as SNAP and housing assistance. In July 2018, Trump's Council on Economic Affairs declared an end to the "War on Poverty" and justified the work requirements. The Department of Education, moreover, is no longer calling on educational institutions to account for the historical exclusion of African-Americans and Latinos from learning opportunities. Trump's base will welcome the cuts aimed at minorities and immigrants.

DeVos even promoted the use of federal grant funds to buy guns for schools. In doing so, DeVos challenged the longstanding federal ban on using federal funds to outfit schools with weaponry, including the congressional school safety bill of March 2018 that prohibited the use of federal money for firearms. Despite the increase in school shootings in the United States, DeVos blocked the Department of Education from studying the role of guns in these shootings.

The only member of Trump's inner circle with a serious reputation in his area of expertise was Gary Cohn, the head of the National Economic Council. But Cohn's disgust with the president's increased tariffs on steel and aluminum, which raised the cost of these products to American producers and consumers, led to his resignation in March 2018. He was replaced by Larry Kudlow, a longtime host on CNBC. Kudlow also criticized the decision on tariffs, but he did not let that stand in the way of occupying an office near the Oval.

Kudlow has a dubious record as an economic forecaster, predicting that President Clinton's tax increases in the 1990s would harm the economy (they did not) and that the economy was booming in late 2007 (it was not). In actual fact, Clinton left office with federal coffers in surplus, and early 2008 marked the beginning of a global financial crash. When a White House official was asked about Kudlow's problems in the past with cocaine and alcohol abuse, he explained that Trump simply wanted an economic adviser who "looks the part."

This nation has survived crises in the past: Civil War; depression; Cold War; McCarthyism; Vietnam; and 9/11. Once again, we are at an inflection point where we will decide what we are as a nation and what we stand for as a people. There are many examples of democracies that have been compromised and even defeated not by military or political coups, but by elected leaders who have taken command of the reins of power in an authoritarian manner. Hitler was elected. So were Chile's Pinochet; Turkey's Erdogan; Philippines' Duterte; and Venezuela's Chavez.

In less than two years in office, President Trump damaged governance in ways that will not be easily reversed. He has used his office to weaken democratic institutions, including regulatory agencies and key institutions within the law enforcement community, and even the credibility and sanctity of our voting system. The FBI is widely discredited, and the CIA is held in contempt. His campaign encouraged violence against his opponents, and he used his office to further polarize the country on racial and ethnic lines. Trump continues to campaign against his predecessor, Barack Obama, one of the most trustworthy presidents in U.S. history, and his fiery and threatening rhetoric against his presidential opponent, Hillary Clinton, is something we expect from a leader of a Third World backwater. He regularly spews out misinformation and disinformation that compromises the credibility of our political institutions and creates cynicism in the electorate.

Public service is also being challenged. Trump has been much too successful in compromising the credibility of virtually every government agency and department. The mainstream media focuses on the corruption and ineptitude of key cabinet officers, but the backstory involves the morale of the men and women who labor in the agencies dealing with housing, education, veterans affairs, and the environment. I experienced the destruction of an intelligence culture at the CIA in the 1980s; today's cultural destruction involves nearly every department of government. Trump's tax bill, which significantly reduces taxes for corporations and wealthy individuals, will make it more difficult to fund non-military agencies.

Trump's greatest long-term impact on governance will be his appointments to the Supreme Court. In the last year of the Obama Administration, the Republican leadership in the Senate disregarded the Constitution of the United States, blocking President Obama's appointment of a moderate lawyer, Merrick Garland, to take the seat of the late Anthony Scalia on the Supreme Court. Senate Majority Leader Mitch McConnell has referred to blocking any vote on Garland as his biggest success as a politician and that the possibility of another conservative on the Court was the single most important factor in "bringing

Republicans home" during the 2016 presidential election.[134] The audacious maneuver could have led to a constitutional crisis, but Democrats had no strategy for dealing with McConnell's extra-constitutional maneuver.

As a result, Donald Trump was the first president in nearly 150 years who was able to nominate a Supreme Court justice in his first days in the White House. To replace the late Justice Anthony Scalia, Trump nominated Neil Gorsuch, a proponent of originalism, the idea that the Constitution should be interpreted as perceived at the time of enactment. And like Scalia, Gorsuch is a textualist, the idea that statutes should be interpreted literally without considering legislative history and the underlying purpose of the law. Justice Anthony Kennedy's surprise retirement in June 2018 provided a second opportunity to move the court to the right, particularly in view of Kennedy's important role for twelve years as the Court's swing vote. In his second year, Trump placed Brett Kavanaugh on the Court, creating the most conservative Supreme Court in U.S. history.

The Supreme Court has accommodated Trump's agenda. The Court upheld the ban on travel from several mostly Muslim countries; blocked public-sector unions from charging non-members for collective bargaining (reversing a 41-year-old precedent to do so); declined to condemn gerrymandering; and upheld various state laws that discriminated against black and Latino voters. Alexander Hamilton called the judiciary the "least dangerous" branch of government, because it relied on "judgment" and lacked "force" and "will," but Trump's court seems armed to join the war on the socially liberal rulings of the past few years.

Trump has dishonored the Preamble to the Constitution, which states "We the people…in order to form a more perfect union, establish justice, insure domestic tranquility, provide for the common defense, promote the general welfare, and secure the blessings of liberty to ourselves and our posterity." The

---

[134] "An Open Letter to Justice Kennedy," editorial, *New York Times*, April 29, 2018. p 10.

rule of law is pivotal to our shared values, which are listed in the Bill of Rights; the institutions of law enforcement that are under attack are also pivotal. Trump has expressed frustration with his inability to control the Department of Justice and the FBI, but the wall of separation between the president and law enforcement, which is currently being tested, should be sacrosanct. Have we become too cynical to recognize the unparalleled nature of the challenge?

As a result of Trump's actions, recent polling finds that only half of American respondents have confidence in democracy as a political system. Trump's autocratic populism is responsible for increased cynicism because of his false claims and outright lies about American politics and policy. Trump is without shame, and is no longer found credible as a leader.

Since the description of "American Carnage" in his inaugural speech, Trump has relied on the politics of fear. He has removed the security clearance of a former CIA director and revoked the press credentials of a reporter who has been critical of the president. Trump tried to undermine the midterm election results in Arizona and Florida, and resorted to the politics of chaos in shutting down the government. The rejection of Trump in the midterm elections of November 2018, however, indicated that Americans may be ready to challenge his authoritarianism.

Benjamin Franklin acknowledged to an inquiring citizen in Philadelphia in 1776 that the Founding Fathers had created a republic, but he said it would be up to the American citizenry to maintain it. He warned that experiments in self-government elsewhere have ended in despotism "when the people become so corrupted as to need despotic government." Too many authoritarians have been elected, and gradually seized power in an incremental and even legal fashion. People everywhere usually wind up with the governments they want and perhaps deserve. Donald Trump wasn't popularly elected, having received three million fewer votes than his opponent, but he received 63 million votes on his way to an electoral college victory that rewarded his authoritarian style. As a result, good governance is at risk.

– 6 –

TRUMP'S WAR ON SCIENCE

"We've spent 40 years putting together an apparatus to protect public health and the environment from a lot of different pollutants. He's pulling the whole apparatus down."
　–William Ruckelshaus, the EPA's first administrator, regarding former EPA administrator Scott Pruitt.

"Science denialism" is an anachronism, the worst aspect of the current political climate, and Trump and Vice President Pence are leading the movement. Trump supports the notion that vaccines cause autism. Recent outbreaks of mumps and measles in the United States are linked in part to those Americans who choose to withhold vaccines from children. Pence denies evolution as a concept.

A key indicator of Trump's hostility to science, his anti-intellectualism, was the delay in appointing a director to the White House Office of Science and Technology, the science adviser to the president. Prior to naming Kelvin Droegemeier, a meteorologist, the president withdrew the United States from the Paris climate accord and entered into negotiations with North Korea on nuclear matters without a science adviser. Droegemeier is a distinguished researcher in his field, but narrowly based for a White House position that involves biological, environmental, and physical sciences.

Until Trump entered the White House, the record for presidents without a science adviser belonged to George W. Bush, who went nine months without one. Finally, on August 2, 2018, Trump announced that he would nominate a

145

meteorologist, whose views on climate change are not familiar to many researchers in the field, marking the longest period the office has not had a director since the position was created in 1976. In January 2019, Droegemeier was finally confirmed, although there was no significant opposition during the confirmation process.

The Office of Science and Technology Policy was authorized by Congress to provide "independent, expert judgment and assistance on policy matters that require accurate assessments of complex scientific and technology activities and policies among federal agencies."[135] The director of the office is appointed by the president and serves as the Science Advisor. President George W. Bush's advisor was John Marburger, the Director of Brookhaven National Laboratory. President Obama's advisor was John Holdren, a physicist and energy policy expert from Harvard. Holdren and Secretary of Energy Ernest Moniz, a nuclear physicist from M.I.T., played key roles in developing the 2015 nuclear agreement with Iran.

The government shutdown that began in December 2018 had a negative impact on scientific research. The shutdown closed laboratories throughout the country; compromised scientific conferences that depend on federal participation; and interrupted the planning and flow of resources needed by the scientific community. The biggest impacts were on the National Oceanic and Atmospheric Administration, which includes the National Weather Service; the Environmental Protection Agency; and NASA, where all scientists were furloughed. Government agencies that dole out research grants, such as the National Science Foundation, canceled review panels and put plans for future spending on hold.[136]

---

[135] Neal F. Lane and Michael Riordan, "The President's Disdain for Science," *New York Times,* January 5, 2018, p. 19.

[136] Alan Blinder, "Toll on Science Mounts as Data Go Uncollected During Federal Impasse," *The New York Times,* January 6, 2019, p. 18.

147 | American Carnage

The first indicator of Trump's war on science, particularly climate change, was the naming of climate deniers to his cabinet: Tillerson to the Department of State; Pruitt to the Environmental Protection Agency; Zinke to the Department of the Interior, and Perry to the Department of Energy. Pruitt opposed environmental legislation, earning a dubious reputation by suing the EPA to reverse numerous regulations; Perry was ignorant of most energy issues. He did not know that the central work of his department was managing nuclear programs, particularly nuclear weapons, not the extraction of oil and gas. In this group of troglodytes, only Perry remained in the Cabinet at the end of Trump's second year in office.

Tillerson had been the CEO of ExxonMobile, known for covering up scientific data on climate change. One of the worst examples of climate denial was the lobbying effort by ExxonMobil to deny the fact of man-made global warming. Tillerson and ExxonMobil argued for years that humans had no impact on climate change and that, even if they had, nothing could be done about it. Tillerson was also a major critic of carbon credits, a system designed to cap the emission of greenhouse gases. In his confirmation hearings, he finally acknowledged the problem of global warming, but offered no ideas regarding reforms or solutions.

Trump's closest supporters argue that climate scientists are frauds; that climate science was fabricated for political reasons; and that climate research was a gravy train for academicians to gain government funding.[137] They charge environmentalists with using land, air, and water regulations as political tools to advance a socialist agenda and create a global green mafia to fund like-minded academicians and progressive businessmen. Trump's war against science includes heavy restrictions on the release of official information as well as resistance to Freedom of Information Act requests.

---

[137] See Michael Savage, *Trump's War: His Battle for America*, New York: Hachette Book Group, 2017. (pp. 179-180)

Since his first days in office, Trump strived to eliminate federal regulations, particularly environmental rules that he believed burdened the fossil fuel industry. The research of various law schools, including those at Harvard and Columbia, concluded that more than 70 environmental rules created by President Obama are threatened.[138] Oil and gas companies no longer have to report methane emissions; the use of hydrofluorocarbons, a powerful greenhouse gas, is no longer prohibited; coal companies can dump mining debris into local streams; and certain uranium mines no longer have to protect groundwater.

The month of August 2018 brought a stunning two-edged attack on climate as a result of natural and political failures. On the one hand, it was a month of heat waves, wildfires, droughts, and Arctic ice melt. On the other hand, the month of August found an aggressive attack on the legacy of the Obama administration in fighting climate change. The Trump administration froze the scheduled increase in fuel economy standards for cars and light trucks, and weakened the Clean Power Plan to reduce greenhouse gas emissions from coal-fired plants. Transportation and the production of electricity are the greatest contributors to greenhouse gas emissions in the United States, accounting for more than half of the total.[139]

The industry's campaign to erode the regulations of the Obama era was led by William L. Wehrum, who spent the past decade fighting the EPA and weakening air pollution rules. As a corporate lawyer, Wehrum represented chemical manufacturers, refineries, oil drillers, and coal-burning power plants; as EPA's top air pollution official, another fox has entered the hen house. The rollback of regulations on emissions from coal plants will benefit the very trade association that Wehrum represented.

---

[138] Nadja Popovich, Kendra Pierre-Louis, and Livia Albeck-Ripa, "78 Environmental Rules on the Way Out Under Trump," *The New York Times*, December 27, 2018, p. F12.

[139] Jason Bordoff, "Another Step Backward for the Climate," *The New York Times*, August 21, 2018, p. 19.

In June 2017, President Trump audaciously declared in the White House Rose Garden that he was "elected to represent the citizens of Pittsburgh, not Paris," presaging his withdrawal from the Paris Climate Accord to cut greenhouse gas emissions. Trump's reference to Pittsburgh was ironic because the city is one of American's great urban success stories. Pittsburgh's civic leaders have dealt successfully with a coal-fed economy that had devastated the environment. Pittsburgh turned its situation around; its citizens oppose U.S. withdrawal from the Paris accord.

Trump's climate deniers have made the United States an environmental "pariah state" in a global community committed to addressing the problem of climate change. The United States is the only nation in the world to reject the deal; even Nicaragua and Syria—the two original outliers—have joined. Nicaragua stayed out of the accord initially because it felt the agreement didn't go far enough. The Obama administration made a great effort in 2014-2015 to get the world's other major polluters—particularly China and India—to reduce their emissions. Trump's policies undermined Obama's rich legacy in the field of environmentalism and isolated the United States in the process.

After Trump's withdrawal from the Paris accord, France announced a program called "Make Our Planet Great Again" in order to recruit the best American scientists to France. Thus far, the program has attracted 24 scientists from the United States and elsewhere to conduct research in France, including Ben Sanderson of the National Center for Atmospheric Research.[140] Sanderson received a $1.8 million, five-year grant to work for Meteo-France, the national weather forecaster.

---

[140] Coral Davenport, "In the Trump Administration, Science is Unwelcome. So Is Advice," *The New York Times*, June 10, 2018, p. 18.

Trump promised to reduce the Environmental Protection Agency to "little tidbits" with his appointment of Scott Pruitt to head the agency.[141] Pruitt, who immediately charged that the "future ain't what it used to be at the EPA," was the worst possible selection as a steward for the environment, having sued the EPA more than a dozen times as the attorney general of Oklahoma. Pruitt immediately targeted the EPA's authority to regulate toxic mercury pollution, smog, carbon emissions from power plants and the quality of wetlands and other waters. He initiated more than a dozen rollbacks of regulations from the Obama era.

The Trump Administration's assault on the EPA and its scientific foundation is unprecedented, a perfect example of Trump's blaming liberals for allowing environmentalists to pass regulations to attack free enterprise, not to protect the environment. President Nixon created the EPA five decades ago to enforce science-based standards that would create a healthier atmosphere. Pruitt's attacks on the budget and the scientific framework of the EPA ensure the return of illness and disease related to pollution. William Reilly, who headed the EPA for President George H.W. Bush, remarked that Pruitt's tolerance for "more exposure to pollution is altogether different from anything we are used to."[142]

Representative Frank Pallone (D-NJ), the leading Democrat on the House Energy and Commerce Committee, noted that his "biggest concern…which runs across the whole spectrum, is science." Pallone and others have noted that Pruitt "wants to put science under the rug, make decisions that are not scientifically based. Get rid of anyone who is scientifically oriented."[143] Pruitt made sure that EPA's scientists were excluded from the decision making process.

---

[141] Brady Dennis and Darryl Fears, "The most consequential environmental stories of 2017," *The Washington Post*, January 2, 2018, p. 11.

[142] Davenport, "Science is Unwelcome," p. 18.

[143] ibid, p. 16.

151 | AMERICAN CARNAGE

Pruitt treated the EPA as an unconstitutional agency that shouldn't exist and, as a result, more than 700 people left the agency. The scientific community within EPA has been hardest hit, with many scientists being offered buyouts. As a result, there are now 14,000 staff members at EPA, the lowest number since the last year of the Reagan Administration in the 1980s. Political appointees are running the agency, and "experts" from industries EPA is supposed to regulate have replaced academic researchers.[144]

The forced resignation of Pruitt in July 2018, and the naming of Andrew Wheeler as acting administrator of EPA meant that Trump's war against the environment would continue but in less abrasive hands. Wheeler, the deputy to Pruitt, has been a lobbyist for energy and mining companies for the past decade, and served as the vice president of the Washington Coal Club. He has been just as vigorous as Pruitt in fighting the regulations of the Obama era but, unlike Pruitt, avoided a brazen misuse of his political position. Wheeler has continued the unraveling of federal restrictions on greenhouse-gas emissions and toxic-waste discharge from coal-fired power plants. He is fighting the ban on a commonly used pesticide linked to neurological damage to fetuses. As Senator Edward Markey (D-MA) said, the Trump administration was merely "trading one fossil fuel friend for another."[145] Wheeler was not confirmed until 2019.

The renunciation of science is a staple of Trump's war on fact-finding. It flies in the face of the U.S. reputation for scientific research on every aspect of medicine and health. An attack on research is an attack on science and the scientists responsible for important breakthroughs in every aspect of human existence. If the "deconstruction of the administrative state" includes a war against the scientific community, then the United States will turn its back on

---

[144] Dennis and Elperin, "Climate Change at EPA," p. 16.

[145] Steven Mufson, "Pruitt out as EPA head amid scandals," *The Washington Post*, July 6, 2018, p. 5.

152 | Melvin A. Goodman

progress. Trump administration "talking points" include instructions for underscoring uncertainties about how human activity contributes to climate change.

The mere notion that an EPA administrator can tell scientists what they must say about basic scientific information violates the Constitution's protection of free speech. Pruitt established "red teams" to challenge the scientific consensus in peer-reviewed journals, a reason why experienced scientists and technicians are leaving the agency in record numbers. In the first several months of the Trump administration, experienced academic scientists have been removed from advisory boards and replaced with industry shills.

Pruitt, a lawyer with no background on climate science, was the most aggressive and authoritarian member of the Trump cabinet. Like the president, he was fixated on overturning every aspect of the Obama legacy. Pruitt soon became the subject of 12 government investigations into his flamboyant travel and security expenses as well as mismanagement of his agency and its staff. By the end of his first year, Pruitt was facing investigations by the EPA's Inspector General, the congressional watchdog Government Accountability office, and even the White House's Office of Management and Budget. The president's spokesman, Sarah Huckabee Sanders, acknowledged an "ongoing" review of various ethics issues, but offered no details.[146] Pruitt may be gone, but several investigations continue.

The investigations involve his "24/7 security detail—a setup that tripled past staffing requirements" and is unheard of outside the national security bureaucracy.[147] He installed biometric locks on his office doors as well a

---

[146] Lisa Friedman and Coral Davenport, "Pruitt's Plan of Defense: Lay the Blame on Others," *New York Times*, April 26, 2018, p. 11.

[147] Brady Dennis and Juliet Eilperin, "In Year under Pruitt, a climate change at EPA," *Washington Post*, January 1, 2018, p. 16.

soundproof booth to make secure calls to the White House and industrial sources. He communicated exclusively by phone and face-to-face meetings in order to avoid email that would be subject to open records laws. Pruitt's Superfund Task Force took no minutes in order to avoid Freedom of Information Act requests. He regularly misused his senior staff to do his personal shopping, including the demand for a used mattress from the Trump hotel empire!

Pruitt is not only a science-denying Neanderthal, but a servant to wealthy corporate interests trying to corrupt a regulatory agency that has contributed to a healthier environment for all Americans. Pruitt's zeal in dismantling Obama's legacy was the key to his popularity with the president. Instead of looking out for the well-being of future generations, Pruitt catered to the very industries that have done the most to pollute our water and air. With the exception of President Ronald Reagan's appointees, previous EPA administrators—both Democrats and Republicans—created a balanced participation from industry, environmental organizations, and the citizenry to improve the environment. When the Trump administration is finished, a massive rebuilding job will be needed that will be costly and time consuming.

Pruitt censored EPA scientists and prevented scientists from attending scientific conferences, particularly on climate change. In October 2017, EPA scientists were scheduled to participate in a conference on the environmental health of Narragansett Bay, the largest estuary in New England and central to the region's fishing and tourism industries. EPA scientists were scheduled to deliver keynote presentations on environmental damage to the bay from climate change. At the last minute, EPA announced without explanation that the scientists scheduled to speak would not be attending the conference. The last time the government conducted a concerted and well-funded effort to distort and silence scientific research was several decades ago when the Reagan administration tried to block the link between cigarettes and cancer.

Key regulations on proven carcinogens have been abandoned without explanation. An ugly example of the EPA's willingness to allow the use of a dangerous chemical involves the pesticide chlorpyrifos. This particular chemical was developed as a nerve gas by Nazi Germany; it has been linked to lung cancer and Parkinson's disease in adults. It can cause brain damage and reduce I.Q. levels in children. The EPA banned chlorpyrifos for most indoor residential use in 2000, which is why it can no longer be used in chemicals sprayed at cockroaches.[148] The EPA was prepared to ban the chemical for agricultural and outdoor use in the spring of 2017, but the Trump administration rejected the ban. The pesticide is produced by Dow Chemical Company, which donated $1 million for Trump's inauguration, and accused the Obama administration of a "lack of scientific rigor."

Fortunately, in August 2018, a federal appeals court ordered the EPA to ban the controversial pesticide chlorpyrifos, which Pruitt had refused to do despite its risks to human health. In a 2-1 decision, the U.S. Court of Appeals for the 9th Circuit said that federal law bans any pesticide that "causes neurological damage to children."[149] The Judge writing for the majority accused the EPA of "stalling" on the decision and accused the agency of an "utter failure" in responding to objections to Pruitt's obfuscation.

Pruitt began his stewardship at EPA by lobbying the White House for withdrawal from the Paris climate accord, a case of kicking on an open door in the Trump administration. Pruitt convened a team of researchers to test the scientific premise of human-caused climate change as well as a "red team-blue team" exercise to challenge mainstream climate science. Andrew Dessler, a professor of atmospheric science at Texas A&M University called the exercise "fundamentally

---

[148] Nicholas Kristof, "Trump's Legacy: Damaged Brains," *The New York Times*, October 29, 2017, p. 9.

[149] Brady Dennis, "Federal court orders EPA to ban controversial pesticide," *The Washington Post*, August 10, 2018, p. 14.

a dumb idea. It's like a red team-blue team exercise about whether gravity exists."[150]

In the wake of heavy lobbying from the chemical industry, the Trump administration is undercutting the way the government determines health and safety risks associated with dangerous chemicals. A law in the final year of the Obama administration required EPA to evaluate hundreds of potentially toxic chemicals to determine if they should face new restrictions or be removed by the market.[151] The EPA decided to exclude from its calculations any potential exposure caused by the presence of chemical substances in the air, water, or ground in order to focus exclusively on direct contact with substances in the workplace. Therefore, the improper disposal of chemicals, which can contaminate drinking water, was not a factor in decisions to restrict use. The Trump administration's appointee to oversee the EPA's toxic chemical unit, Nancy Beck, previously worked as an executive at the American Chemistry Council, a major lobbying group.[152]

The EPA is changing the methodology for assessing scientific findings in order to restrict the work of research scientists in writing environmental regulations. On April 24, 2018, EPA announced a new regulation to restrict the use of scientific studies for the development of policy. No longer would the EPA be allowed to use scientific research based on raw data that is not available publicly for industry groups to examine. This policy will permanently weaken the agency's ability to protect public health.

Under the new measure, EPA requires that underlying data for scientific studies to formulate air and water regulations must be publicly available. In effect,

---

[150] Brad Plumer and Coral Davenport, "EPA Chief Is Planning a Test of Climate Science," The New York Times, May 16, 2017, p. 11.

[151] Eric Lipton, "EPA Eases Way It Evaluates Risk From Chemicals," The New York Times, June 8, 2018, p. 1.

[152] Lipton, "EPA Eases Way It Evaluates," p. 16.

regulators will not be able to use seminal environmental research that links air pollution to premature death or that measures human exposure to pesticides and other chemicals because such information is based on personal health information protected by privacy rights or agreements of confidentiality. This provision will limit the number of studies for consideration because such studies rely on confidential health data. This is a classic Catch-22 situation as Pruitt—the fox-in-the-henhouse administrator—cunningly contended that the new approach is designed to promote transparency.

Public health and environmental groups have vowed to challenge the move in court. Richard J. Lazarus, a professor of environmental law at Harvard, said EPA would be "walking into a judicial minefield" if it no longer considered certain studies during any agency rule-making.[153] In a letter to Pruitt, Senator Tom Carper (D/DE) and several Senate colleagues warned, "Your proposed new policy violates several laws with which EPA must comply."

Any restrictions on applying established science to EPA rules will allow the agency to weaken or even repeal existing regulations on clean air and water. According to Dr. Ivan Oransky, co-founder of Retraction Watch, an independent blog that monitors scientific journals, Pruitt was bent on introducing an element of doubt into areas of public health where none exists.[154] "Data that Pruitt doesn't like will get disqualified," concluded Oransky.

Pruitt's major effort to weaken the Obama-era regulations on water pollution took place in June 2018, when he submitted a proposal to narrow the interpretation of the Clean Water Act to prevent regulation of seasonal tributaries, streams, and wetlands that flow into larger bodies of water such as the Chesapeake Bay. The Obama rule prevented farmers from dumping chemical

---

[153] Lisa Friedman, "EPA Sets Rules on Research; Scientists Promise to Fight It." *New York Times*, April 24, 2018, p. 17.

[154] Lisa Friedman, "Narrower Scope for E. P. A. Rules, *New York Times*, March 27, 2018, p. 13.

fertilizers and pesticides into such waters. The Pruitt rule would benefit golf course owners and real estate developers such as the Trump Organization, which owns more than a dozen golf resorts in the United States. According to Jonathan Devine of the Natural Resources Defense Council, the new ruling would "make it easier for polluters to dump" in streams and other waters.[155]

In addition to restricting scientific research, Pruitt was an outspoken salesman for the nation's fossil fuels industry, and blocked advocacy groups such as the Sierra Club and Environmental Working Group from access to EPA. In 2017, he met more than 200 times with representatives from the fossil fuels industry and other regulated industries, while meeting with environmental and public health groups a dozen times. Soon after taking office, Pruitt cancelled the EPA's request that nearly 20,000 oil and gas companies gauge their emissions of methane, a potent greenhouse gas.

Pruitt challenged the fuel economy standards for automobiles, compromising one of President Obama's singular achievements. This decision could lead to creating one set of rules for such states as California that have put stringent requirements in place and another set for the rest of the country. Pruitt argued that easing the regulatory burden on automakers will lead to cheaper trucks, vans, and sport utility vehicles. According to the director of Harvard's environmental economics program, Robert Stavins, the "result will be more gas-guzzling vehicles on the road, greater total gasoline consumption and a significant increase in carbon dioxide emissions."[156]

California received a waiver from the Clean Air Act in 1970 that allowed it to enforce stronger air pollution standards than those set by the federal government,

---

[155] Coral Davenport, "Pruitt Plans to Roll Back Obama-Era Rules on Water Pollution and Tailpipe Fumes," *The New York Times,* June 15, 2018, p. 17.

[156] Coral Davenport and Hiroko Tabuchi, "U.S. Set To Blunt Pollution Rules For Automakers," *New York Times,* March 30, 2018, p. 1.

a holdover from the state's history of setting its own air pollution regulations before the federal government got into the game. Twelve other states representing 40 percent of the domestic auto market, including New York, Massachusetts, and Pennsylvania, have followed California's lead. The Obama Administration actually toughened tailpipe pollution standards to match California's.

The Trump administration is rolling back efficiency rules for cars, known as the Corporate Average Fuel Economy Standard or CAFE standard. The Department of Transportation and the EPA drafted a new set of regulations on planet-warming emissions to undercut Obama's standards. In April 2018, Pruitt weakened Obama's stringent vehicle fuel economy standards that was to double the average fuel economy of new cars, SUVs and light trucks by 2025. In July 2018, the White House approved the plan to freeze national fuel-efficiency standards for six years. Part of Obama's legacy, the CAFE standard would have required automakers to nearly double the average fuel economy of new cars and trucks to 54.5 miles per gallon by 2025.[157]

According to EPA projections, this standard could cut oil consumption and reduce carbon dioxide pollution by about six billion tons over the lifetime of the affected cars. In June 2018, Pruitt's EPA moved to gut Obama's rulings to reduce climate-warming pollution from vehicle tailpipes. Obama's rules would have put the United States, typically a laggard in fuel economy regulations, at the forefront in the global manufacture of electric and highly fuel efficient vehicles. Pruitt fought the wavier arrangement that allows California and other states to work around the new standards; Wheeler is continuing Pruitt's fight.

Pruitt's proposal would freeze fuel-economy standards at 2020 levels for cars and light trucks, which would slow progress in reducing auto emissions. Since

---

[157] Davenport and Tabuchi, "U.S. Set To Blunt Pollution Rules," p. 15.

automakers already have the technology in place for their 2020 models, the proposal would freeze CAFE standards and prevent any further regulation of fuel economy. Ann E. Carlson, a professor of environmental law at the University of California, Los Angeles, said that this would be tantamount to telling the auto industry that "We aren't going to regulate you anymore. You're already geared up to meet the standards and we're finished."[158] A protracted court battle is likely.

Pruitt's proposals challenged California's authority to impose its own vehicle standards. The auto industry favors weakening California's greenhouse gas standards, but federal courts have sided with the state government. California is committed to its stricter Obama-era regulations, and automakers are shying away from a collision course that could lead to regulatory chaos within the industry. The White House also approved challenging the right of California and other states to set their own standards. Once again, chaos is Trump's *modus operandi*.

Not even major automakers are lobbying to lower the CAFE standards. The president of Ford Motor Company, Executive Chairman Bill Ford, said that he supports "increasing clean car standards through 2025" and is "not asking for a rollback.[159] Honda Motors issued a separate statement in favor of flexibility to address the problem of California, but "without a reduction in overall stringency."

The governor of the so-called Republic of California, Gavin Newsome, is also proposing a plan to allow his state to directly negotiate prescription drug prices with manufacturers to benefit consumers. Senate Democrats favor a bill to allow the federal government to directly negotiate drug prices under Medicare, but face stiff resistance from Republicans. The Trump administration supports the idea of

---

[158] Hiroko Tubuchi, Brad Plumer and Carol Davenport, "Plan to Loosen Emission Limits Disputes California's Right to Set Its Own," *The New York Times*, April 28, 2018, p. 15.

[159] Juliet Eilperin and Brady Dennis, "Trump officials debate fuel-efficiency goals," The Washington Post, March 30, 2018, p. 19.

a plan to lower drug prices, but major manufacturers such as Pfizer and Allergan continue to raise prices.

Andrew Wheeler has been no less tenacious than Pruitt in reversing course at the EPA. At the very least, Wheeler should recuse himself from energy and environmental issues in view of his energetic lobbying on behalf of various extractive industries. Norman Eisen, the chairman of Citizens for Responsibility and Ethics in Washington, helped draft the 2009 executive order that set rules for administration officials who have worked as lobbyists; he believes recusal is in order.[160] Ironically, one of Trump's first executive orders in 2017 seconded the 2009 executive order as part of his promise to "drain the swamp."

Scientists have confirmed that climate-related factors worsened storm surges and flooding during major hurricanes in the Gulf of Mexico. The year 2017 overall was a year of devastating weather in the United States, not only hurricanes but deadly wildfires. Hurricane Harvey in September 2017 was marked by a record-setting storm surge, high winds, precipitation and flooding. The hurricane would have taken place without global warning, but experts believe climate change helped to produce the extreme conditions that will cost more than $180 billion to repair. Fifteen of the biggest fires in California history have occurred in the past two decades. We have a president who believes that "raking" the forests is the answer.

Only a matter of weeks before Harvey hit the coast, President Trump dumped a series of rules from the Obama administration that reduced the risks of flooding in the United States. The Obama rules included new standards for the construction of roads, housing, and other infrastructure projects that received federal dollars. Cathleen Kelly, who served on the White House Council on Environmental Quality from 2010 to 2011, said that Obama placed climate

---

[160] Lisa Friedman, "EPA Chief Details Past Advocacy for Big Utilities and Mining Companies," *The New York Times*, August 2, 2018, p. 18.

change "front and center with the recovery and rebuilding process" in order to reduce future risk."[161]

Trump's deniers ignored the abnormal warming of the ocean, which provided energy for the storm. Several anomalies increased the destructiveness of these storms, including an elevated sea level; atmospheric pressure that contributed to storms stalling over the coast; and atmospheric water vapor that produced greater moisture for precipitation. A strongly warming Atlantic Ocean; higher seas along the Gulf Coast; and the fact that Hurricane Harvey stalled over Houston contributed to the devastation.[162] Hurricanes Maria, Harvey, and Irma cost the United States over $265 billion in damages.

Another Obama-era rule required construction projects funded by the Federal Emergency Management Agency to build structures at least three feet above the 100-year flood elevation in an expanded flood plain. A companion ruling required that projects funded by Housing and Urban Development, such as multi-family housing projects, be built two feet higher in an expanded flood plain. President Trump rescinded these rules on August 15, 2017, two weeks before Hurricane Harvey hit the Gulf Coast.

In 2015 President Obama toured a mixed-income development in New Orleans on the site of a housing project destroyed in Hurricane Katrina. It was built two feet above base flood elevation, and when the neighborhood was threatened in August 2017, it resisted the deluge. A former HUD official, Marion McFadden, noted that "countless money" was saved because of the regulations on new construction.

---

[161] Juliet Eilperin, "After storm, Trump administration reconsiders flood rules it just dropped," The *Washington Post*, September 2, 2017, p. 12.

[162] Noah S. Diffenbaugh, "How We Know It Was Climate Change," *The New York Times*, December 31, 2017, p. 10.

California's wildfires brought greater devastation because of climate changes that produced strong, dry winds; a protracted drought that killed millions of trees that created substantial fuel; and an extremely wet winter followed by severely hot, dry conditions that produced additional fuel for fires. Global warming has increased aridity in the West, meaning that fires are more likely to encounter large amounts of dry fuel. Heat waves are responsible for lower crop yields; by 2050, the midwestern United States could see agricultural productivity drop to its lowest level in decades.[163]

Persistent warming in the Arctic is pushing the region into "uncharted territory" and increasingly affecting the continental United States. The "Arctic Report Card" of the National Oceanic and Atmospheric Administration documented that the Arctic has been warming at twice the rate as the rest of the planet and, as a result, there were severe storms in the United States and a bitter cold spell in Europe known as the "beast from the East."[164] The surge of Arctic warmth produces algae species in the Arctic Ocean that can poison marine life and people who eat contaminated seafood.

A warming Arctic heats up the U.S.-Russian military rivalry in a theater of operations where Russian warships outclass the U.S. Navy. The Arctic represents the shortest flight path for each side's intercontinental ballistic missiles and nuclear armed intercontinental bombers in the event of conflict. With the prospect of continuing Arctic warming, the Arctic Ocean and its periphery becomes one more theater in Russian-American military rivalry. The Arctic region is also important to Russia for its energy resources. China has discussed adding a "Polar Silk Route" to its Belt and Road initiative.

---

[163] John Kerry, "Forget Trump. Act on the Climate," *The New York Times*, December 7, 2018, p. 23.

[164] John Schwartz and Henry Fountain, "Scientiests Warn of a 'Rapid Unraveling' of the Arctic," *The New York Times*, December 3, 2018, p. 8.

An environmentally sustainable economy would produce more jobs than the reliance on fossil fuels. Robert Pollin documents in "Greening the Global Economy" that an investment in clean energy would create three times as many jobs as continuing the lethal addiction to fossil fuels.[165] According to Pollin, "investing $1 million in renewable energy and energy efficiency will create three times as many jobs as spending $1 million on our existing fossil fuels infrastructure." Job losses in the fossil fuel sector could be addressed with "retraining and relocation support for individual workers" as well as pension protections and re-employment guarantees. Since the number of workers in fossil fuels extraction is at an all-time low, the cost of a "just transition" would be limited.

EPA will not be the only federal agency facing the task of rebuilding. The Department of Energy, like EPA, has downgraded the work of its scientists, leaving Rick Perry to make decisions on the development and safeguarding of nuclear weaponry for which he is totally unqualified. In the past, secretaries of energy had the support of presidential science advisors, who were typically physicists who could address the sophisticated problems of nuclear weaponry and technology. President Trump's reckless decision in 2017 to decertify Iran's compliance with the Iran nuclear accord was made without advice from the scientific community at the Department of Energy or elsewhere. As many have warned, no president has greater need of scientific support than Trump, but this is a president who wants no support.

Perry is doing his best to cut regulations, to end support for renewable subsidies, and to revive the coal industry. There are nuclear and coal plants that are unable to compete with renewables and natural gas, but Perry is doing his best to keep them open. Employment in coal mining increased by 2.5 percent in 2017

---

[165] See Robert Pollin, *Greening the Global Economy*, New York: Boston Review of Books, 2015.

compared to 1.8 percent growth for all private jobs.[166] Secretary of Energy Perry endorsed Pruitt's "red team-blue team" idea in order to weaken regulations, although he has not been as aggressive as EPA's Pruitt in politicizing the department.

No government agency is immune from the Trump administration's attack on science. The Department of Agriculture introduced a plan to overhaul two federal offices responsible for food and agricultural research in order to reduce spending on projects connected to climate control, nutrition, and other key concerns. In August 2018, Secretary of Agriculture Sonny Perdue announced a plan to move the key research office—the Economic Research Service—into the Office of the Secretary, which is a political branch of the Department of Agriculture.[167] Perdue's plan would move the research service and the National Institute of Food and Agriculture out of Washington in 2019, which would weaken their influence on policy. Many top economists and scientists will resign if they face a move out of Washington.

In the early 1980s, when CIA director Bill Casey and the director of intelligence, Bob Gates, wanted to weaken the influence of the office of Soviet analysis, they moved the group out of the Headquarters Building in McLean, Virginia to an obscure location in Vienna, Virginia. Casey and Gates were more able to politicize intelligence on the Soviet Union as the role of the Soviet analysts was significantly weakened; eventually they returned to the McLean headquarters.

The Department of Agriculture is redefining part of its core mission, the scientific monitoring of food safety, in order to promote exports of American farm products. The office devoted to food safety was moved from the Food Safety and

---

[166] *The Wall Street Journal*, editorial, "Rick Perry's Obama Imitation," June 6, 2018. 16.

[167] Caitlin Dewey, "Scientists fear overhaul of USDA could curtail research," The Washington Post, August 17, 2018, p. 12.

Inspection Service to the new Trade and Foreign Agricultural Affairs office, thus undermining the "mission that the U.S. has for science-based standards for food," according to the former chief scientist at the agency from 2010-2017.[168] The Union of Concerned Scientists has warned that moving the research service into the office of the secretary will lead to politicization of a key function of the department.

The appointment of Zinke to run the Department of the Interior was another blow to the environment. From the outset, Zinke stressed he would open public lands to extract oil, gas, and coal, and would sidetrack the examination of health risks to fossil fuel workers. His first act as secretary set the tone as he removed a colorful picture of a western landscape from the Bureau of Land Management's website and replaced it with a black wall of coal.[169] Zinke announced in November 2017 the largest Gulf lease for oil and gas exploration in U.S. history: 77 million acres on the east coast from New Jersey to Florida. This led to opposition from the attorney generals from the affected states as well as from lawmakers and the Department of Defense.

Trump campaigned on the basis of "drill, baby, drill," and his Secretary of the Interior opened large tracts of previously protected land to coal excavation in the West. The 2018 tax bill paved the way for additional leases for exploration; the Arctic National Wildlife Refuge was the first victim. In expanding offshore drilling, Zinke gave a political exemption to Florida, a swing state, to help Republican Governor Rick Scott defeat Senator Bill Nelson (D-FL) in the November 2018 election. The exemption enhanced Scott's campaign against the incumbent. Florida's exemption led to challenges from state officials throughout

---

[168] Davenport, "Science is Unwelcome," p. 18.

[169] Dennis and Fears, "Consequential environmental stories," p. 11.

the South and the Pacific coast for similar exemptions. As a result, Zinke's home state of Montana was exempted from oil and gold mining.

Just as California is leading the fight to save fuel-economy standards, New Jersey is leading the resistance to the expansion of offshore drilling. The state became the first Atlantic state to adopt a legal barrier in the form of a law that would prohibit oil exploration in state waters, which extend three miles from shore. An amendment to the law went even further, barring the construction of infrastructure such as pipelines in federal waters, where state waters end. New York has passed a similar law, and the Delaware legislature is considering one.[170]

Zinke shrank two major monuments in Utah—Bears Ears and Grand Staircase-Escalante—by two million acres. Citing Theodore Roosevelt's Antiquities Act, the Clinton and Obama administrations created both national monuments in Utah in order to protect Native American cultural sites. Utah Republicans have long protested the efforts of Clinton and Obama to expand the nation's national monuments, and in April 2017 President Trump announced a review of 27 land and marine monuments in order to end presidential "abuses" and give control of the land "back to the people."[171] In 2018, Zinke announced the review of other monuments in the Atlantic and Pacific Oceans as well as in the West.

In May 2018, Zinke's National Park Service blocked rules from the Obama era that prevented hunting on federal land in Alaska that scientists and conservationists called cruel and inhumane. The new rulings allowed bear cubs to be killed alongside their mothers; the hunting of wolves and their pups in their dens; and the targeting of animals from airplanes and snowmobiles. The National

---

[170] Darryl Fears, "N. J. leads resistance to offshore drilling," *Washington Post*, May 28, 2018, p. 10. While the Trump administration caters to the oil and gas industry, it is worth noting that Germany with the world's fourth largest economy announced in 2017 that it has met more than one-third of its power needs with renewable resources.

[171] Dennis and Fears, "Consequential environmental stories," p. 11.

Parks Conservation Association called the proposal a "shocking reversal of common-sense wildlife management."[172]

Not even the Department of Interior's Bureau of Land Management escaped Trump's war on science. Early in 2018, the Bureau blocked more than 14 of its staff archaeologists from attending a major scientific conference to debate whether archaeological sites should be protected on public lands. The meeting involved the largest organization of professional archaeologists in the Western Hemisphere, the Society for American Archaeology. The Bureau only authorized three of its staff to attend the conference, and the limited participation by government scientists forced the Society to cancel the panel on "Tough Issues in Land Management Archaeology." The Bureau's unwillingness to allow its archaeologists to participate fully was another attack on science and Obama's legacy.

In 2017, the Department of the Interior directed the U.S. Geological Survey to delete language from a news release that discussed the role of climate change in raising the level of the Earth's oceans. It removed two top climate experts at Montana's Glacier National Park from a delegation scheduled to show Facebook founder Mark Zuckerberg a park studded with shrinking glaciers.[173] Several scientists resigned from the department as a result of the actions to compromise research, creating an additional brain drain of American scientists from the government to private agencies, including those operating abroad.

Early in his administration, President Trump, who calls climate change a "Chinese hoax," eliminated policies and institutions designed to assess the impact of climate on infrastructure planning. In March 2017, he revoked the climate

---

[172] Darryl Fears, "Park Service moves to end ban on Alaska hunting practices considered cruel," *The Washington Post*, May 25, 2018, p. 3.

[173] Dino Grandoni and Juliet Eilperin, "Interior agency blocks group of archaeologists from attending conference," *Washington Post*, May 4, 2018, p. 16.

guidance of the National Environmental Policy Act, which instructed agencies to review the impact of climate on the construction of bridges, roads, pipelines and other projects. In the summer of 2017, key departments in the National Institutes of Health were instructed to drop references to "climate change" from NIH's website.

Trump catered to industries that would benefit from the lack of regulations regarding infrastructure spending. The National Home Builder Association was sharply critical of the HUD proposal to impose new requirements for building in flood-prone areas as well as efforts by the Obama administration to expand the range of the flood plain. In October 2016, when the HUD rule was proposed, the NHBA argued that it would "increase construction costs and project delays for single-family homes…to serve low- to moderate-income buyers."[174] This is reminiscent of the major airliners that pushed back against creating safer cockpit doors in the 1970s because of increased costs to passengers or the efforts of the Ford Motor Company to resist the introduction of seat belts in the 1960s.

When President Trump scrapped Obama-era rules in 2017, he referred to the "over-regulated permit process" as a "massive, self-inflicted wound on our country" Speaking at Trump Tower in New York City on his infrastructure program, Trump referred to Obama's rules as "disgraceful—denying our people much-needed investments in their community." Trump challenged scientific evidence and relevant federal analysis that projected an increase in heavy downpours and a rise in sea level in the United States as a result of climate change.

The disastrous appointments of Zinke and Pruitt to the Interior Department and EPA, respectively, is reminiscent of President Reagan's appointments of James Watt and Anne Gorsuch Buford to the same institutions. Watt was an unabashedly pro-industry voice who was determined to loosen government

---

[174] ibid, p. 12.

control over public lands. He started out by promising that "we will mine more, drill more, and cut more timber," and he offered up the entire U.S. coastline to oil and gas leases.[175] Watt, a loose-lipped racist and political liability, was forced to resign.

In two years, Buford, the mother of Supreme Court Justice Neil Gorsuch, cut the EPA budget by 21 percent and staff by 26 percent, which meant a massive retreat on all environmental programs.[176] She played a role as well in the discrediting of science. The corruption of the Superfund toxic waste cleanup program forced Buford to resign. Zinke and Pruitt did more damage than Watt and Buford.

No American president in history has demonstrated such disdain for science and technology and the role of the Science Advisor as Donald Trump. The advisor is essential to the president for gathering relevant information and evaluating often conflicting advice from other senior officers and Cabinet secretaries, and for formulating evidence-based options for decision making. In the recent past, the Science Advisor was essential to decision making on 9/11; the subsequent anthrax attacks; the Fukushima nuclear nightmare in 2011; the Ebola and Zika outbreaks; and various cyber-attacks.

The lack of scientific advice abetted Trump's attacks against health and environmental regulations; his departure from the Paris accords; and his challenging of the public health case for vaccinations. A former science advisor to President Bill Clinton, Neal Lane, noted that Trump ignored the negative impact of his immigration bans on science and technology in the United States.[177] There was no input from a science advisor on the 2019 budget, which listed draconian

---

[175] www.rollingstone.com, April 1983.

[176] *Washington Post*, June 7, 1983.

[177] Lane and Riordan, "Disdain for Science," p. 19.

cuts at the EPA, the Department of Energy, the National Institutes of Health, the National Science Foundation, and the National Oceanographic and Atmospheric Administration. There would be severe long-term consequences from any cuts, and short-term consequences from the government shutdown in 2018-2019.

Trump's attack on science and fact-finding is unprecedented in a country that prides itself on innovation and development. The United States leads the global community in Nobel prizes for science and math, and no country has registered more patents for research and the application of theoretical ideas. U.S. educational and research institutions are some of the finest in the world, and regularly attract foreign scientists to its classrooms and laboratories. The impact of Trump's campaign will compromise not only the important work of public service, but will affect the quality of life in the United States.

The Trump administration is committed to finding evidence to support its actions against the environment regardless of the source. In March 2018, Peter Navarro, Trump's trade adviser, told Bloomberg News that his job as an economist is to "try to provide the underlying analytics that confirm [Trump's] intuition. And his intuition is always right in these matters."[178] There has never been an administration with so many principal officials appointed on the basis of servile loyalty to the president and willingness to ignored established fact. Throughout the decision-making community, there are "yes men" adhering to presidential directive and ignoring experts.

The Union of Concerned Scientists conducted a survey in 2018 of more than 63,000 federal scientists from 16 government agencies. With more than 4,200 responses, the survey concluded that the Trump Administration is doing its best to stymie scientific analysis.[179] Major areas of scientific inquiry have already been

---

[178] Ben Terris, "From Know-How to Kowtow," *Washington Post*, Style Section, March 29, 2018, p. 3.

[179] Pamela Worth, "Federal Scientists Speak On the State of Science Under President Trump," *Union of Concerned Scientists*, Fall 2018, p. 12.

compromised by virtue of hiring freezes, staff cuts, and budgetary pressures, let alone the government shutdown. Half of all respondents reported that political interests are hindering the ability to base policy decisions on science, and that self-censorship is worsening the problem. The survey confirmed that the Trump administration is making every effort to roll back environmental and public health safeguards.

Any weakening of the role of science in government will hurt our most vulnerable citizens. Low-income populations are the hardest hit when regulatory policies are compromised or existing rules and standards are weakened. The rollback of the Stream Protection Rule, designed to protect people living near mountaintop-removal coal mining operations from toxins in their drinking water, was reversed shortly after Trump was inaugurated.

Many of the efforts of the Trump Administration to rollback the Obama-era regulations remain in draft form and will have to face a public comment phase. The final versions of these rollbacks will probably not be issued until late 2019, but the EPA is being particularly secretive about its filing plans. EPA alone has challenged dozens of environmental rules in the first years of the Trump administration as well as the scientific basis of these rules. Overall, it raises serious questions for those people willing to serve in an anti-intellectual Trump administration where experts and expertise have limited influence.

Trump has created an era of anti-enlightenment, and it is up to the scientific community to lead the opposition to his administration. Science is one of the sources of truth, and Trump's war on truth has been destructive.

— CONCLUSION —

TRUMP'S CARNAGE: WHAT CAN BE DONE?

"If we do not provide against corruption, our government will soon be at an end."
—George Mason, Constitutional Convention, 1787.

"Power and those in control concede nothing...without a demand. They never have and they never will...each and every one of us must keep demanding, must keep fighting, must keep thundering, must keep plowing, must keep struggling, must speak out and must speak up until justice is served because where there is no justice there can be no peace.
—Frederick Douglas, March 1857.

There were no successes in domestic or foreign policy for the United States in the first years of the Trump presidency. Trump and his base boast about the largest defense bill in U.S. history; a tax bill that benefitted the wealthy; the abrogation of the Paris and Iran accords; the bizarre summits with North Korea and Russia, and the appointment of two conservative justices to the Supreme Court. Trump's election exploited the cynicism of millions of Americans, many angered by economic inequality; a pathetic infrastructure that Democrats and Republicans ignored; and a weakening middle-class unable to enjoy social mobility.

The Trump administration has demonstrated a mindless indifference to our environmental problems, our national debt, and our third world transportation system. A bloated military budget has diverted hundreds of billions of dollars from the domestic economy and the needs of the middle class. The richest one percent of Americans now own 40 percent of the nation's wealth, which is corrosive and unconscionable.

Instead of addressing these issues, Trump created chaos in the domestic and international arenas. One would have to turn to Andrew Johnson's administration after the Civil War to find the level of animosity and polarization that exists in U.S. politics. Despite the lies and deceit in the political arena, Republican leaders and too many Americans remain unconcerned about the damage to U.S. influence abroad and our democracy at home. The midway point in Trump's first term, however, surfaced evidence of Republican impatience and public criticism.

A new low was reached in the first half of 2018 when President Trump and Attorney General Sessions used children from Central America as hostages to gain leverage for a border wall. Nearly all of Trump's policy initiatives at home and abroad—the travel ban; the tariff war; the bilateral summits—were accompanied by controversy and uncertainty, but the separation of children and babies from parents revealed a lack of humanity not seen since the end of slavery and the era of Jim Crow. Trump's immigration policy is racist; if blond and blue-eyed children had been crossing our borders, they would have been treated humanely. The adoption and implementation of his inhumane policy—like the policy of sadistic torture and abuse in the Bush era—is an indictment of every member of the administration who took part.

As of December 2018, the Department of Health and Human Services identified nearly 3,000 children who were separated from their parents at the border with Mexico, but several thousand more may have been separated before the courts required the Trump administration to maintain an accounting of separations. The lack of coordination between HHS and the Department of Homeland Security worsened the problem that the administration created to "deter" immigration. According to HHS's assistant inspector general, the separations may have taken place a full year before the court order was issued.[180]

The government shutdown of 2018-2019 did serious harm to the air transportation system as well as to national security in view of the furloughs at the FBI, the Coast Guard, and Customs and Border Protection. Those agencies that collect important economic information, such as the Weather Service and the Forest Service, were hard hit. The federal workforce lost more than 17,000 employees in Trump's first 18 months; more will be lost as a result of the shutdown with those departments that help the poor, such as the Departments of Housing and Urban Development and Education, having the greatest losses. Trump and his inner circle welcome the idea of a smaller government.

There has never been a time in U.S. history when the global community has reacted with such anxiety toward a U.S. president. Presidents Franklin D. Roosevelt and John F. Kennedy were seen as heroes by friends and had the respect of foes. President Harry S. Truman received royal treatment in Europe because of the Marshall Plan and the Truman Doctrine. Donald Trump is the only American president who has been so vilified by allies and adversaries alike. His ignorance and coarseness are only part of the problem.

Our closest European allies are alarmed. An early signal took place in May 2017, when German Chancellor Angela Merkel warned that the "times in which we could totally rely on others are to some extent over."[181] She had returned from a state visit to Washington, and received a huge ovation in Berlin when she urged Europeans to "take our fate into our own hands." French President Emmanuel Macron is showing independence and diffidence. The anti-Trump mood in Europe is morphing into anti-Americanism.

---

[180] Miriam Jordan, "Many Families Split at Border Went Untallied," *The New York Times*, January 18, 2019, p. 1.

[181] *The Economist*, June 3, 2017, "Europe and Trump: Don't let him get to you," p. 45.

175 | AMERICAN CARNAGE

Miro Cerar, the foreign minister of Slovenia, a small Balkan country, warned about the lack of U.S. leadership in Europe, which is allowing Russia and China to gain influence. Russian foreign aid has tripled over the past decade, and China's belt and road initiative involves infrastructure projects in Africa and Latin America. Cerar cited the U.S. withdrawal from the Iran nuclear accord, the Paris climate accord, and the Global Compact on Migration.[182] His views are commonplace among foreign ministers in West and East Europe.

In addition to creating problems with European allies, Trump has offended allies in Japan and South Korea needed in the strategic effort to denuclearize the Korean peninsula. In the midst of North Korea's nuclear testing in 2017, Trump—the bull in the china closet—pressured Tokyo and Seoul on their trade relations with the United States. Japan is the fourth largest trade partner for the United States in terms of total trade; South Korea is the sixth largest.[183] Despite the opposition of some of his national security team as well as his economic advisers, Trump is determined to roll back free trade agreements such as the North Atlantic Free Trade Agreement.

Trump's ignorance of nuclear issues, exemplified by policies toward Iran and North Korea, worsens relations with global allies and rivals such as Russia and China. Trump pursues a form of "nuclear diplomacy," priding himself on "ripping up" the Iran nuclear accord, which he called "the dumbest deal...in the history of

---

[182] Carol Morello, "Slovenian diplomat warns of waning U.S. interest in Europe," *The Washington Post*, December 17, 2018, p. 13.

[183] South Korea is the sixth-largest trade partner with the United States, accounting for $112 billion in two-way trade in 2016. U.S. companies exported $42 billion in goods to South Korea, and imported $70 billion, creating a trade deficit of $28 billion. China is our leading trade partner, and any trade war could risk a serious setback to American GDP, perhaps a loss of 4% in U.S. GDP. In 2016, the United States exported $170 billion in goods to China, and China exported $480 billion in goods to the United States.

deal-making."[184] In the case of North Korea, it meant threatening Pyongyang with "fire and fury like the world has never seen." Iran has received similar warnings.

Members of the administration, primarily the generals such as the former secretary of defense, the national security adviser, and the chief of staff, have been critical of the president, citing his self-absorption, his instability, and his lack of curiosity. In 2017, there was great criticism from the left regarding the appointment of general officers to sensitive positions, so it is ironic that the loss of the so-called moderate generals drew regret from conservatives and liberals. There was alarm following the Mattis resignation, which left decision making influence in the hands of neoconservative loyalists such as Secretary of State Pompeo and National Security Adviser Bolton.

AMERICA AND THE WORLD ORDER: THE TRUMP EFFECT

For the first time in history, a U.S. president has better rapport with the world's authoritarian leaders than with democratic partners. Throughout the presidential campaign of 2015-2016 and the first years of his presidency, Trump praised authoritarians such as Russia's President Putin, Philippines' President Duterte, Turkey's President Erdogan, Egypt's President al-Sisi, Saudi Arabia's deputy crown prince Mohammed bin Salman, and Malaysia's Prime Minister Najib Razak. Israeli President Netanyahu, a quasi-authoritarian, is a special friend. North Korean leader Kim Jong Un, described as "smart" and "skilled," is Trump's newest friend.

---

[184] Jessica T. Mathews, "Nuclear Diplomacy: From Iran to North Korea," *New York Review of Books*, August 17, 2017, p. 18.

The common denominator for these heads of state is their authoritarian and bellicose tendencies. Duterte is responsible for the deaths of thousands; Erdogan and Sisi have jailed tens of thousands; the judiciary in both Turkey and Egypt has been shredded; the Saudis have tortured thousands and embarked on a burnt-earth war in Yemen; and Putin has amassed a private fortune and compromised free press and free speech. The North Korean regime is the most brutal in the international community.

Trump's nativist instincts are reversing the bipartisan post-war foreign policy that centered on U.S. international activism. Since World War II, U.S. leaders have taken the high ground on international agreements and mediation, particularly with regard to arms control and disarmament. There have been exceptions, of course, particularly President Clinton's lack of enthusiasm for U.N. agreements on nuclear test limitations and land mine prohibitions as well as President George W. Bush's abrogation of the Anti-Ballistic Missile Treaty. But no president since the Spanish-American War has brandished such a "garrison-state mentality" as Trump, who ended the American-led international order.

Trump has sponsored "unilateral retrenchment," compromising international pacts and multilateral organizations that Democratic and Republican presidents built over the past 70 years. American influence in the World Bank and the International Monetary Fund is at stake; American dominance of NATO may be challenged as well. The political and diplomatic achievements of the Marshall Plan and the Truman Doctrine, sources of national pride, have been forgotten. Trump's attack on international trade agreements is an attack on American values that viewed "prosperous trade among nations" as an essential element in "enduring peace."[185] We have a President who is isolated in the international arena, unlike any other in more than 100 years.

---

[185] Paul Krugman, "Fall of the American Empire," *New York Times*, June 19, 2018, p. 24.

In pursuing a policy of isolation, Trump has created an international vacuum of power that awaits a new leader. Merkel and Macron favor a European-driven international order, but both face domestic political obstacles as well as the emergence of authoritarian leaders in East Europe. China is pushing into the South China Sea, and is gaining greater influence throughout Asia. Russia hopes to regain its superpower status, but its heavy-handed actions in Syria, Crimea, and Eastern Ukraine have not attracted supporters outside the Middle East. Meanwhile, Beijing and Moscow have taken advantage of the chaos in the Trump Administration to forge their closest relations since the 1950s.

Trump has created, moreover, a huge credibility problem for the presidency and the nation the next time the United States faces a geopolitical crisis. During the Cuban missile crisis in 1962, President Kennedy dispatched high-level personnel to European capitals to make the case for a naval blockade of Cuba. His emissaries carried sensitive surveillance photographs of Soviet missile deployments in Cuba. A former colleague of mine at the CIA, John Whitman, accompanied Secretary of State Dean Acheson to inform President Charles de Gaulle. When it was time to present the French president with the photographic evidence, de Gaulle waved away the chance to examine the photography, saying that "the word of the President of the United States is enough for me."[186] It is impossible to imagine any respect for the word of Trump.

The election of Trump exposed the weakness of the guardrails of our democracy. For the second time in 16 years, a president was elected despite losing the popular vote. Al Gore garnered 500,000 more votes than his opponent, George W. Bush, and Hillary Clinton exceeded Trump's vote by nearly three million. As a result, four of the five conservative justices on the Supreme Court were appointed by presidents who failed to win the popular vote. Bush's election,

---

[186] Conversation with John Whitman, March, 1972.

moreover, was tainted by the role of the Supreme Court, which politicized the election results in Florida. Trump's election was aided by the intervention of Russia, including the hacking of the Democratic National Committee and Clinton's campaign manager, John Podesta.

The congressional dysfunctional over the past ten years has demonstrated an inability to legislate public policy in an effective and timely manner. Narrow interest groups have taken over a Republican Party devoted to overturning the social and economic policies of the past 80 years. Despite overwhelming popular consensus, legislation on many issues is stymied. Large majorities favor the institution of more rigorous gun control, but not even the horrific disaster at a Florida high school on Valentine's Day in 2018 budged the congressional process. Large majorities believe that campaign spending by corporations and other private groups needs to be regulated, but *Citizens United vs the Federal Election Commission* is the law of the land due to a 5-4 vote in the Supreme Court. There are popular majorities that favor the legalization of marijuana and a higher minimum wage, but Republican majorities in the Senate stand in the way.

Trump has convinced many that a "deep state" of military officers, intelligence officials, and even judges is determined to keep the president from governing. It is ironic that Trump gave the military so much influence in the making of foreign policy in view of his attitudes toward the military and the "deep state." For the past two years, Trump has been at war with the Department of Justice, the FBI, and the CIA, undermining the integrity and credibility of the law enforcement and intelligence communities. Trump's questionable behavior in trying to block the investigations of Special Counsel Mueller has suggested a case for obstruction of justice.

Even before the election of Trump, the United States was witnessing the compromise of civil liberties typically at risk during permanent war. The Founding Fathers warned about the risks to liberties during times of war; President Dwight D. Eisenhower's trenchant Farewell Address in 1961 echoed these warnings. This country has been in permanent, and even undeclared war since the 9/11 attacks, and, as a result, we have witnessed attacks on our Bill of Rights. The Fourth Amendment, protecting against illegal seizures and searches, was violated by massive surveillance of Americans by the National Security Agency, a violation of it's charter. The Eighth Amendment forbidding torture was violated by the U.S. military and the CIA as they abused captives in secret prisons in East Europe and the Middle East.

The Supreme Court is not serving as the judicial guardrail that the Founding Fathers created. It regularly defers to the federal government in cases, such as the travel ban and the use of military force, making it difficult to use the judicial branch to pursue violations of the Bill of Rights and the congressional War Powers Act. The Trump administration has worsened the problem by limiting access to public information; neutralizing public affairs officers at government agencies; blocking the process of Freedom of Information; and censoring specific words and phrases that invite political reform. Press conferences at the White House and the Departments of State and Defense have become infrequent events.

Russian meddling in the 2016 presidential election threatened our democratic electoral process. The dumbing down of the American electorate facilitated Russian efforts to gain leverage in the process. Russian techniques were an updated form of a disinformation campaign that the two sides have pursued against each other since the end of WWII. But social media and the cyber world presented a new platform for fake news, false identities, and other tactics to reach an expanded audience that gets most of its news on Facebook or other social media. Too many people on the right and left believed outrageous propaganda on a "deep state" or Hillary Clinton's child kidnapping ring.

Russian disinformation exploited the fears and anxieties within the American populace that have grown over the past decade due to the pressures of immigration, social change, and economic inequality. The Russians were trying to compromise American democracy, but so was the home-grown Tea Party movement that gained traction in 2009. Too many Americans believed that President Obama was born in Kenya or that Obamacare would create "death panels" to decide the fate of elderly Americans. The fact that Americans were willing to believe the worst accusations against their own government made it easy for Russian troll factories to exploit U.S. cynicism and polarization. Trump's lies have created additional confusion about our elections and our judicial system; his charge of "fake news" has compromised the credibility of the media.

The problem is compounded by a U.S. president without respect for the rule of law and the rights of minorities. The decline in political rights and civil liberties started before Trump's inauguration, but the president has accelerated the decline. The Trump campaign encouraged the use of violence, denigrated the worth of Trump's opposition, and engaged in race baiting with dog whistle accusations. Donald Trump is following Stephen Bannon's exhortation to "flood the zone with shit" by dispensing lies, half truths, and alternative facts to create confusion among voters.

Trump conducts his policies on the basis of his faith in "might makes right." His predecessors in the White House struggled with the relationship between power and principle. Trump does not struggle; he has taken a wrecking ball to our relations with allies and our democratic institutions. His message in his inaugural address was a simple one: America was facing "carnage;" the global community was a mess; and U.S. foreign policy was a total failure. He stated during his campaign that only he "could fix it." He has done exactly what he said he would do regarding the Paris climate agreement; Iranian nuclear accord; trade and tariffs; and total support for Israel regardless of the regional implications.

Trump is an international bully who rejects any notion of world order that previous presidents understood as vital to U.S. security. Past iterations of the "Nuclear Posture Review" emphasized the importance of reducing our nuclear arsenal, but Trump's review focused on new weapons and new missions, and endorsed his worst impulses. For the first time in history, the greatest danger to the United States does not come from a foreign threat, but from the president himself. We learned in January 2019 that the FBI initiated an investigation of Trump as a witting or unwitting agent of Russia. As Pogo said, "We have met the enemy and he is us."

Prior to Trump's election, Senate majority leader Mitch McConnell (R-KY) conducted his own "war" against the Constitution and the judicial branch of government, holding a Supreme Court seat hostage for political reasons. This placed the court in a position of "real institutional peril," according to Yale University's Linda Greenhouse, who covered the Court for *The New York Times* for several decades.[187] Former Justice John Paul Stevens noted in the wake of the presidential election of 2000 that the *Bush v Gore* decision had compromised the credibility and integrity of the Court. The elimination of the filibuster for nominees to the Court has permitted a dangerously narrow path for Trump appointees.

Even if the Mueller investigation should lead to an indictment of the president or provide grounds to impeach, Trump will defend his self-proclaimed innocence regarding "no collusion," perhaps pardoning himself. Trump's lawyer, Rudy Giuliani, stated that the president could do so. The political use of the presidential power to pardon would mark one more step in Trump's campaign against our democracy. The threats to the Department of Justice and the FBI suggested efforts to obstruct justice. Labeling the press as the "enemy of the people" was out of the totalitarian playbook.

Over the past several decades, two presidents have dealt with possible impeachment. The mere threat of impeachment led to Nixon's resignation. His last days were filled with tragedy, including a tear-filled goodbye to his closest

---

[187] "An Open Letter to Justice Kennedy," editorial, *New York Times*, April 29, 2018, p. 10.

colleagues, who were told, "I hope you won't feel I have let you down."[188] Nixon asked Kissinger to join him on his knees in prayer in the Lincoln bedroom in the White House before announcing his resignation in a televised address to "spare the nation further pain." Nixon's farewell talk to his White House staff was painful and unforgettable. I watched the speech in the crowded office of the assistant secretary of state for European affairs; there were few dry eyes in the room as we witnessed Nixon's palpable sense of shame.

Clinton's insecurities were well hidden. There was little evidence of sadness and regret in the way he fought the issue of impeachment to the bitter end. When the impeachment motions failed in the Senate, where a two-thirds vote was required, Clinton thanked those who helped him "fight off the right-wing coup" or, in the words of a New York businessman, the "demonizing mullahs in our midst."[189] There was no hint in his later behavior or his memoir that his actions in the White House and the charge of obstruction of justice probably cost Al Gore the election in 2000 and enabled the collateral damage of a Bush presidency, particularly the invasion of Iraq.

Special Counsel Mueller may hold potential evidence for the impeachment of Donald Trump, but Congress holds the key to whether he will be impeached. The firing of FBI Director Comey, who was investigating the Trump campaign's connections with Russia, and the forced resignation of Attorney General Sessions suggested obstruction of justice. Failing to divest himself of his wide-ranging business interests pointed to a violation of the emoluments clause of the Constitution, but no president has been charged with such a crime. The indictment and prison sentence for Trump's lawyer, Michael Cohen, pointed to a charge against the president as an unindicted co-conspirator, similar to the

---

[188] John A. Farrell, "Richard Nixon: The Life," New York: Doubleday, 2017, p. 531.

[189] Bill Clinton, *My Life*, New York: Vantage Books, 2005, pp. 845-846.

Grand Jury description of Nixon during Watergate. Trump benefitted from Russia's interference in the presidential election, but there is no proof that he colluded with the Kremlin. There may not be a presidential resignation or impeachment, but the rhythms of Watergate are dominating the Trump presidency.

WHAT IS TO BE DONE?

The odds do not favor the possibility of Trump being convicted of impeachment or indicted and, unlike Nixon, we do not have a president with a sense of shame. In view of Trump's bizarre behavior, however, there is an unusual alternative in the 25th Amendment that has no precedent in U.S. history.

In 1963, following the assassination of President Kennedy, there was a bipartisan effort by Senators Kenneth Keating (R/NY) and Estes Kefauver (D/TN) to create a procedure to replace a president unable to discharge the powers and duties of the office. The proposal was based upon a recommendation of the American Bar Association in 1960, and resulted in the enactment of the 25th Amendment in 1967. Trump's mental state raises the possibility of resorting to the 25th Amendment that deals with presidential succession and disability.

Prior to the 25th Amendment, there were occasions in our history when a president was incapacitated, most prominently Woodrow Wilson and Dwight D. Eisenhower, but there was no procedure for enhancing the role of the Vice President. Many psychiatrists believe that the combination of Trump's malignant narcissism, paranoia, and lack of impulse control has created the potential danger of a president ordering a reckless use of military force. According to the 25th Amendment, the Vice President and a majority of Cabinet officers would have to initiate the process. Two-thirds majorities in both the House and the Senate are then required to allow the Vice President to assume the duties of the President. The use of the amendment is even more unlikely than impeachment or indictment.

It is unlikely that Trump will be removed from office before 2020, so it is imperative to focus on ways to contain his worst impulses and protect the country. With the Democrats in control of the House of Representatives as a result of the November 2018 election, there are initiatives that could be pursued. At the very least, the fact that President Trump is being investigated by more than a dozen entities points to limits on his political leverage if not his political longevity.

The presidential assault on governance and the meanness of Trump's social and economic policies will require conciliation to ameliorate the political damage that has been done. We cannot simply wait for a more trustworthy occupant in the White House in view of Trump's efforts to reduce non-military spending and bludgeon important federal programs and regulations. Trump is not conducting "government reform" any more than the tax bill was "tax reform." Trump vowed during the campaign that his "reforms" would address the needs of "working men and women," and that he would "drain the swamp" to do so. There is no evidence that government has been made more effective as a result of Trump's policies. It will be necessary to review, reinvigorate, and reinvent the entire federal government in the wake of the destruction caused by the Trump presidency.

Congress must establish an independent and nonpartisan entity to oversee the process of "real reform" in order to repair the damage wrought by Trump's ideological appointees, who weakened and even destroyed government programs. President Clinton gave such a task to Vice President Gore in 1993 in the "National Partnership for Reinventing Government." We will need another round of "reinventing government" so that departments can be reinvigorated, and important rules and regulations can be restored. The Environmental Protection Agency and the Consumer Financial Protection Bureau will have to be rebuilt.

A blue ribbon commission must conduct a serious accounting of the damage Trump's political appointees have done to our participatory democracy, particularly voter suppression. This effort would resemble the truth and reconciliation commissions that were created after the tragic developments in Africa and East Europe after the Cold War.[190] Such a commission could educate the American public on the importance of dedicated public servants at FEMA, the Coast Guard, and law enforcement, who provide the essential services that citizens favor.

A commission is needed to evaluate the Trump administration's damage to civil rights laws of the past fifty years, particularly the dilution of federal rules against discrimination in education and housing. The Department of Housing and Urban Development has weakened regulations that prohibit discrimination on the basis of race or religion. In my own state of Maryland, a Republican governor shifted transportation money from a light-rail project that would have helped African-American residents of Baltimore. The money went to infrastructure projects that served white residents elsewhere in the state.

In order to renew a functioning and participatory democracy, it will be necessary to create a time of internal reflection. We must end the ugliness of our civil discourse, avoiding discussion of "deep state," "fake news," "witch hunts," and "secret societies" in order to revive our political culture. It would take clinical psychologists and psychiatrists to analyze the political and psychological chaos of Trump's first two years in the White House.

Our way of governing, our democracy, will have to be strengthened to correct the ills of voter suppression and gerrymandering. There are far too many Americans eligible to vote who are not registered, which begs for easier voter registration, perhaps using information already provided to Departments of

---

[190] See Kevin Baker, "Nothing in All Creation is Hidden: Why America Needs Truth and Reconciliation After Trump," *The New Republic*, June 2018, p. 30.

Motor Vehicles. A new Voting Rights Act is needed to stop voter suppression and to provide adequate and accessible polling places. A law is needed to ensure that candidates for the presidency (and the Congress) release their tax returns. The role of the Electoral College and the Citizens United decision that opened the door to big money in our elections, must be challenged.

Trump's lies and false statements weaken democratic governance. Numerous fact checkers have compiled lists of Trump's falsehoods since he assumed the office of the presidency, but they have ignored the corrosive aspect of the president's deceit.[191] One of the reasons for the collapse of the Soviet Union in 1991 was the fact that the Soviet people no longer believed in their leaders; their cynicism was corrosive. The United States is not going to collapse, but presidential mendacity is weakening the credibility of our leaders, our institutions, and our democratic governance. We have a president who cannot be believed.

Polls taken over the past several decades document a decline in American confidence in key institutions, particularly in the presidency, the Congress, and the media. Trump cannot be blamed for this trend overall, but he is a large part of the recent decline. Surveys once revealed overwhelming trust in the "federal government to do what is right;" current responses cluster around a dismal 20 percent.[192]

Congress itself must be rebuilt and restructured. The institutional support for Congress has been weakened, particularly the Government Accountability Office, the Congressional Research Service, and the Congressional Budget Office. Representative Newt Gingrich's war on Congress in the 1990s led to the defunding of the Office of Technology Assessment, an essential think tank for

---

[191] Fact checkers at The *Washington Post* have recorded more than 7,500 false statements from the president in 2017-2018; *The Toronto Star* tabulated nearly 4,000.

[192] Robert J. Samuelson, "Our unhappy new year," *The Washington Post*, December 31, 2018, p. 15.

technological problems. Congress no longer has the resources or the will to cope with the growth of corporate lobbying that finds corporations devoting far more resources to lobbying Congress than Congress spends to fund itself.[193]

There are other large issues to address. Donald Trump is not the cause but a symptom of systemic problems associated with social and economic inequality, and the growth of cynicism toward government due to this inequality. While the lower and middle-classes lack advocates in Washington to deal with the high cost of health insurance and college education, there has been an increase in corporate lobbying that enhances the wealth of the richest people in the United States. U.S. economic output has doubled over the past forty years, but the bulk of the bounty has gone to the very rich.

The fact that fewer people have trust in government leads to the anger and discouragement that resulted in the election of a demagogue and an authoritarian such a Trump. Previously, a political personality such as Trump would not have survived the nomination filters and political guardrails in his own party, let only a presidential election that garnered him 63 million votes.

The corruption in government finds former lawmakers and government officials remaining in Washington to lobby for corporate clients who helped to craft the tax bill that benefitted the rich in 2017, and to increase defense spending at the expense of non-defense priorities. For the past 25 years, Representative Gingrich and his "Republican Revolution;" the Tea Party; and Trump's campaign to "Make America Great Again" have focused on demonizing government and reducing its role, outsourcing important functions of governance to private enterprise. The antigovernment campaign began in the Reagan administration, but Democrats also have not been helpful. They have campaigned against Washington's bureaucracy, making it easier to scapegoat civil servants.

---

[193] Bill Pascrell Jr, "Why is the Congress so dumb?," *The Washington Post*, January 13, 2019, p. B2.

Accompanying this demonizing of the bureaucracy is what Senator Elizabeth Warren (D/MA) has termed the "privatization of lawmaking" that finds K Street lobbyists drafting our laws and legislation. During the 2017 battle over the tax bill, there were more than 6,000 registered tax lobbyists dealing with 130 aides on the Senate Finance Committee and the Joint Committee on Taxation. Even worse, there were no congressional hearings on the tax bill, and no public hearings on the renegotiation of the North Atlantic Free Trade Agreement.[194]

Senator Warren understands that the Founding Fathers devoted themselves to building a system that would be safe from moneyed influence. She has targeted both the efforts of Republicans, the Tea Party, and Trump to reduce the role of government as well as the influx of corporate money and the influence of lobbyists to draft our laws. As a result, Warren has called for an end to the revolving door between public service and lobbying; a ban on lobbying on behalf of foreign governments; and demanding that presidents and vice presidents release their tax returns and cooperate with conflict-of-interest laws.[195]

Upon taking office, Trump moved immediately against Warren's signature achievement, the creation of the Consumer Financial Protection Bureau to launch investigations into corrupt institutions and practices. In November 2017, he appointed his director of the Office of Management and Budget, Mick Mulvaney, to be the acting director of the CFPB. Mulvaney, in turn, fired the Bureau's Consumer Advisory Board, which was required under the 2010 Dodd-Frank financial law that addressed the financial crisis of 2007-2008. Mulvaney also stripped the enforcement powers of the office responsible for pursuing discrimination cases and weakened regulations that dealt with payday lenders guilty of financial scams. Corporate interests applauded all of the measures

---

[194] Pascrell, "Why is Congress so dumb?," p. B2.

[195] Senator Elizabeth Warren, "A Radical Anti-Corruption Platform," *The Intercept*, August 21, 2018.

designed to weaken the Bureau's jurisdiction over banks, credit unions, and securities firms.

The problem of student debt must be addressed, particularly the Trump administration's efforts to erase efforts to make for-profit institutions more accountable. The typical student borrower will obtain nearly $7,000 in a single year, averaging around $25,000 in debt by graduation. The Congress needs to address college affordability, and to create more educational opportunities for low-income students. A college education should not be a debt trap for American students. There must be more funding and support for vocational education and two-year community colleges.

Senator Bernie Sanders (I/VT) has addressed the problem of inequality by introducing measures that would promote Medicare for all and the elimination of college tuition. It has been difficult to attract co-sponsors for these measures, but 24 progressive and health care advocacy groups have supported a comprehensive single-payer system similar to most industrial countries. Of course, Trump would veto such measures, but it is time for Congress, Commissions, and the citizenry to be doing the planning and positioning to restore good governance in 2021.

The steady erosion of checks and balances in U.S. governance over the past several decades, particularly the decline of Congress, has allowed Trump to create the very swamp that he campaigned against. The constitutional requirement for oversight of the executive branch has been observed in the breach. Congressional committees have been particularly inept in monitoring U.S. foreign policy and defense policy. The Senate committees responsible for oversight of national security—the Foreign Relations Committee and the Armed Services Committee—have held fewer hearings than in the past. As a result, the defense budget does not receive the scrutiny that it needs, and American wars in the Middle East and Southwest Asia have become interminable. The longest war in U.S. history involves a nation, Afghanistan, that has no relevance to American national security.

Congress has been dysfunctional, refusing to address, let alone challenge, the harm that Trump has done in the fields of national security, particularly issues of war and peace; trade, particularly protectionism; and foreign policy. As a result, the Pentagon has been funded at record levels with no real congressional oversight. The defense budget for 2019, which was named after the late Senator John McCain, who never encountered a weapons system he could not support, set a new record at $716 billion. Meanwhile, the Department of State is no longer a major force in conceptualizing and implementing American foreign policy.

The disappearance of bipartisanship on the congressional intelligence committees has been harmful. The former chairman of the House intelligence committee, Rep. Devin Nunes (R-CA), went rogue, providing sensitive exculpatory intelligence documents to the White House, the subject of a congressional investigation. The chairman of the Senate intelligence committee, Senator Richard Burr (R-NC), has been derelict in using his subpoena power in the investigation. As a result, Senator McCain believed the Congress "no longer had the credibility to handle" the possibility of collusion between Russia and the Trump administration, and the cover-up of the contacts.

Although Obama campaigned for the presidency on the basis of transparency and accountability, he ignored the transgressions of the Central Intelligence Agency and worked actively to diminish the role of the Office of the Inspector General throughout the national security arena, particularly at CIA. A statutory Inspector General was created at the CIA in 1989 due to the crimes of Iran-Contra, but Obama made sure there was no IG in place at the CIA during most of his eight-year presidency. The decline of oversight throughout the government has enabled the Trump administration to weaken governance in the regulatory agencies and the national security process.

Trump has been derelict in making credible political appointments to the federal bureaucracy, but hyperactive in naming judges to the federal bench. He persistently maligned the civil service during the campaign with ludicrous demands to "drain the swamp" and the charge that the "civil service was the problem." As president, he imposed a hiring freeze, involuntary transfers of senior executives (many of whom were replaced by political appointees), and a halt in cost-of-living increases. The government shutdown in 2018-2019 worsened the serious morale problem that the Trump administration created.

The selection of so many political appointees led directly to an exodus of experienced senior executives. As of October 2018, only 357 of 705 key executives requiring Senate confirmation were filled. At the same point in Obama's presidency, 700 appointees had been confirmed.[196] The Trump administration is clearly responsible for driving out some of the best and the brightest in the bureaucracy, marking a loss of expertise and mentoring for junior officials, which will be felt in the near term.

While the mainstream media have focused on the appointments of Neil Gorsuch and Brett Kavanaugh to the Supreme Court, less attention has been given to Trump's nomination of 36 court of appeals judges and 99 district judges. The Senate confirmed 24 of Trump's picks for the federal bench in Trump's first 18 months. As a result, two circuit courts—the Sixth and the Seventh—have been flipped from liberal to conservative; and two more—the Eighth and the 11th— will soon follow.[197] Senate Democrats under the leadership of Chuck Schumer (D/NY) have been insufficiently aggressive in fighting confirmations that are occurring at a record pace.

At this rate, President Trump will have replaced nearly one-third of the nation's judges by the end of his first term in 2020. These judges will have an impact on the lives of all Americans for several decades. No president since Franklin D. Roosevelt has been more successful in shaping the judicial branch of

---

[196] Joe Davidson, "Top civil servants are leaving administration quickly," *The Washington Post*, September 12, 2018, p. 14.

[197] Jason Zengerle, "Warfare on the Courts," *The New York Times Magazine*, September 26, 2018, p. 33.

government. In the Roosevelt era, the Supreme Court was moving to the right as the administration and the nation were moving to the left; in the Trump era, the nation is moving to the left on a variety of social and political issues as the president moves to the right.

Federal courts serve as the most important guardrail for our democracy, confronting the administration on myriad political, economic, and social issues. These issues include the Muslim travel ban, which required intervention from the Supreme Court to allow the Trump administration to keep its ban on the basis of national security. There were three significant Federal court rulings in the summer of 2018, however, that rolled back executive actions that weakened access to health care and reined in federal unions. In June 2018, a Federal District Court in Washington stopped a Kentucky plan to introduce work requirements that would have caused 95,000 low-income people to lose Medicaid coverage.

In August 2018, the same court struck down a set of executive orders that would have made it easier to fire employees and weaken their representation. For the past several years, the Republican Party has made a special effort to rein in public-sector trade unions by ending mandatory union dues for government workers. The judge in the case, Ketanji Brown Jackson, determined that most of the key provisions of Trump's executive orders "conflict with congressional intent in a manner that cannot be sustained."[198] Federal courts also blocked Trump's efforts to close a program that shielded some 800,000 young undocumented immigrants from deportation and to deny federal money to so-called sanctuary cities.

In January 2019, a U.S. district judge in New York blocked an attempt by the Trump administration to add a citizenship question to the 2020 census that Judge

---

[198] Noah Scheiber, "Judge Strikes Down President's Efforts to Set a Bridle on Unions," *The New York Times*, August 26, 2018, p. 13.

Jesse Furman considered "arbitrary and capricious."[199] The Trump administration wanted the question to isolate immigrant communities. For the past 70 years, the census has not included a citizenship question. A federal judge in Pennsylvania stopped the Trump administration from restricting the ability of some women to obtain birth control at no charge because their employers objected on religious or moral grounds.

The most important federal ruling involved a lawsuit against President Trump. A federal court made history in August when Judge Peter J. Messitte allowed a lawsuit to go forward against the president that alleged he violated the Constitution by conducting business with foreign and domestic governments.[200] This is the first time in history that a federal judge ruled on the meaning of the "emolument" clauses in the Constitution. These clauses forbid presidents from using their office for "profit, gain, or advantage." The Founding Fathers introduced these clauses to create an obstacle against corruption in the executive branch.[201] Ironically, the president revoked the security clearances of a former director of the CIA for "monetizing" his access to classified materials. Meanwhile, no president in history has "monetized" the office of the presidency in Trump's fashion.

The charges against senior members of the Trump campaign as well as the trials of his campaign manager, Paul Manafort, and his lawyer, Michael Cohen, point to the need for a new Office of Public Integrity to make sure government works for all American citizens. Overall, the Senate Ethics Committee has failed to monitor and punish members of Congress who are guilty of ethics violations.

---

[199] Tara Bahrampour, "Judge rules against citizenship question on census," *The Washington Post,* January 16, 2019, p. 6.

[200] Judge Peter Messitte also made history on August 1, 1993 in Bethesda, Maryland where he married the author and Carolyn McGiffert Ekedahl.

[201] Alexander Hamilton warned in Federalist 73 that a president's business interests might allow foreign actors to "tempt him by largesses, to surrender at [his] discretion his judgment to their inclinations."

The Senate has done a poor job of ensuring that the large lobbying firms file the required forms with the Senate Office of Public Records and has failed to pursue lobbyists who do not register.

Several years ago, there was a bipartisan effort led by Republican Senators McCain and Susan Collins (ME) and Democratic Senator Joe Lieberman (CT) to create an independent Office of Public Integrity, but the chairman and and ranking minority member of the Ethics Committee's opposed such legislation. Two-thirds of the Senate voted against the measure. The Federal Election Commission, with 400 employees and a $54 million budget would be able to monitor campaign contributions that are not properly scrutinized.

As long as Congress defers to the president on the conduct of national security; the Supreme Court intervenes to prevent any challenge to the power of the president; and the media defer to official and authorized sources, it will be difficult to correct the transgressions and deceit of the Trump administration. As a result, the role of the whistleblower has become particularly important in view of the recklessness of the president on both domestic and international issues. Trump's attitudes toward nuclear forces, nuclear proliferation, the use of force, and the creation of a space force demand greater scrutiny throughout the legislative process as well as a national constituency that applies pressure on the legislature. Whistleblowers are particularly important due to the overuse of secrecy, which limits national debate on foreign policy and deprives citizens of information needed to participate in genuine life-or-death issues. There cannot be serious investigative journalism without whistleblowers.

Meanwhile, the international community is not waiting for Trump's successor in the White House; serious efforts are underway to enhance traditional world order and to maintain the effectiveness of important political and economic institutions. In Europe, Prime Minister Macron's government created a "Paris Peace Forum" as well as a European Intervention Initiative. It is noteworthy that Washington's notification of withdrawal from the Paris climate accord has inspired greater efforts at cooperation by the remaining 194 members. No nation joined the United States in leaving the accord. European leaders are also trying to hold together the Iran nuclear accord, which has been threatened by Trump's withdrawal.

The European Union has been particularly active in the wake of Trump's designation of the EU as a "foe." It signed a major free trade initiative with Japan that covers more than 600 million individuals and represents nearly one-third of global GDP. The EU held serious discussions with China on trade issues. Canadian Prime Minister Trudeau, who Trump vilified as "dishonest and weak," has also been busy, organizing a Lima Group with 16 Latin American countries to address issues such as restoring democracy in Venezuela.

More needs to be done in Asia where China, the major beneficiary of Trump's American First policy, is holding a strong hand that includes formation of the Shanghai Cooperation Organization and the Asian Infrastructure Investment Bank. Japan and Australia, with great concerns about the power and influence of China, have reinvented the Trans-Pacific Partnership; they have also held joint military exercises and have negotiated reciprocal access agreements with India. In order to counter China militarily, however, the United States must play a part. And to counter China economically, the United States requires the support of its allies.

There has never been a better time for the United States to change course and seize the high ground on matters of international security. An obvious place to start would be the promotion of a trilateral conference of the major nuclear powers—China, Russia, and the United States—to reinforce the idea that a nuclear war cannot be won and must never be fought. There needs to be greater communication between the national security officials of these countries as well as between NATO and Russia to reduce the tensions that have been created in the first two years of the Trump administration. The absence of any mechanism for a serious diplomatic dialogue with Russia on arms control and disarmament as well as differences over Ukraine and Syria have created Cold War conditions.

The nuclear nations must ensure that nuclear materials don't fall into the hands of non-nuclear powers and non-state actors, particularly terrorist and insurgent groups. This dialogue should include discussion of the cyber dangers to strategic warning systems that are designed to prevent accidental warfare. The false nuclear alert in Hawaii in January 2018 was not a mistaken or accidental act, but a failure of leadership and technology that could have had terrible consequences.

It is hard to imagine the United States conducting successful multilateral diplomacy because it has been so inept at conducting even bilateral diplomacy, particularly summitry. There have been several meetings between Trump and Russian President Putin, but the national security team has no idea of what took place at these meetings. According to U.S. officials, there is no detailed record of Trump's interactions with Putin, which is highly unusual.[202] This handicaps the entire national security team, and allows Russia to dominate the discussion and interpretation of the face-to-face meetings that took place in 2017-2018.

On balance, the international reaction to Trump and his "war cabinet" has been far more energetic and imaginative than the response of the Democratic Party to Trump and his minions. There is an absence of leadership at the top of the Democratic Party, and the early concentration on the 2020 presidential election has blocked discussion of domestic programs needed to revive our democracy and to address the needs and aspirations of the American public.

The weakening of the U.S. democracy did not begin with the election of Donald Trump. Prior to his election, extensive gerrymandering, voter suppression and the sanctioning of corporate money in the electoral process

---

[202] Greg Miller, "Officials in dark on Putin's talks," *The Washington Post*, January 13, 2019, p. 1.

contributed to the U.S. decline in governance. Gerrymandering and voter suppression did far more damage to U.S. democracy during the presidential election of 2016 than the Russian effort to compromise our democracy and defeat the Democratic candidate Hillary Clinton. Unfortunately the legal tension between the Supreme Court and the federal court system on the issue of gerrymandering has blocked the ability to deal with one of the most serious threats to democratic representation in the United States.

Gerrymandering refers to the efforts of a Massachusetts governor, Elbridge Gerry, to use his electoral victory in 1810 to create an unusually shaped congressional district in the shape of a salamander to benefit his party. In recent times, the Republicans in the state of Wisconsin captured the State Assembly and drew new districts in 2011, which allowed the Republicans to capture 65 percent of the seats in the assembly with 45 percent of the vote. A similar development took place in Pennsylvania where Republicans won 13 of the 18 seats in the House with less than 50 percent of the vote. The Republican Party in North Carolina won 10 of the 13 seats in the State Assembly with less than 50 percent of the vote. Democrats garnered ten million more votes than Republicans in the 2018 congressional election, and should have gained more than the 41 seats they acquired.

In August 2018, a federal three-judge panel repudiated North Carolina's outrageously gerrymandered congressional map, declaring that the Constitution "does not allow elected officials to enact laws that distort the marketplace of political ideas so as to intentionally favor certain political beliefs, parties, or candidates and disfavor others."[203] The judges ruled that several constitutional provisions were violated, including Article I, which "preserves inviolate the right

---

[203] "The right move on gerrymandering," editorial, *The Washington Post*, August 30, 2018, p. 16.

of the People to elect their Representatives;" the First Amendment; and the equal protection clause that declares the State must govern "impartially."

Nevertheless, the Supreme Court took no action with previous cases against gerrymandering in Wisconsin and Maryland, where Democrats benefitted from the reshaping of a congressional district. The Court also upheld congressional and legislative maps in Texas that discriminated against black and Latino voters, according to the lower courts. Gerrymandering on the face of it is a violation of the equal protection clause of the 14th Amendment, which assures "one person/one vote," but the Court believes that the answer to the problem rests with the Legislative branch of government, not the Judicial branch. Addressing the Duke Law School summer program in Washington in August 2018, Justice Ruth Bader Ginsburg argued that the issue would come before the Court again and that plaintiffs should be able to establish they suffered direct injury from gerrymandering.[204]

If the Supreme Court fails to address the problem, then gerrymandering could be addressed by independent redistricting commissions, which have been established in California, Michigan, and Colorado. Chief Justice Earl Warren wrote in the 1950s that the "right to exercise the franchise in a free and unimpaired manner is preservative of other basic civil and political rights."[205]

The Supreme Court's recent decisions on voting rights favored entrenched Republican majorities. In January 2013 in *Shelby County v. Holder*, the Court struck down the heart of the Voting Rights Act of 1965 that required certain states and local governments to obtain federal clearance before implementing changes to voting practices. In the "Federalist Papers," Alexander Hamilton called the judiciary the "least dangerous" branch of government, because it relies on

---

[204] Adam Liptak, "Forecast and Highlights After 'Divisive' Court Term," *The New York Times*, August 7, 2018, p. 10.

[205] Jeffrey Toobin, "Winning Votes," *The New Yorker*, November 26, 2018, p. 21.

"judgment" instead of "force" and "will." The increasingly ideological Supreme Court has found ways to weaponize its judgment, however, beginning in January 2010 with the *Citizens United* ruling that gave the green light to corporations and unions to spend unlimited amounts of money on advertising and other political tools. Even before the confirmation of Kavanaugh, the Trump administration had the votes on the Supreme Court to uphold voting restrictions, gerrymandering, and the purging of voter registration rolls.

In the wake of the *Shelby County v. Holder* decision, the federal government has been less active in protecting voter rights for minorities. According to the head of the United States Commission on Civil Rights, Catherine E. Lhamon, discrimination against minority voters has become "enduring and pernicious," and is not being addressed by federal law.[206] The Congress must return to the Voting Rights Act of 1965 in order to expand the protections of the Act and restore some of the enforcements powers nullified by the Supreme Court. The Court's decision in 2013 ended the Department of Justice's power to block and litigate changes in voting rules in 15 states, mostly in the south. Since the decision, more than 60 lawsuits have been filed regarding election practices that violate the Voting Rights Act, but only four of these suits were brought by the Justice Department, all under President Obama. The lack of enforcement to protect voting by the disabled is even more egregious than the failure to protect minorities.

While a majority of the Supreme Court has been given over to the Republican party by the Trump administration, the federal appeals courts have issued important rulings to limit the damage that Trump has caused. In addition to the decision to ban the controversial pesticide chlorpyrifos, the courts may eventually block the Trump administration's efforts to deny green cards or citizenship to any

---

[206] Michael Wines, "Civil Rights Report Finds Few Protections for Voters," *The New York Times*, September 13, 2018, p. 20.

immigrant who has ever benefited from safety-net programs such as the Children's Health Insurance Program (CHIP) or health insurance purchased on the Obamacare exchanges. This policy would even apply to immigrants in the United States legally, which reflects the cruelty of the president and his administration. There has never been greater need for the rule of law in this country against the willful and casual cruelty of a president.

In the wake of a federal court decision in Texas in December 2018 against the legality of the Affordable Care Act (ACA), the Supreme Court will be needed to save health care for 20 million Americans, including compulsory coverage for Americans with pre-existing conditions and young adults who are covered by their parents' insurance until the age of 26. Republican politicians at the federal and state level have been trying to kill the ACA since 2010. The law is embedded in American society, so there would be additional political chaos if the federal court decision were allowed to stand.

Unfortunately, fewer Americans are tracking the political details and controversies that surround appointments to the Supreme Court and the decisions of the Court. Since a majority of our citizenry relies on social media, particularly Facebook, for news, there is much to be done about the dumbing down of America. This trend has allowed Trump to benefit from the "poorly educated" he so roundly thanked during the campaign in 2016. A Russian disinformation campaign on social media took excellent advantage of the lack of political sophistication in the United States in order to wage a campaign in favor of Donald Trump in the 2016 election. Russian intelligence officers introduced millions of "news" items to exploit the backlash against immigration and ethnic diversity. The Trump campaign exploited such factors as the impact of globalization, technological change, and immigration to win the election.

The Trump Administration will come to an end one of these days, but repairing the damage to our democracy will be a difficult long-term struggle. In short order, the candidate who promised to "drain the swamp" became the president who filled it instead. This time of reckoning will require stamina and vigilance as well as greater enthusiasm about simply going to the polls. President Trump is not alone in the cockpit: he has a compliant Senate, a sympathetic Supreme Court, and an enabling number of voting constituents who do not seem to object to the authoritarian behavior of a commander-in-chief who has weakened our democracy. Not even Trump's misogyny blocked his ability to secure the votes of a majority of white women in the 2016 presidential election.

Trump has politicized the military, and compromised the norms of civilian-military relations that ensure a subordinate place for the military in democratic governance. At the same time, he has perplexed the military leadership with three senior general officers leaving his administration in 2018, the so-called "adults" in the room. When he announced the withdrawal from Syria and Afghanistan, General Joseph Dunford Jr., the chairman of the Joint Chiefs of Staff and the senior military adviser to the president, was not present. Retired General Stanley McChrystal, who led U.S. forces in Afghanistan, described President Trump as dishonest and immoral. "I don't think he tells the truth," McChrystal stated.[207]

Eventually the American populace will learn whether Donald Trump was a comet across the sky or someone who changed this nation forever. We will learn about all the details of Trump's corrupt world from the investigations of his White House, his campaign, the transition, his charities, his businesses, and even his inauguration. For the present, we know that on the basis of the qualities for judging presidential leadership, such as political skill, cognitive style, vision, public communications, organizational skill, and emotional intelligence, Donald Trump is arguably the worst president in the history of the United States and unfit to serve.

---

[207] "This Week," ABC News, December 30, 2018.

In the meantime, the American people must make sure that we are not too late in learning the lessons of Trump's rampant corruption. We cannot wait for the Mueller investigation to expose the various facets of the corruption of Donald Trump and his minions. Cynicism and apathy have already compromised democratic government in many ways. As Benjamin Franklin left the Constitutional Convention in Philadelphia in 1787, an anxious citizen asked, "Well, Doctor, what have we got, a republic or a monarchy?" With no hesitation whatsoever, Franklin responded, "A republic, if you can keep it."

ABOUT THE AUTHOR

Melvin A. Goodman was a Soviet analyst at the CIA and the Department of State for 24 years, and a professor of international relations at the National War College for 18 years. He served in the U.S. Army in Athens, Greece for three years, and was intelligence adviser to the SALT delegation from 1971–1972. Currently, Goodman is the Director of the National Security Project at the Center for International Policy in Washington, DC, and adjunct professor of government at Johns Hopkins University. He is the national security columnist for *Counterpunch.org.*

Goodman has authored, co-authored, and edited eight books, including *Whistleblower at the CIA: An Insider's Account of the Politics of Intelligence, National Insecurity: The Cost of American Militarism, Gorbachev's Retreat: The Third World; The Wars of Eduard Shevardnadze; The Phantom Defense: America's Pursuit of the Star Wars Illusion; Bush League Diplomacy: How the Neoconservatives are Putting the World at Risk,* and *Failure of Intelligence: The Decline and Fall of the CIA.* His articles and op-eds have appeared in numerous publications, including the *New York Times, Harper's, Foreign Policy, Foreign Service Journal, The Baltimore Sun,* and *The Washington Post.* He lives in Bethesda, Maryland.

INDEX

A

Azar, Alex, 120

B

Bannon, Stephen, i, v, 7, 12,27, 40,117, 185

Bezos, Jeff, xi

Block, Herbert ("Herblock"), x

Bolton, John, ii, vi, 12-14, 16, 62, 64, 78, 108, 114

Brennan, John, 21, 89, 93, 111

Buford, Anne Gorsuch, 172

Bundy, McGeorge, 107

Bush, Barbara, iv

Bush, George H.W., 80, 81

Bush, George W., 14, 25, 36, 66, 76, 106, 117, 140

C

Carson, Ben, 122, 139

Cheney, Dick, 27, 63, 66, 80

Clapper, James, 7

Clinton, Bill, 25

Clovis, Sam, 24

Coats, Daniel, 21, 96

Cohen-Watnick, Ezra, 13

Cohen, Michael, iii

Cohen, William, 26

Collins, Susan, 199

Colson, Charles, ix, 3

Comey, James, xii, 187

D

Dean, John, ix, 3
Department of Justice, i
Department of State, 22, 26
DeVos, Betty, 134, 138, 143
Droegemeier, Kelvin, 148

E

Ehrlichman, John, 5
el-Sisi, Abdel Fattah, 180
Environmental Protection Agency, vii, 3
Erdogan, Recip Tayyip, 78, 180

F

Fleitz, Fred, 109
Friedman, David, 75
Flynn, Michael, iv, 6-8, 11, 13, 91

G

Gates, Robert, 66, 95, 106
Gerry, Elbridge, 203
Gerson, Michael, 10
Gingrich, Newt, 192
Goldwater-Nichols Act, 26
Gorbachev, Mikhail, 74
Gore, Al, 187, 190
Gorka, Sebastian, 12
Gorsuch, Neil, 145, 172, 197
Goss, Porter, 105
Greenblatt, Jason, 75
Guiliani, Rudy, iv

H

Haig, Alexander, xi, 9 63

Haley, Nikki, 36, 41, 43
Haspel, Gina, 20 62, 101-103, 112, 114
Hicks, Hope, 19

I
Ignatius, David,10
Intermediate-range Nuclear Forces Treaty, vi, 30, 64, 82
Iran Nuclear Accord, 15

J
Johnson, Lyndon Baines, 4

K
Kavenaugh, Brett, 197
Kelly, John, 8, 16, 17, 19, 128
Keogh, James, x
Kerry, John, 46
Khashoggi, Jamal, 86
Kissinger, Henry A., xi, 2, 63, 83, 187
Kristof, Nicholas, 10
Kislyak, Sergei, 10, 97
Kudlow, Larry, 31, 143
Kurshner, Jared, 75, 112

L
Lavrov, Sergei, 97
Lewandowski, Corey, 19
Lieberman, Joe, 199
Logan Act, 10
Long, Huey, iii

M
Manafort, Paul, iii
Mattis, James, ii, 6, 8, 16, 17, 46, 61, 62, 65, 77

McCain, John, iv, x, 195, 199

McCarthy, Joseph, iii, 40

McChrystal, Stanley, 207

McConnell, Mitch, 145, 186

McFarland, K.T., 12

McGrory, Mary, ix

McGurk, Brett, ii, 61

McMaster, H.R., 10-12, 25, 97

Messitte, Peter, iv, 194

Miller, Stephen, iv, v, 27

Mnuchin, Steven. ii, 8, 51, 121

Morell, Mike, 103

Mueller, Robert, iii, 99, 181, 187

Mulvaney, Mick, ii, 133, 134, 142, 194

N

Naubert, Heather, ii

Navarro, Peter, 31, 51

Netanyahu, Benjamin ("Bibi"), 49, 180

Nielson, Kirstjen, 121

Nixon, Richard, viii, xiii, 2, 3, 23, 91, 187

North American Free Trade Association, 32, 51

North Atlantic Treaty Organization (NATO), 32, 33

Nunes, Devin, 196

O

Obama, Barack, 25, 80, 165, 185, 196

P

Palin, Sarah, v

Panetta, Leon, 20, 102, 108

Papadopoulos, George, 24

Poindexter, John, 11

Pompeo, Mike, ii, vi, xii, 9, 20, 39, 42, 43, 71, 78, 94, 100, 110

Powell, Colin, 11, 64, 66
Price, Thomas, 123m 124
Priebus, Reince, 9
Pruitt, Scott, 121, 122, 154, 155, 158, 160-162, 172
Putin, Vladimir, i, 5, 32, 33, 49, 59, 95, 202

R
Razak, Najib, 180
Reagan, Ronald, 26, 82, 106
Rumsfeld, Donald, ix

S
Sanders, Bernie, 195
Schorr, Daniel, ix
Schumer, Charles (Chuck), 18, 197
Scowcroft, Brent, 11, 13, 80
Sessions, Jefferson, v, xii, 131
Shine, Bill, ii
Shulkin, David, 123, 140, 141
Spicer, Sean, 126
Stevens, John Paul, 186

T
Tillerson, Rex, 8,11, 22, 23, 35, 36, 38, 41, 57, 64, 70, 71, 80
Trans-Pacific Partnership, vi, 15
Trudeau, Justin, 31, 55, 201
Trump, Donald, i-iii, 2, 16, 19, 23, 30-32, 45, 47-51, 55, 59, 60, 64, 65, 68, 75, 82, 84, 85,
    87, 89, 91, 93-95, 119, 127, 131, 136, 145, 152, 171, 175, 182, 183, 186, 207
Turner, Stansfield, 106

U
Un, Kim Jong, xii, 34, 68, 113, 180

W

Warren, Elizabeth, 193-194
Watt, James, 173
Wheeler, Andrew, 122, 162

X

Xi Jinping, 69

Z

Zinki, Ryan, 119, 123, 131m 132, 150, 168-170, 172